D1566863

TECHNOLOGY AND CAPITAL IN THE AGE OF LEAN PRODUCTION

A Marxian Critique of the "New Economy"

Tony Smith

State University of New York Press

Published by
State University of New York Press, Albany

© 2000 State University of New York

All rights reserved

Printed in the United States of America

For information, address State University of New York Press
State University Plaza, Albany, New York 12246

Production by Dana Foote
Marketing by Patrick Durocher

Library of Congress Cataloging-in-Publication Data

Smith, Tony, 1951–
Technology and capital in the age of lean production : a Marxian critique of the "New
Economy" / Tony Smith.

p. cm. — (SUNY series in radical social and political theory)
Includes bibliographical references and index.
ISBN 0–7914–4599–2 (alk. paper) — ISBN 0–7914–4600–X (pbk. : alk. paper)
1. Production (Economic theory) 2. Marxian economics. 3. Capitalism. 4. Labor.
5. Employees—Effect of technological innovations on. I. Title. II. Series.

HB241 .S65 2000
335.4′12—dc21
00–028520

10 9 8 7 6 5 4 3 2 1

Contents

PREFACE

Once again, and surely for the last time, Marxism has died. This, at least, is the common consensus. Marxism may continue to be studied as an episode in the history of ideas, as one studies Bishop Berkeley's idealism or phrenology in the nineteenth century. And it may continue to attract the interest of students of political history, eager to examine a current that briefly diverged from the main flow of history and then dried up. But few hesitate when asked what is living and what is dead in Marxism. Nothing, and everything, is the reply.

Jacques Derrida has refused to let this confident judgment persist unquestioned. In his view we can no more escape Marxism than Hamlet could escape the specter of his father's ghost. Instead of celebrating the triumph of neoliberal right-wing thought, we should mourn the demise of Marxism. Most importantly, we must recognize that Marx's writings bestow "access to an affirmative thinking of the messianic and emancipatory promise as promise" (Derrida 1994, 52). This messianic thinking "belongs to the movement of an experience open to the absolute future of what is coming, that is to say, a necessarily indeterminate, abstract, desert-like experience that is codified, exposed, given up to its waiting for the other and for the event" (Ibid., 55).

Derrida's refusal to join his voice to the chorus of capitalist triumphalism is to be applauded. And it is surely correct to stress the emancipatory promise at the center of Marxism, as Walter Benjamin did in his day and liberation theologians do in ours. But if this is all that speaks to us today in Marx's writings, then it is really Heidegger, not Marx, whose thought remains of contemporary importance.[1] If Marxism qua Marxism is to have a future, it must involve far more than this. Marx's thought is indeed dead if it does not help us understand determinate and concrete features of our social world, and if it does not offer a hope for the future rooted in that understanding.

There are two main reasons for the widespread dismissal of Marxism today. The collapse of the Soviet Union has convinced most people that Marxism has led to a dead-end in social evolution. And many hold that recent developments in capitalism have made Marx's framework outmoded. These misgivings cannot be removed by reference to a "messianic promise" in Marxism. They must be confronted directly.

The greater portion of the present work is devoted to a critical examination of "the new economy thesis," the view that capitalism is evolving in ways that make Marxian categories such as "class struggle," "exploitation," and "alienation" passé. I shall term theorists who accept this perspective "new capitalist utopians."[2]

The notion of the "new economy" is quite elastic, often encompassing a wide variety of financial, political, psychological, and cultural dimensions. In the present work, however, I shall concentrate on recent developments in the production and distribution of commodities. Questions of psychology and culture will be bypassed, while finance capital and the state will be considered only in passing. I do not wish to suggest that production and distribution are always more important than other spheres of human life, let alone that these other spheres are mere epiphenomena of economic processes. Some focus is necessary. Concern with the fate of Marxian thought dictates that the focus be on production and distribution, for this is where the heart of Marx's social theory is found.

Chapter 1 begins with a sketch of the "Fordist" model of mass production and distribution, an ideal type capturing many significant features of the form of capitalism dominant in the so-called "long Twentieth Century" (Arrighi 1994, 239ff.). In the late '60s and early '70s a "crisis of Fordism" broke out in the capitalist global system. This crisis set off an extended period of economic restructuring over the last decades. Four main candidates have been proposed as likely results of this restructuring: postindustrialism, flexible specialization, the diffusion of the lean production model developed in Japan, and neo-Fordism. The first two can be dismissed relatively quickly. Most of the remainder of chapter 1 is devoted to an extended reconstruction of the debate between those who hold that lean production is destined to triumph as a qualitatively new stage in the history of capitalism, and those who believe that the dominant trend in the contemporary economy is the intensification of practices associated with Fordism.

"Lean production" can be provisionally defined as a system of production and distribution involving work teams, the elimination of non–"value adding" positions in production (quality control, cleaning, middle management), the use of just-in-time deliveries from suppliers and to distributors, mass customization (that is, relatively short product runs aimed at narrowly defined market segments), and the cooperation of different enterprises within networks. I believe that neo-Fordist theorists have convincingly shown that there are a great number of continuities between Fordism and certain dimensions of lean production. They have also established that some of the most emphasized aspects of lean production have not as yet been institutionalized on anything approaching an economy-wide scale, and that much of the rhetoric regarding the advantages of lean production over Fordism has been overblown. Neo-Fordists have also proposed numerous warranted criticisms of utopian claims defended by advocates of lean production, many of which will be incorporated in the present work. Nevertheless, in my opinion they have failed to substantiate their claim that lean production is simply the latest variant of Fordism, or else a mere thought construct without empirical relevance. In this work lean production will be taken as the part of the so-called new economy devoted to the production and distribution of commodities.[3]

Defenders of lean production in the scholarly and popular business press believe that its diffusion is likely to successfully resolve the crisis of Fordism and inaugurate a new period of extended prosperity in the capitalist global system. Consideration of this claim is postponed until chapter 6. These theorists also hold that the technologies and social organization of lean production tend to result in a profound transformation of social relations. The heart of the present work, chapters 2–5, is devoted to an immanent critique of this claim.

Advocates of lean production assert that the interests of capital and labor can be harmoniously reconciled in the "new economy," that true consumer sovereignty is finally in the process of being instituted, and that there are levels of trust and cooperation within networks of lean production firms beyond anything seen thus far in the history of capitalism. In stark contrast, Marx held that social antagonisms are inherent in capital/wage labor relations, capital/consumer relations, and intercapital relations. If the assessments of the "new capitalist utopians" are correct, then Marxian theory is indeed hopelessly irrelevant to the world of contemporary capitalism. I attempt to show, however, that structural tendencies are built into the lean production model that significantly limit the extent to which the goals of overcoming labor antagonism, instituting consumer sovereignty, and extending economic cooperation can be fulfilled.

Chapters 2 and 3 explore contemporary capital/wage labor relations in light of changes in the technologies and social organization of the workplace. A number of social theorists in the Marxian tradition have asserted that the history of technical change in the capitalist workplace is a history of management attempts to use technology to deskill the workforce. According to these theorists, the introduction of technologies now associated with lean production is merely the latest chapter in this story. Chapter 2 begins with a presentation of this view. I then consider arguments against the deskilling thesis in general and specific criticisms of the claim that technical changes in lean production further accelerate deskilling. After examining the responses that could be made to these arguments by defenders of the deskilling thesis, I conclude that this thesis is a very insecure foundation for a defense of the contemporary relevance of Marxian thought.

In the beginning of chapter 3 I point out that the deskilling thesis is in fact not the central component of the Marxian analysis of labor relations in capitalism. In the first volume of *Capital*, Marx focussed more on three different notions: structural coercion, exploitation, and real subsumption.[4] He argued that those without access to means of production and subsistence are forced to sell their labor power to those who own the means of production and subsistence; that those who own and control capital are generally able to appropriate surplus value produced by wage laborers; and that these owners and controllers also necessarily tend to transform the labor process in order to increase the accumulation of surplus value. For Marx, these three notions define the social context within which the technologies of the workplace are introduced. Marx derived the claim that there is a fundamental conflict of interests between capital and labor from these three notions. In chapter 3 I analyze the strongest arguments made by the new capitalist utopians implying that structural coercion, exploitation, and the real subsumption of labor will be overcome in lean production. I contend that these arguments are not convincing. In the course of this discussion the gender and racial dimensions of the lean production system are considered.

In chapter 4 the focus shifts to the realm of consumption. The proponents of the "new economy" claim that a series of technological advances now allow consumer sovereignty to become a reality for the first time in human history. These advances include information technologies allowing manufacturers to track consumer desires on the individual level, and flexible production technologies (computer-aided design, computer-aided manufacturing, and so on) allowing production to both meet individual wants on a mass level ("mass customization") and adjust rapidly to shifts in consumer desires. The new capitalist utopians argue that capital and consumers will be united in a "co-destiny" relationship that overcomes consumer alienation. I argue in response that the asymmetry in economic power between units of capital and consumers is if anything yet more pronounced in lean production; that the effects of consumption on the subjectivity of consumers are ever-more pernicious; and that relevant knowledge conveyed to consumers by the price form remains limited. Further, talk of consumer sovereignty mystifies an economic system where the imperatives of capital accumulation continue to be the alpha and omega of social life. As long as this is so, Marxian theory will remain the starting point for any serious attempt to comprehend the social dynamic of the capital/consumer relation.

Chapter 5 examines the manner in which advances in information technologies—especially EDI (electronic data interchange) and Internet software—enable lean production firms to be bound closely together in networks. The new capitalist utopians claim that relationships within these networks are characterized by trust and cooperation. One pivotal manifestation of this trust is a sharing of information, which contributes to a faster rate of diffusion of innovations. I argue that this view ignores the asymmetry of power between the firms at the core of networks and the smaller subcontractors and distributors located on their ring. I point out that any increase in trust and cooperation within networks comes at the cost of displacing conflicts to relations among networks. I also contend that the new utopians overlook how the flow of certain relevant types of information is seriously restricted within lean production networks. Finally, I suggest that the technologies associated with lean production have been used in a way that shifts the balance of power between private units of capital and public authorities, exacerbating problems of trust and harmony within society as a whole.

The beginning of chapter 6 returns to a question posed in chapter 2: how likely is it that lean production will inaugurate a new period of extended expansion in global capitalism? Discussion of this question leads to a consideration of a number of perspectives on globalization. The two leading mainstream views may be termed "neoliberalism" and "competitive regionalism." Adherents of both positions agree that the global diffusion of the "new economy" may well set off a long boom in twenty-first century capitalism, while disagreeing on the proper role of government and other matters. Theorists holding a third perspective, "global underconsumptionism," do not share this optimism. In their view the new economy places extreme pressure on wages in both the richer and the poorer countries. The likely result is that effective demand for the commodities produced in the global economy will not be sufficient to avoid extended economic slowdowns. I agree that the new economy, like the old, will be beset by recurrent economic crises whose greatest burdens will be borne by those who benefited least from periods of expansion. But the root of these crises lies less in problems of effective demand than what Robert Brenner describes as "the unplanned, uncoordinated, and competitive nature of capitalist production, and in particular individual investors' unconcern for and inability to take account of the effects of their own profit-seeking on the profitability of other producers and of the economy as a whole" (Brenner 1998, 8). The root of the problem, in brief, lies with what Marx termed "the law of value," a law that remains in force in the age of lean production.

This conclusion leads to the question what an international system of production and distribution beyond the law of value might look like. And this query in turn forces us to confront the second main reason for the widespread dismissal of Marxism today, the collapse of the Soviet Union. Even if we suppose that the objections to the lean production model proposed in chapters 2–6 can withstand scrutiny, this in itself does not refute the new capitalist utopians. Defenders of the "new economy" could simply concede that some of their stronger claims cannot be fully redeemed, while insisting nonetheless that the economic arrangements they advocate remain the best feasible alternative. Hasn't history shown, after all, that attempts to construct a socialist alternative to capitalism invariably end in failure?

In order to deal with this line of thought I take a somewhat round-about path in the seventh and final chapter. A number of factors underlying the collapse of the so-called Soviet model are examined, concentrating especially on shortcomings regarding processes of technological change. I then consider the sorts of social transformations that would be required for the promises of lean production to be fulfilled, arguing that a transition from capitalist market societies to a democratic form of socialism would be necessary. In the third section of the chapter I attempt to show that this democratic form of socialism could in principle avoid the shortcomings that doomed centralized bureaucratic planning. The work concludes with an extension of this socialist model to the international level.

This work would not have been completed without a grant from the National Science Foundation, which allowed me to immerse myself in the literature on lean production at Berkeley for a year. Various drafts of chapters have been read by Paul Adler, Sebastian Budgen, James Dickinson, Peter Drucker, Fred Evans, John Exdell, Don Ihde, James Lawler, James Marsh, Joseph McCarney, Kim Moody, Mike Parker, Christopher Phelps, Ed Royce, Harley Shaiken, Justin Schwartz, Frank Thompson, Richard Walker, Robert Went, and the members of the philosophy department at Iowa State University. Earlier versions of chapters 3 and 4 were read by the participants at an annual working conference on Marxian theory held at Mount Holyoke College: Chris Arthur, Martha Campbell, Mino Carchedi, Paul Mattick Jr., Fred Moseley, Patrick Murray, and Geert Reuten. I am very grateful for the many helpful comments and suggestions I received from these scholars and friends, as well as for the many constructive suggestions offered by the blind reviewers for SUNY Press. None of these people deserve the least blame for the shortcomings of what follows. I am also grateful to International Studies in Philosophy for permission to use material from an earlier paper, "Flexible Production and Habermasian Social Policy" (27.4 [1995]: 85–100), and to St. Martin's Press and Macmillan Press for premission to incorporate material from my essay "The Capital/Consumer Relation," which appeared in The Ciculation of Capital, Arthur and Reuten, eds. (1998, 67–94).

The book is dedicated to Bridgit and Conor, our bright spirits.

CHAPTER ONE

From Fordism to Lean Production

Our story begins with the "crisis of Fordism," considered in the first section of this chapter. In the second section I argue that there are good reasons to consider lean production the most significant form of capitalist restructuring undertaken in response to this crisis. I then briefly sketch the main ways in which lean production represents a serious challenge to Marxian thought.

A. Fordism

It has become customary to refer to the form of capitalism dominant in the mid-twentieth century as "Fordism." There are a number of problems with this practice. It is certainly true that many features of the Fordist model have their roots in nineteenth century capitalism (Hounshell 1984; Clarke 1991, 114). It is also true that this model appeared in anything close to a pure form only in the United States, and that even here there were numerous sectors where few of its characteristic features could be found (Walker 1989; Tolliday and Zeitlin 1992; Jessop 1991; Webber and Rigby 1996).

In general, the dangers of employing ideal types such as "Fordism" are obvious and serious. Out of the indefinite number of ways in which different phenomena can be brought together in thought, which should be selected? What ensures that an ideal type will not obscure profound differences among the divergent empirical phenomena it brings together? How do we know that these differences are not more important than the shared features emphasized in the ideal type? Conversely, how do we know that features shared by two ideal typical models are not more significant than the distinctions drawn between them? What guards against these sorts of issues being decided arbitrarily by the social theorists constructing the ideal types in question? What guards against dominant cultural values and ideologies determining how these questions are resolved?

I believe that there is no way to resolve these sorts of difficulties *a priori*. But we should remember that if we abandon the use of ideal typical models to concentrate entirely on case studies of individual events and processes, we would soon be adrift in countless contingencies. Some sort of conceptual framework is necessary if we are not to lose ourselves in the ontological infinitude of the world; this is the price that must be paid for focusing on the part of the world most relevant to our theoretical and practical concerns (Weber 1959). Ideal types, in brief, are necessary to orient empirical work. This remains true even when empirical work documents aspects of the world that do not fit neatly under those types.

In the case at hand if the only ideal types at our disposal were those that held for capital generally, it would be extremely difficult to study capitalism as the sort of system we know it to be, a system that regularly undergoes significant restructuring. And so ideal types at an intermediate level of analysis between the general logic of capital and individual case studies must be employed. "Fordism" is such an intermediate category (as is "lean production").

There are certain general questions to consider when constructing an ideal type on this intermediate level. However vague and open-ended these questions may be, they can still provide some protection against theoretical arbitrariness.

1. Does the ideal typical model capture essential features of the most pervasive empirical phenomena of the historical period in question?
2. Does the proposed ideal type capture the essential features of the leading economic sectors of the relevant period, that is, the sectors where growth rates are highest, the greatest amount of surplus profits are appropriated, and so on?
3. Does the model focus attention on the social institutions and social agents of most relevance to future historical development? Does the ideal type in question define "best practice" cases that undergo rapid diffusion? Does it help pick out social agents with a capacity to bring about significant social transformations in the given historical context?
4. Does the model capture the framework to which appeal was most often made in legitimations of the social order during the period in question?[1]

The answers to these questions may conflict with each other. An ideal type of the numerically most prevalent phenomena in a given period may differ from a model of the phenomena most closely associated with leading sectors of the economy. Ideal types capturing either of these concerns may well differ from thought constructs emphasizing the social forces most responsible for historical transformations, which in turn may diverge from the models used to legitimate the social order of the day. All we can say is that any ideal type relevant to one or more of the above considerations in principle may be helpful for grasping essential features of particular periods in economic history.

I believe that the use of the category "Fordism" can be justified by these criteria, at least in certain contexts. During the mid-twentieth century more and more leading firms in more and more sectors took on the characteristic features of "Fordism," including those in the most economically dominant industries. The internal dynamic of Fordism also provides a helpful framework for grasping significant historical transformations in capitalism. The dynamic between Fordist firms and the mass production worker of Fordism, for example, is crucial for understanding both the potential for social change in this historical period and the contradictory ways in which that potential was actualized. Lastly, the Fordist model played a central role in the chief legitimations of the social order formulated during this period (Smith 1992, chapter 8).

There are certainly many theoretical and practical contexts in which a more fine-grained empirical analysis than that provided by the relatively abstract Fordist model would be necessary, as critics of the model have correctly insisted. Further, there are many contexts in which it would be fully warranted to stress the profound continuities connecting earlier periods of capitalism and the Fordist epoch (Glick and Brenner 1991).[2] Nonetheless, if one wishes to examine the dominant structural features of mid-twentieth-century capitalism, I know of no better alternative. It should be possible to avoid the pitfalls here, as long as we do not forget that we are dealing with thought constructs rather than concrete phenomena, and as long as we do not confuse general features of the logic of capital with features distinguishing one particular period in capitalism from another.[3] It is now time to turn to the main features of this ideal type.[4]

Since Fordism is a particular variant of capitalism, its basic features can be introduced in terms of the circuit of capital accumulation (M-C-P-C'-M').[5] The first phase in this circuit is M-C, the use of investment capital (M) to purchase two sorts of commodities (C), means of production and labor power. In Fordism, control of initial investment capital was largely centralized in the hands of large firms. The most important means of production purchased by these firms were large-scale single purpose ("dedicated") machines. These machines demanded extensive supplies of raw materials and considerable energy resources (especially oil).

The Fordist firm sought a high degree of vertical integration in the hope of obtaining significant economies of scale. As a result, many inputs were produced within the firm itself prior to final assembly. But this vertical integration was never complete; some purchase of raw materials and parts from suppliers was always required. The relationship between a manufacturer and its suppliers was a "hands-off" one. Manufacturers wanted low prices from their suppliers, and were quick to change to new suppliers when they were willing to undercut previous prices. In this sense the boundaries separating firms were obvious and fixed.

Besides means of production, the other sort of commodity purchased as an input into production was labor power. In the early years of the Fordist epoch, firms regularly resorted to violence to resolve wage disputes. Gradually, however, labor relations became more institutionalized. Most leading Fordist firms were eventually unionized, and wage levels became the subject of routinized negotiations leading to regular wage increases for the (mostly white and male) workers in the unionized sector.

In the next phase of the capital circuit, P-C', means of production and labor power are set in motion to produce (P) new commodities (C'). The single purpose machinery characteristic of Fordism allowed the mass production of standardized products. Unit costs decreased with each additional product, and so product runs tended to be extended as far as possible. This tendency was reinforced by the fact that the machinery was difficult to replace without shutting down production for an extended period of time. Facing relatively limited competition in their national markets, Fordist oligopolies could extend product runs and plan extensively for the costly and time-consuming switch from one product line to another.

Turning to the labor process, the classic Fordist arrangement revolved around assembly lines in which each worker was assigned a specific task to be performed repeatedly. This was similar to the detail labor Marx described as holding in nineteenth-century "machinofacture." What was new to Fordism was the way labor was subjected to "scientific management." In the initial version of scientific management, termed "Taylorism" in honor of Frederick Taylor, its founder, the goal was to fragment the labor process and deskill the laborer with the aid of time/motion studies undertaken by industrial engineers. In this manner management's control over the labor process could be increased (Braverman 1974). Soon, however, the illusory goal of complete and direct management control was abandoned as a result of worker resistance, the inherent need for the active cooperation of labor in production, and the continued dependence of management upon certain skills in the workforce. Elements of Taylorism were instead combined with a system of formal job classifications and work rules regulating the labor process. These classifications and rules provided the workforce with some protection against especially arbitrary managerial interventions into the work process. They also institutionalized a seniority system holding out hope for advancement to higher levels of status and remuneration. These advantages came at a cost to the workforce, however. The classifications and rules were premised upon a strict separation of mental and manual labor.[6]

And decisions regarding the development and implementation of new technologies were defined as "management prerogatives" exclusively. This complex system of control and compliance was administered by a bureaucratic apparatus of supervisors and middle managers. Conflicts over work rules and classifications were resolved in routinized arbitration with labor unions, whose bureaucratic organization mirrored that of management. Bureaucratization within Fordist firms also involved the separation of functions into distinct divisions within the organizational structure. Responsibility for the quality of the produced goods and services was assigned to a quality control department separate from the production process itself. Responsibility for developing innovations was located in a R&D lab physically removed from the production site. Product design, manufacturing, and marketing were all undertaken by separate divisions operating in quasi-autonomy.

The height of the Fordist era coincided with the first period of the so-called computer age. Beginning in the 1950s corporations introduced mainframe computers for data processing. This form of computing fit neatly into the organizational structure of Fordism. The computing intelligence was located in a "host" computer (typically a mainframe or, later, a minicomputer), while the local or remote terminals were "dumb," that is, totally dependent on the availability of the host computer to function (Tapscott and Caston 1993, 122, 209). This host-based hierarchy computing paralleled the centralized command and control organization of Fordism. Computing strategies also followed the same "bigger is better" philosophy found in the search for economies of scale in Fordist production and distribution. It was thought that the cost of processing would fall as more applications were combined on a single computer. This reasoning led the biggest Fordist firms to undertake a series of multimillion dollar upgrades of their mainframes (ibid., 128). Finally, computing did not challenge the balkanization of the Fordist firm into separate divisions. Organizational barriers separated data-processing departments from engineering, production, marketing, and administration divisions, each with their own separate data bases (ibid., 61).

Throughout the chain of production the operative precept of Fordism was "just in case." Raw materials and parts were stockpiled just in case provision by suppliers was interrupted. Partly finished goods were amassed at each step of the production process just in case problems in production arose later. Reserves of labor were hired just in case there were absences. Finished goods piled up as inventory just in case sudden orders from distributors came in.

In the final phase of the circuit of capital accumulation, C'-M', the new commodities (C') resulting from the process of production are (hopefully!) sold for more money (M') than the initial money invested. I have already

noted that the technologies associated with Fordism allowed the mass production of commodities, and that as the product runs of these commodities
were extended, unit costs declined. This allowed a decline in prices,
fulfilling one condition for the emergence of a mass consumer market. The
other precondition was a broad growth in disposable income. The routinization of class struggle played a central role here, bringing regular wage
increases to many categories of workers.[7] Once these wage increases were
won, the oligopoly position of the largest Fordist firms allowed them to pass
on rising wage costs to consumers. Higher prices simply led to another
round of wage increases, and so mass production and mass consumption
could remain roughly in sync.

This completes the sketch of Fordism. As with all ideal types, it is always possible to eliminate certain features of the model and to add others.
The theoretical and practical interests motivating the inquiry provide the
only standard for assessing whether such subtractions and additions are warranted. There are certainly circumstances in which the model described
above would need to be significantly modified. But for present purposes the
above sketch provides a fairly helpful way of articulating the characteristic
features of mid-twentieth-century capitalism. This conclusion holds despite
the fact that many features of the model were neither unique to mid-twentieth-century capitalism, nor exemplified always and everywhere during this
period.

By the mid-1970s a "crisis of Fordism" was well underway in the global
capitalist system, measured by a general decline in the rate of profit.[8] At the
risk of some slight repetition the factors alleged in the scholarly and popular business press (and much of the left press as well) to have hampered capital accumulation in Fordism can be grouped under six headings.

1. Difficulties connected with *constant capital*[9] included:

- high raw material costs (especially oil);
- high inventory costs; and
- the use of machinery that discouraged rapid shifts in product lines.

2. *Circulation time and costs* were another relevant factor in the crisis of
Fordism. Factors resulting in an extension of circulation time and an increase of circulation costs included:

- lengthy delivery times between suppliers and assemblers;
- extended interruptions in production due to the need to retool;
- the length of the time required to make decisions within an extensive corporate bureaucracy;
- the time required to correct quality problems;

- the time demanded to work off previous inventories; and
- the length of the time required to institute innovations, due to the institutional separation of design engineers and production personnel.

3. A third difficulty concerned the connection between *science and the capital form*. The separation of research and development departments from other divisions in the Fordist corporate structure has already been mentioned as a factor increasing circulation time. This also limited the degree to which science could be effectively subsumed within the circuit of accumulation.

4. Regarding *the capital/wage labor relation* we can mention:

- mounting unproductive expenses connected with the supervision of the workforce;
- worker resistance at the point of production, taking both overt and indirect forms (e.g., strikes and absenteeism, respectively);[10]
- wage increases not always matched by productivity advances; and
- quality problems stemming from the separation of quality control to a separate department (this also involved mounting unproductive expenses).

5. The *capital/consumer* relation was also characterized by certain shortcomings:

- a host of factors prevented a quick response to shifts in consumer demand; these included high levels of inventories, bureaucratic decision making, the need to have long product runs to amortize fixed capital investment, delays in the innovation and diffusion process, and so on;
- the mass production of standardized products did not allow producers to produce commodities fitting the needs and wants of individual consumers;
- consumers were negatively affected by quality problems in production.

6. Finally, *relations among units of capital* were also beset by a series of difficulties:

- the institutional separation between engineers in supplier firms and in assembly firms prevented close co-operation, thereby increasing both circulation time and the costs of circulation;

- competition among suppliers on the basis of price encouraged suppliers to cut costs, generating yet more quality problems;
- the hands-off relationship between suppliers and assemblers discouraged the latter from sharing innovations with the former, thereby increasing the time it took for innovations to diffuse.

In chapter 6 I shall return briefly to the question of the causes of the global crisis of Fordism and question certain aspects of the above account. For now the key point is simply this: by a certain point in time (the early 1970s) the above sorts of difficulties appeared to most observers to reach a critical mass in those regions and sectors where the closest approximations of the Fordist model could be found.[11] The crisis of Fordism then set off a significant restructuring of capital that continues to this day. How ought we to conceptualize this restructuring? Opinions here are sharply divided.

B. Responses to the Crisis of Fordism: Some Alternative Perspectives

Economic restructuring is a vast process, with many dead-ends, reversals, and contradictory developments. Stephen Wood's assessment is surely correct: "There do not appear to be powerful homogenizing forces to push work organizations and market strategies down one channel" (Wood 1989, introduction 26). But even if a number of distinct social structures coexist in a given period, this surely does not mean that they are all of equal interest in every theoretical and practical context. Is it possible to pick out a dominant trend in the contemporary economy among the vastly divergent forms we see around us? Four attempts to do so will be considered in the present section. Some social theorists hold that the notion of a postindustrial economy allows us to grasp the basic direction being taken in response to the crisis of Fordism. Others continue to make the industrialization process central to their analysis, disagreeing on the way recent developments ought to be categorized. Three main competing options here are "flexible specialization," "lean production," and "neo-Fordism." Defenders of the postindustrialist, flexible specialization, and lean production viewpoints hold that a new stage in the economic evolution of capitalism is emerging in response to the crisis of Fordism, an assertion denied by defenders of the neo-Fordist perspective. All four perspectives emphasize the close connection between forms of social organization and technical developments in microelectronics.[12]

The first two positions can be discussed rather quickly; the crucial debate for our purposes is between advocates of lean production and neo-Fordism.

1. The Postindustrial Model

Defenders of the postindustrialist thesis assert that we are entering a period in which the service sector will predominate in the economy. Certainly the so-called service sector has grown in importance. But many activities ordinarily characterized as services are in fact industrial processes. McDonald's assembly line, for example, involves the material transformation of inputs as much as any Fordist automobile plant. Also, a great many "services" are themselves a part of manufacturing, such as writing computer programs to run machine tools. Other services are auxiliary to manufacturing, and would vanish if the manufacturing activities were to disappear. Examples include bank lending to manufacturers, the advertising of manufactured products, and the drawing up of legal contracts between suppliers and assemblers. Finally, information-intensive activities are commonly taken to be the core of the postindustrial economy. But information-intensive activities require information technologies, and these, of course, must be produced in an industrial sector.

In the light of all these considerations it makes far more sense to say that the contemporary economy is characterized by *increasing* industrialization than it does to speak of a sudden shift to a postindustrial economy (Cohen and Zysman 1987; Sayer and Walker 1992). On this point the remaining three positions all agree.

2. Flexible Specialization

The theory of flexible specialization was developed by Piore and Sabel (1984) as part of an extended study of "industrial divides." This term refers to historical periods in which there is an open choice between economic development based on craft production and a path of mass production. Contingent factors then determine which option is selected. Once one or the other option has been institutionalized, it may be reproduced for an extended period of time, pushing the other option to the margins of economic activity. At some later point, however, a new set of historical contingencies may arise that brings society to a new industrial divide, where the choice between craft production and mass production is once again open.

In the nineteenth century Proudhon formulated a vision of a society based on small-scale independent worker cooperatives and craft labor. For Piore and Sable, Proudhon's vision was a viable option; European society faced an industrial divide at that juncture. But Proudhon's proposals went unheeded. Small scale co-ops lost out to the factory system, in which wage laborers were hired for mass production. The Fordist model discussed in the previous section counts as the most developed stage of this system. According to Piore and Sabel, the crisis of Fordism has now brought us to another industrial divide.

Piore and Sabel suggest that matters may be resolved differently than they were in the nineteenth century. For one thing, mass production markets are now saturated. Consumers have grown tired of standardized products, and sudden shifts in demand are becoming more and more frequent. Second, technologies have arisen that allow new products to be developed without massive amounts of additional investment. With the flexible multipurpose technologies of the microelectronics revolution we are moving closer to a time when a new product line can be introduced simply by typing in a new program. As a result "economies of scope" can be attained, as opposed to economies of scale; short runs of diverse products can be produced just as efficiently as extended runs of standardized products. Finally, the costs of these flexible technologies has been declining rapidly. They are now within the reach of most small-scale enterprises.

Of course, not all organizational forms are equally capable of instituting flexible responses to sudden shifts in consumer demand, even when the right sorts of technology are employed. In Piore and Sabel's view, decentralized worker-run firms are in the best position to make use of microelectronics technologies in this manner.[13] Small worker cooperatives are not hampered by slow-moving bureaucratic hierarchies, and they possess a more committed workforce. Piore and Sable point with approval to regions in Northern Italy and elsewhere where new forms of craft production have arisen. In these regions small-to-medium batch production by skilled workers has replaced the mass production of standardized goods by a deskilled workforce. Work is organized by self-directed teams responsible for quality. This arrangement both reduces rigidity and increases productivity.

The regional organization of these small firms into flexible networks bound together by relations of trust completes the flexible specialization model. In Northern Italy and elsewhere, temporary affiliations of firms arise in order to produce specific products, to be replaced by different alliances when consumer demands shift. This flexibility requires long-term bonds among the firms in an extensive regional network:

> Sabel and others stress that the widespread development of flexible specialization will depend on co-ordination and long-term links between firms, each of which will be specialized in one part of the total production process (including design and distribution). Flexibility is thus provided as much by this overall arrangement as by anything one firm does (Wood 1989, Introduction 24).

There are a number of problems with the flexible specialization perspective. Most striking is the absence of a strong tendency in the contemporary economy to move to decentralized worker cooperatives of the sort they describe (Williams et al. 1987). While Fordist firms have certainly been "downsizing," they have hardly been fragmenting into small worker-run firms. Differences in size and relative economic power among enterprises remain quite striking. While the decentralization of production is no doubt occurring in many areas, economic power is hardly becoming less concentrated. It remains disproportionately in the hands of a relatively small number of global firms. The reach of these firms is increasing, not decreasing; their ability to organized production on the global level is growing, not shrinking, even if they allow somewhat greater autonomy to local units (Harrison 1994). And in the regions where small firms once dominated in a manner consonant with the flexible specialization model, successful firms have tended over time to increase in both size and relative economic power. Northern Italy is itself an example of this; Benetton, for instance, has become a giant firm dominating a network of small suppliers (Wood 1989, introduction 24–25).

Another difficulty for the flexible specialization model is that there is little evidence that mass production markets have become saturated; demand for autos and televisions remains a high percentage of overall consumer demand. And it has not been proven that economies of scale suddenly disappear with the computerization of manufacturing. Taking both points together, it follows that there is little reason for asserting that large firms producing for mass markets are about to disappear.

This conclusion is reinforced if we consider the question of innovation. Small-scale workers' cooperatives do indeed mobilize the intelligence of laborers on the shop floor. As a result flexible specialization appears to be well suited to two types of innovation, incremental product innovation and incremental process innovations. But other sorts of innovation must be considered as well, such as system innovations that take a number of related technologies and fit them together, and the development of hybrid technologies that take previously unrelated technologies and merge them in a new way (recent examples include opto-electronics and mechatronics). For these types of innovation to occur more is generally required than just a close connection between manufacturing and design work within the same organization. They appear to demand large-scale enterprises in which people working in one technical area have regular formal and informal contact with those concerned with quite different matters. For this reason Florida and Kenney (1990) argue that large-scale corporations are likely to be more successful than small-scale ones in an economy based upon the ceaseless commercialization of innovations.[14]

There is also the question of the costs of technical innovation, especially those associated with microelectronics, the technology of most importance to the flexible specialization model. Processing power per dollar invested has indeed fallen drastically, putting fairly advanced computer equipment within the reach of many small enterprises. But the development costs connected with each successive generation of microelectronics technology has increased geometrically.[15] Small firms are simply not able to devote the funds necessary for fundamental innovations in this area.

Other advantages of large firms must be mentioned here as well. Large firms including both a consumer electronics division and a division devoted to high technology products have a considerable advantage; the consumer electronics division provides a large internal market for the high technology products.[16] The income from this internal market can then fuel further high tech research. This arrangement also allows a rapid diffusion of the results of high tech research to other divisions, rejuvenating sectors that had previously appeared to be "mature" (Kenney and Florida 1993, 73). It would seem that large enterprises are not likely to disappear anytime soon, a point recognized by advocates of both of the two remaining perspectives.

3. Lean Production

Due to a series of historical contingencies the leading firms in postwar Japan never completely embodied the Fordist paradigm. They instead evolved the lean production system, which many take to be a new variant of capitalism. The authors of an influential study of the global automobile industry, *The Machine That Changed the World: The Story of Lean Production*, believe that this new model is in the process of proving its superiority in the global market:

> [I]n the end we believe lean production will supplant both mass production and the remaining outposts of craft production in all areas of industrial endeavor to become the standard global production system of the twenty-first century. (Womack et al. 1990, 278)

A composite picture of lean production will now be presented, based upon the writings of those who defend the "lean production thesis" articulated above by Womack and colleagues. Critical remarks will be postponed until subsequent chapters. Once again we may use the different phases of the general circuit of capital as an ordering device to bring out the salient features of the proposed model.

In the first stage of the circuit of capital, M-C, investment capital is used to purchase means of production and labor power. In the model of lean production the means of production employed are "flexible," that is, they can be shifted rapidly from one configuration to another.[17] To some extent this can be done with conventional technologies. While U.S. manufactures chased the dream of full automation, the Japanese learned how to create what were in effect "multifunctional" machines through combining low-cost conventional machines in manufacturing cells (Warner 1989, 276). It is clear, however, that lean production systems tend to evolve such that conventional machines are replaced by programmable multifunctional machines, capable of switching from one production application to another at low cost (Ohno 1988; Maleki 1991). Computer numerically controlled (CNC) machine tools, robots, and networks of desktop computers are the most important examples of such machines. In this manner computing intelligence is dispersed throughout the enterprise, rather than being centralized in a host computer only. The lean production model thus represents a second age of information technology, beyond the host-based computing that fit so easily within Fordist structures (Tapscott 1996).

I would like to postpone consideration of the labor market in lean production to the following two chapters, and move immediately to the next stage in the capital circuit, the production of new commodities (P-C′). One goal of lean production in this context is the reduction of indirect labor costs. All forms of labor that do not add "value" to the final product are targets.[18] This includes supervisory labor, quality control, maintenance work, cleaning, and so on. Many of these positions can be eliminated if the operator on the shop floor (or office) becomes a multiskilled laborer capable of self-direction, as opposed to the detail laborer of past epochs of capitalism. The multiskilled worker incorporates quality concerns (often involving relatively sophisticated forms of statistical reasoning), machine maintenance, and cleaning assignments into the labor process.

In lean production it is assumed that multiskilled workers have a unique perspective on the labor process. They are therefore in a unique position to formulate insights regarding how to manage the complexity that arises at the point of production. The model thus includes attempts to mobilize workers' insights in a process termed "kaizen" ("continuous improvement") by the Japanese. Developing, testing, and sharing insights is an inherently intersubjective matter. And so the model also includes work teams, which provide a forum for such intersubjective relations.

According to the advocates of lean production, this new form of production overcomes the functional boundaries characteristic of Fordism. Close ties are established between R&D and manufacturing, and between both and marketing, as representatives of all three divisions regularly serve on the same work teams. With these closer ties across divisions the rate of both process and product innovations tends to increase.

In lean production firms concentrate on areas of production that match their "core competencies." Aspects of the work process that distract attention from these core concerns are "outsourced" to specialist firms. More and more enterprises, for instance, no longer hire janitors or security guards themselves, but contract these jobs out to specialized agencies. The same point holds for an increasing range of inputs to final assembly. The lean production model thus includes a variety of subcontracting arrangements, spin-offs,[19] joint ventures,[20] and so on.

Turning to the C'-M' phase of the capital circuit, in which finished commodities are offered for sale to consumers, the lean production model incorporates a variety of information technologies allowing firms to track consumer behavior in great detail. This allows them to grasp both nuances in consumer demand and shifts in demand to a much higher extent than was possible in Fordism. The production technologies and organizational innovations mentioned above then allow producers to respond to this information much more quickly as well. As a result a greater range of products is offered to consumers than in Fordism, and product runs tend to be of significantly shorter duration.[21]

The enhanced significance of consumer demand is reinforced by another crucial feature of the model, the "just-in-time" mode of organizing the various stages of production and distribution. In Fordism high levels of inventory would pile up in the hope that it could be sold later. In lean production inventories are kept low, and only replenished after information regarding sales establishes that this is warranted. When information to that effect arrives, a chain of events is set off: information that a completed product is needed by a customer is transmitted back to final assembly; requests for the different parts required for final assembly are transmitted back to the sites where partially finished goods are produced; and so on, all the way back to the transmission of requests to suppliers to deliver raw materials and other inputs to the plant. Each step in the production and distribution process completes its task on an as needed basis, that is, "just-in-time" for the results to be used by the next stage in the process. Once again, it is consumer demand that sets off this chain of events, thereby integrating consumer activity into the production and distribution process much more than was the case in Fordism.

The just-in-time approach obviously implies that relations between assembly firms and their suppliers and distributors cannot be of the "hands-off" variety characteristic of Fordism. Defenders of the lean production thesis hold that suppliers, assemblers, and distributors now form networks within which information and technologies are shared. This allows new practices such as "concurrent engineering," in which design engineers working for suppliers collaborate closely with engineers from core assembly firms.

Advocates of lean production insist that scale and volume have hardly become irrelevant in the contemporary economy.[22] Nonetheless, the greatest profits today are won from tailoring goods or services to the specific needs of particular customers in a way that cannot be easily duplicated by others.[23] This requires a quickness of response and commitment to continuous experimentation that firms with an extensive bureaucratic apparatus have great difficulty attaining. And so in lean production the bureaucratic apparatus tends to shrink relative to the norm in Fordism. Developments in information technologies aid this process. I have already mentioned that the lean production model reflects a "paradigm shift" from host computing to distributed (or "networked") computing. Host computing was based on centralized computing power, as more and more applications were added to mainframes in a search for economies of scale. In contrast, network computing is based upon the relative price/performance advantages of microprocessors dispersed throughout the enterprise. As computing resources are moved closer to the operational areas of business, the traditional centralized command and control approach tends to break down. The monopoly on information that propped up much of the prestige and power of corporate bureaucracies is undermined, and the autonomy of work teams is furthered. Also, "cooperative processing involves spreading application components across multiple platforms and using the network to link these components" (Tapscott and Caston 1993, 125). This means that information technologies now aid in breaking down the bureaucratic barriers separating design, production, marketing, and administration functions. Before each division had its own data base, which few the outside the division could access without going through bureaucratic channels. Now someone engaged in any one of these functions has relatively easy access to information gathered in the course of any of the other activities.

This concludes the provisional sketch of lean production as articulated by the model's leading advocates.[24] It should be noted that other terms have been used to refer to this model. Some authors speak of "the Japanese model." I consider that to be a profoundly misleading appellation, implying as it does that the practices just described are an expression of cultural attributes supposedly unique to Japan, such as cultural homogeneity, a predisposition to obedience, groupism, and paternalism. Lean production practices have been institutionalized successfully in a great variety of different national settings (Babson 1995b, passim.), albeit with regional variations (Kochan et al. 1997). This shows that lean production does not depend upon cultural factors specific to Japan.

Sayer and Walker refer to the "just-in-time" model (1991). Strictly speaking, this refers to a part of the new system rather than to the model as a whole. Kenney and Florida speak of "innovation-mediated production," and this too seems to describe certain aspects of the model rather than the whole (Kenney and Florida 1993, 4). "Flexible production," another term often used, has a number of problems as well. As Sayer and Walker correctly point out, the reference to "flexibility" is potentially misleading. In some respects and in some contexts the Fordist approach may be *more* "flexible" than lean production. The hands-off relation between assemblers and suppliers in Fordism, for instance, often granted firms more room to maneuver than they have in lean production networks. The term "flexible" is also quite ambiguous in itself. It can be used to refer to a myriad of quite distinct phenomena, including pay flexibility, flexible technologies, the flexible use of technologies, organizational flexibility within firms, flexibility in subcontracting work outside of firms, work flexibility ("functional flexibility"), flexibility in numbers of people employed, flexibility in firing, flexibility in alliances with other firms (start-ups, strategic alliances, etc.), flexibility in product mix, and so on (Wood 1989, introduction 1). Firms that are committed to "flexibility" in one or more of these dimensions need not pursue it in any of the remaining dimensions. Even worse, the pursuit of flexibility in one dimension may demand a sacrifice of flexibility in one or more of the other areas.

A much more accurate term in this context has been coined by David Harvey: "flexible accumulation" (Harvey 1989). This expression conveys that the flexibility that ultimately matters here is flexibility in the strategies employed to accumulate capital. In Harvey's usage, however, the term refers primarily to the strategies of finance capital, specifically, the awe-inspiring ingenuity with which ever new forms of fictitious capital (that is, paper wealth and assets) are deployed. The importance of these phenomena in the contemporary economy cannot be overstated (Henwood 1997a). The intricacies of finance capital, however, demand a separate investigation, and will only be referred to in passing here.

I have decided to use the phrase "lean production" simply because this term appears to be becoming fairly established in the literature. I take it to refer to a central component of the so-called new economy. I am hopeful that the analysis of the model does not stand or fall with the choice of the term used to refer to it.

The lean production model includes a number of features discussed by postindustrial theorists and defenders of the flexible specialization perspective. The model incorporates the growing importance of service-related activities (design, marketing, customer service, etc.) emphasized by postindustrialist theorists. The importance of rapid product cycles, multi-purpose machinery, changed work relations, and interfirm networks emphasized by Piore and Sabel is found here as well. But the lean production viewpoint is clearly distinct from either of these perspectives. The notion of lean production is based on the assumption that the process of industrialization continues to be an essential feature of the economy, and that large-scale firms seeking economies of scale continue to be of central economic importance. The thesis that lean production is emerging as a response to the crisis of Fordism appears to incorporate many of the strengths of these two competing accounts, while avoiding their greatest weaknesses. From the standpoint of a fourth perspective, however, the lean production model is itself fatally flawed, both conceptually and empirically.

4. Neo-Fordism

In my estimation the strongest case against the view that lean production represents a new stage in capitalism is posed by those who believe that the heightening of Fordism is the most significant form of contemporary capitalist restructuring. For defenders of this "neo-Fordist" view there is indeed something new in the contemporary economy. In leading industries and regions of the mid-twentieth century something of a class compromise was in place that allowed certain sectors of the workforce to enjoy improved living standards. Falling rates of profit led many units of capital to reject this dimension of traditional Fordist practices. An all-out attempt to weaken labor organizations and roll back labor gains has been undertaken, an offensive that includes a shift from full-time permanent workers to part-time and temporary workers, wage cut-backs, the reduction if not elimination of benefits, job speed-ups, forced overtime, legal and illegal harassment of labor activists, and so on. None of this implies that a qualitatively new form of production has emerged; Fordism with a strong capital offensive remains Fordism. All of the talk of lean production as a new epoch in capitalism thoroughly obscures this state of affairs (Pelaez and Holloway 1991).

The debate between defenders of the lean production thesis and neo-Fordists can be considered in the light of the four criteria for assessing the historical significance of a model of production introduced at the beginning of the chapter:

1. The number of empirical instances illustrating the model in question
2. The extent to which the most dynamic sectors and regions of the given period illustrate the model in question
3. The extent to which the model points towards the most likely path of future capitalist development
4. The extent to which the model was (is) employed in the most significant attempts to legitimate the social order of the day.

(1) Regarding the question of the number of empirical instances illustrating lean production, neo-Fordists make two quite different sorts of arguments. The first is that most so-called lean-production firms retain basic elements of Fordism, and therefore should count as examples of Fordism rather than as instances of some new type of economic model (Dohse, Jurgens, and Malsch 1985; Williams et al. 1992; Williams et al. 1995). The sec-

ond grants that lean production is distinct from Fordism in principle, but denies that there are sufficient instances of the former to justify proposing the emergence of a new stage in capitalist development.

Steve Babson summarizes the first argument in the following passage:

> From this alternative perspective, lean production, rather than marking the end of Fordism, extends it by modifying certain features and retaining essential elements of the Fordist regime: jobs are still subdivided into narrowly defined tasks (though workers sometimes rotate through a few tasks within their immediate area); work is still regimented by the assembly line and by strict adherence to standardized procedures (though workers are expected to suggest refinements and solve minor problems); mass production at high volumes still characterizes the system's output (though ar somewhat lower levels and shorter runs per model than the peak years of the past); and management retains fundamental control of the overall production process. (Babson 1995a, 14)

There are a number of problems with this argument from the standpoint of proponents of lean production. For one thing, its force rests on terms such as "sometimes," "few," "minor," and "somewhat" found in the parentheses. These terms are inherently imprecise. Who gets to decide when such terms are appropriate, and when stronger terms should be used instead? It seems obvious that those working in self-proclaimed lean production enterprises have as good a claim to decide this as anyone. If lean production were not qualitatively distinct from traditional Fordism we would expect these workers to be indifferent to the prospect of returning to traditional Fordist practices. More relevant to an assessment of the neo-Fordist thesis, if lean production were no more than a hyperintensive version of Fordism we would expect laborers in lean production facilities to desire a return to more traditional Fordist arrangements. Yet it is all but impossible, claim the defenders of the lean production thesis, to find members of the workforce in these facilities who wish to return to old Fordist arrangements (Adler 1995, 214). To my knowledge no neo-Fordists have ever disputed this claim. This suggests that in the lived experience of those most directly affected by capitalist restructuring, workers at the point of production, differences in the new system clearly outweigh continuities with Fordist practices. If this is so, by what right are these differences to be dismissed as "minor"?[25]

A second difficulty in the neo-Fordist argument is that it assumes that (supposedly) slight changes (those mentioned in the parentheses of the Babson passage above) have only slight effects. But there is no reason to hold that this is so. It is quite possible that even slight initial changes in a number of domains simultaneously might set off significant adjustments throughout the entire system, resulting in a qualitative transformation of the system of production as a whole. The neo-Fordist argument does not take the possibility of such nonlinear effects into account.

Of course a defense of the lean production thesis based on the first of the four criteria must go beyond showing that lean production facilities are in principle qualitatively distinct from Fordist ones. It must be demonstrated that such facilities are predominant in the contemporary economy. At this point neo-Fordists make a second move. As of now, they insist, there are relatively few empirical examples of anything approaching the full lean production model described above. A University of Southern California survey of three hundred major U.S. corporations found, for example, that only one in ten had set up work teams covering more than 20 percent of their workforce (Lawler et al. 1992). These results are corroborated by Appelbaum and Batt in the course of a comprehensive overview of recent studies of workplace practices:

> Summing up these diverse surveys is difficult, but it seems reasonable to conclude that between one-quarter and one-third of U.S. firms have made significant changes in how workers are managed and about one-third of large firms have serious quality programs in place or have experienced significant gains from their quality programs. (Appelbaum and Batt 1994, 68)

Since these programs affect only a portion of the employees of these firms, only about 10 to 15 percent of workers in the United States have been touched by "the high performance workplace" advocates of lean production speak of.[26] According to Edward Lawler, a managment professor who has tracked 216 Fortune 1000 firms at three year intervals beginning in 1987, no more than 12 percent of the U.S. workforce were in "high involvement" jobs as of 1998 (quoted in Ross 1998). Fordism, in brief, appears to remain the dominant form of capitalism in the United States, at least. Bloated bureaucratic hierarchies remain a feature of the corporate landscape, microelectronics is often used to exacerbate (rather the eliminate) the split between conception and execution in the workplace, and so on (Gordon 1996). After all, if capital were really serious about creating the "high performance workplace" eulogized by lean production spokespersons, why do U.S. employers devote only 1.4 percent of payroll to training, or increase the money they spend on formal staff development at less than the rate of inflation (Tapscott 1996, 299)? In places such as Canada and Great Britain the story is much the same (Gordon 1996).

Some advocates of the lean production thesis dispute these empirical estimates. Paul Osterman of the Massachusetts Institute of Technology, for example, asserts that nearly 80 percent of industrial employers in the United States have adopted total quality management, team-based systems, quality circles, or some combination of the three (cited in Hammonds et al. 1994, 84). MacDuffie and Pil's more recent survey of the auto industry in the United States, Europe, and Japan corroborates this conclusion: "[The] data reveal that the direction of the changes in work organization is clearly convergent toward high-involvement practices" (MacDuffie and Pil 1997, 38). Osterman and Macduffie and Pil would certainly grant the relative paucity of instances of the lean production model in anything like its pure form. And along with many other theorists, they would grant the regional variations that have emerged in the course of the diffusion of lean production (Kochan et al. 1997, Introduction, Conclusion; Streeck 1996). But in their view this does not refute the thesis that lean production is the most significant form of capitalist restructuring today. This debate has not concluded.

Of course, other matters are surely relevant here besides the quantitative question of how many instances of a model can be documented in a given period. To make a historical analogy, when Marx wrote *Capital* there were far more instances of agricultural production on small landholdings than there were of machinofacture. Yet for Marx the latter, not the former, defined the most significant form of capitalism in the second half of the nineteenth century. Machinofacture was the most dynamic sector of the economy, there were good reasons to think that this sector would have the greatest influence in determining the future course of capitalist development, and it played a central role in the most significant legitimations of the social order of the day. In an analogous fashion the number of lean production facilities operating today by itself does not necessarily answer the question of the historical significance of the model.

(2) It is worth noting that the same University of Southern California survey that documented how few firms have adopted team systems also documented that 60 percent of the companies surveyed plan to increase the use of "self-managing" teams in the near future. Of course, neo-Fordists are unlikely to be impressed by such a statement of intention. Fads come and go; the fact that firms announce plans to do something doesn't mean much; a new fad may come along in the meantime. While the basic structures of Fordism have an abiding presence, on this view lean production is just the latest in a series of management vogues. It too will be abandoned as soon as the advantages promised to management do not materialize.

With this move we have left behind the question of how many concrete instances of lean production can be counted and turned to the question of the dynamic of contemporary capitalism. Besides arguing that the non-Fordist aspects of lean production are empirically insignificant, neo-Fordist theorists insist that the advantages of these non-Fordist aspects for management have been wildly overstated, while the strengths of a heightened

Fordism for capital have been underestimated. If true, these claims would undercut the thesis that lean production practices will tend to be clustered in the most dynamic sectors and regions of the contemporary economy. MIT researchers have claimed that lean production auto plants can be up to twice as productive as traditional Fordist plants (Krafcik 1989). Williams and his collaborators ridicule this figure for a number of reasons. In order to get a comparative ratio of labor input to physical output one must correct for differences in output characteristics and the amount of work undertaken. The correction techniques employed necessarily and arbitrarily abstract from many relevant differences among plants, leading to imprecise and untrustworthy conclusions. According to Williams and colleagues, (1995), certain lean production firms such as Toyota have indeed enjoyed a competitive advantage in the auto sector. But in other lean production firms (e.g., Nissan) value-added per employee is *below* the average of traditional U.S. plants. Further, most of the advantages enjoyed by successful lean production enterprises have been due to relative wage levels, the greater number of hours employees are forced to work, differences in capacity utilization, the relative immaturity of the domestic market, ease of manufacturability, and structural differences in different regions (such as the availability of high-quality low-price suppliers outside the auto sector, lower pension costs, etc.), and not to non-Fordist labor practices. Advocates of lean production promise improvements if management commits itself to introducing the new paradigm, but in the real world managers face constraints that limit what can be accomplished by changes in management practices (Williams et al. 1995).

MacDuffie and Pil have responded to this line of criticism of the lean production thesis. They do not deny that the attempt by MIT researchers to measure labor productivity is inherently imprecise, as are all attempts to measure complex phenomena. But they do insist that ever-more accurate techniques have been employed to factor out variables such as wage differentials, differences in hours worked per employee, ease of manufacturability, product differences, and capacity utilization. Very large performance differentials still result in their view. In 1989–1990, when most Japanese auto firms had instituted lean production practices and U.S.- and European-owned firms mostly continued more traditional ones, they estimate that labor hours per vehicle was 16.8 hours in Japan, 24.9 hours in North America, and 35.3 hours for plants owned by European capitals in Europe (MacDuffie and Pil 1995, 194). Even if we suppose that these calculations are off by 10 to 20 percent—an assessment MacDuffie and Pil would strongly reject—a significant productivity gap would remain. They conclude that there is thus ample reason to expect that there will be a tendency for more and more firms in more and more sectors to adopt the superior lean production approach.

This part of the debate is by no means resolved. But it does appear that MacDuffie and Pil's case is not without some plausibility. A firm like Toyota has certainly taken advantage of lower wage levels, a rapidly growing domestic market, and so on. But can such matters alone account for the following astounding fact: Japanese auto production was under one percent of U.S. auto output in 1955, while twenty-five years later it surpassed the U.S. (Babson 1995a, 7)? It seems unlikely that a shift of this magnitude could have arisen unless the Japanese had discovered more productive ways of implementing technologies and organizing labor. After all, many countries enjoying low labor costs and expanding domestic markets did not experience anything remotely like this rate of growth. The fact that not all Japanese firms benefited equally from this growth does not appear to be a convincing counterargument, since no one has ever said that the rise of lean production automatically equalizes growth rates within sectors. Nor does the extended economic downturn that has plagued Japan throughout the 1990's necessarily refute the claim. Even if the industrial sector of a nation has introduced a more advanced form of production, that nation may still suffer from serious economic downswings due to other factors (for example, speculative bubbles in the financial sector) or poor macroeconomic state policies, or global overcapacity.

Other studies have corroborated the MIT researchers' claim that introducing the innovations of lean production is correlated with productivity gains. Levine and Tyson's (1990) examination of twenty-nine studies found a decisive positive correlation between on-line work teams and productivity outcomes. Kelley and Harrison's (1992) survey of 1,015 plant managers has established that employee participation along the lines of the lean production model had a significant positive effect on productivity in unionized workplaces, a result duplicated by Cooke (1990).[27]

It should also be recalled that the transformation of the labor process is only one dimension of the lean production model. For the neo-Fordist case to hold it would have to be plausible to maintain that the innovations of lean production have only minor impact in the other dimensions as well. There are at least two significant areas where it would appear to be difficult to maintain this position. The first concerns quality matters. The NUMMI plant set up in California along lean production lines by Toyota and General Motors has enjoyed striking gains in this dimension:

> The J. D. Power and Associates Initial Quality Study of the number of problems per one hundred vehicles experienced by customers within ninety days of purchase show that NUMMI progressed from 116 per 100 vehicles in 1989 (compared to an industry average of 148 for all cars sold in the U.S.) to 93 in 1991, and to 83 in 1992 (versus an industry average of 125 for all cars sold in the U.S., an average of 105 for

Asian nameplates, 136 for U.S. nameplates, and 158 for Europeans). (Adler 1995, 213)

Quality improvements of this magnitude appear to be typical after the introduction of lean production. Another crucial matter has to do with rates of product innovation. Howes states that lean production firms in Japan bring products to market in half the time required of Western firms employing traditional Fordist practices, a result comparable to that found by MacDuffie and Pil (Howes 1995, 159; MacDuffie and Pil 1995, 188).[28] This too would seem to undermine the neo-Fordist claim that lean production does not bring any special advantages over Fordism. If labor productivity and quality levels are higher, while product development and time to market are lower, it is at least plausible to hold that lean production firms are among the most dynamic in the contemporary economy.

In their conclusion to a recent volume of papers examining trends in Japan, the United States, Canada, Germany, the United Kingdom, Spain, France, Italy, Sweden, Australia, South Africa, Brazil, and Korea, Kochan and his colleagues note various factors that have led companies to not adopt lean production, such as decisions to stress cost reductions and to maximize the production of popular models. They insist, however, on the following point:

> Those facilities that must compete on both cost and quality criteria with products from around the world experience the greatest pressure to adopt lean production principles. The reason is quite simple. Introducing an integrated bundle of flexible human resource practices and lean production techniques leads to higher levels of quality and productivity than can be achieved with traditional mass production techniques. Lean production plants also are able to manufacture a wider product mix within the same facility than more traditional plants. They also achieve higher levels of performance than plants that invest heavily in technology and automation without transforming mass production work systems and human resource practices. (Kochan et al. 305)

Whatever the ratio between the number of lean production enterprises in the global economy vis-à-vis non–lean production facilities, the empirical evidence in their view thus suggests that the former are likely to be far more dynamic over time, given the likelihood of increasing global competition.

The case for the lean production thesis is further strengthened by contrasting the relative strengths of national economies over the past decades. The United States, Canada, and Great Britain are the three countries where the empirical plausibility of the neo-Fordist thesis is greatest; in these countries more than elsewhere capital's response to the shortcomings of Fordism has been heightened Fordism.[29] Gordon terms this the "low road" of capitalist development. He has established that national economies where most units of capital have taken this "low road" have consistently underperformed nations where labor practices have been fundamentally transformed:

> Those [countries] with the most cooperative approaches [to labor management] feature *both* the most rapid wage growth *and* the smallest corporative bureaucracies. Those with the most adversarial approaches to labor relations, notably including the United States, manifest *both* much slower wage growth *and* much top-heavier corporate structure. . . . [W]hen we compare relatively cooperative and conflictual economies, those driving the high road enjoy more rapid productivity growth, more buoyant investment, and a better combination of inflation, unemployment, and trade performance. There may be many reasons their greater macroeconomic successes over the past twenty years, but at least one of them appears to be that their approach to labor-management pays off not merely for their workers but also for their entire economy. (Gordon 1996, 6–7)

In specific, Gordon estimates for the business sector that in the period from 1973 to 1989 "(i)n the five cooperative economies [Japan, Germany, the Netherlands, Norway, and Sweden], productivity grew at an average annual rate of 1.9 percent over those sixteen years. In the . . . conflictual countries [the United States, the United Kingdom, and Canada], the average productivity growth rate was a much more moderate 1.1 percent, barely more than half as fast" (ibid., 148).[30] This data suggests that while numerous cases of neo-Fordist arrangements continue to be found in contemporary economies, the leading edge of capitalist development may be located elsewhere.

These statistics do not necessarily show that it is lean production that holds a privileged place in the contemporary economy. Gordon lumps together a number of quite disparate national economies (Japan, West Germany, Sweden) when he considers the aggregate accomplishments of nations taking the so-called high road of development. A case could be made that the lean production model extrapolated from Japan should be sharply distinguished from the German and Swedish approaches (Appelbaum and Batt 1994, chapter 4; Berggren 1992). From the standpoint of capital accumulation, the German "Diversified Quality Production" approach to capitalist development and the Swedish "Sociotechnical System" variant both have certain strengths and weaknesses relative to the lean production model first introduced in Japan. But I do not believe it can be disputed that the rate of diffusion of lean production is far more rapid than the rate of diffusion of either of these alternatives. In Sweden itself leading enterprises are abandoning their experiments with sociotechnical systems and turning to lean production (Henriksson 1994). Similarly, ever-increasing numbers of units of capital based in Germany are adapting lean production methods.[31]

Against this entire line of thought neo-Fordists point out the advantages capital can win through moving from a class-compromise version of Fordism to new variants of Fordism based on victories in an offensive against labor. In the United States, for example, the rent, dividends, and interest that owners of capital earned jumped 65 percent in the 1980s. The reasons for this, defenders of the neo-Fordist thesis argue, had next to nothing to do with lean production, and everything to do with declining levels of unionization, cuts in pay and pension and health care benefits, forced overtime, job speed-ups, illegal firings, and so on.[32]

Neo-Fordists would also point out that while the German and Swedish systems do appear to be unstable, it is not at all clear that they are being transformed to the lean production version of "the high performance workplace." Instead the same sorts of assaults on labor are now being undertaken in these countries that we saw beginning in the United States in the 1980s. And even in Japan itself we now see increasing levels of standardization, longer product runs, less variety of models and options,[33] more layers of management, and other features that bring the system closer and closer to traditional Fordism (Miller, Woodruff, and Peterson 1992).

At this point we have moved from attempts to estimate the relative dynamism of sectors and regions that have adopted lean production vis-à-vis sectors and regions that have taken the neo-Fordist path, to the closely related issue of the most likely path of future capitalist development, the third of our four criteria for evaluating the usefulness of an ideal type in this context.

(3) When we attempt to envision the most likely path(s) of future economic evolution in capitalism there are a great number of possibilities to consider. Any list of the main candidates would include the following:

a) The long-term benefits from lean production are such that the full lean production model will diffuse throughout the global capitalist system with relatively minor variations.

b) The long-term benefits from lean production are real. If short-term management and labor perspectives prevent lean production practices from spreading to the point where they become more significant than neo-Fordist approaches, government policies can intervene to counteract them.[34]

c) Both the short and the long-term benefits to capital from neo-Fordism are greater than those obtainable through lean production, so that the former is doomed to remain relatively insignificant in the economy as a whole. Or,

d) In specific circumstances the neo-Fordist option is more advantageous to capital than moving to lean production, with neither path emerging as the dominant trend.

The defenders of lean production insist that either (a) or (b) capture what the capitalist global system is most likely to look like in the twenty-first century. Their opponents reply that contemporary trends suggest that (c) or (d) point in more probable directions.

The strongest argument in favor of the proponents of lean production can be formulated as follows. In many sectors and regions, at least, the wage and benefit cuts, forced overtime, and layoffs of neo-Fordism will provide at best a merely temporary boost to corporate profits. This implies that at some point many units of capital that have taken the neo-Fordist option will be forced to consider a restructuring that involves more than "Fordism without a human face." Henry Conn, head of the research institute of the management consulting firm A.T. Kearney Inc., has stated that "We're not going to downsize our way to prosperity." More important than squeezing labor costs, according to Conn, is the generation of ideas that will produce revenues. This requires the active participation of the workforce (quoted in Wysocki 1995, 1). Batt and Appelbaum report that others share these views:

> Recent studies by the American Management Association and management consulting firms such as the Wyatt Company, however, show that downsizing usually fails to produce anticipated productivity gains because of the harm to employee morale and motivation. In other words, there are limits to strategies based on squeezing labor. (Batt and Appelbaum 1993, 7; see also Tapscott 1996 3, 4, 28)

This analysis appears to be supported by figures from the Economic Policy Institute. Between 1979 and 1989 per capita GDP grew an average 1.5 percent a year in the United States, where the strategy of neo-Fordism was pursued the most aggressively. In contrast, the average was 2.3 percent for eight comparable industrialized countries (Noble 1994, 23). This suggests that the short- and long-term benefits of the neo-Fordist route may be limited.

Perhaps the most striking argument made by the opponents of the lean production thesis in this context is that in matters such as length of product cycles and number of products offered Japan is moving closer to Fordism in response to recent economic downswings in the Japanese economy. Doesn't this suggest that Fordism is alive and well today, and will continue to be alive and well tomorrow? An alternative view is that these changes are relatively minor, so that "the key features of the classic lean production system are still in place in the major plants" in Japan (Kochan et al. 1997; see Ishida 1997; Ohtani et al. 1997). Empirical studies have also documented that traditionally Fordist auto companies have adopted far more of

Toyota's lean production practices than Toyota has adopted practices of theirs (Parker and Slaughter 1994, section II). Here too the debate is ongoing.

(4) One final question must be asked before concluding this discussion. Which ideal type plays a greater role in the legitimations of the social order characteristic of our day, the lean production model or the neo-Fordist model? The answer to this question obviously should not influence our assessment of the empirical significance of either model. But if lean production can be independently shown to be empirically significant, and if it also plays a central role in legitimations of the contemporary social world, the case for subjecting it to close analysis would be reinforced. The answer to the question is clear: *the most significant contemporary attempts to legitimate the contemporary social order all invoke the lean production model.* This can be seen in works ranging across the political spectrum. In the United States, for instance, examples include Tapscott's *The Digital Economy* (1996), written for a conservative audience of corporate executives; the writings of liberal public policy specialists such as the former U.S. Secretary of Labor, Robert Reich; and Bluestone and Bluestone's *Negotiating the Future* (1992), which articulates the official position of the U.S. labor movement. In all three perspectives contemporary capitalism is justified not because of its capacity to perpetuate Fordist practices, but due to the possibilities apparently opened up by lean production. It is certainly striking that *Business Week,* the magazine of corporate America, ran a cover story on "Rethinking Work" (October 17, 1994) whose conclusion is indistinguishable from that of "The New American Workplace," the 1994 report of the AFL-CIO Committee on the Evolution of Work.[35] Both documents culminate in the claim that a "new labor-management partnership" based on the work teams, quality programs, new technology, and just-in-time delivery of lean production will reconcile the interests of labor and management. No other model of capitalism comes remotely close to playing this role in contemporary legitimations of the social order.

This concludes the examination of the lean production thesis and the neo-Fordist alternative. What conclusions ought to be drawn? Any assessment must be provisional. The future holds many unexpected twists and turns, any of which may call into question our judgments about our own age. Capitalism certainly does not follow some pre-ordained sequence of stages; it always follows a number of paths simultaneously, each of which is continuously subject to contingencies. No model provides the ultimate goal toward which all developments in capitalism tend; social action is always capable of reversing the course of events, thereby pushing historical change in quite unexpected directions.[36] Nonetheless, the contingency of the future does not lessen the need to make sense of the present.

Neo-Fordist theorists have convincingly shown that there are a great number of continuities between Fordism and lean production, that some of the most emphasized aspects of lean production have not as yet been institutionalized on anything approaching an economy-wide scale, and that much of the rhetoric regarding the advantages of lean production over Fordism has been overblown. Neo-Fordists have also proposed many warranted criticisms of utopian claims defended by advocates of lean production, many of which will be incorporated in the following chapters. Nevertheless, I believe that the lean production model warrants close scrutiny.

There are two main reasons justifying this modest conclusion. The first has to do with the importance of lean production in contemporary legitimations of capitalism. Critics of contemporary capitalism who wish to address the strongest case of their opponents must confront the advocates of lean production. The second consideration is that whatever one might think of the model of lean production defended by the new capitalist utopians, *some* version of lean production is clearly becoming the hegemonic form of capitol. Kim Moody, a prominent critic of lean production, bases this conclusion on the testimony of workers and union officials. In Canada, "lean-production methods . . . are widespread"; Britain "was the beachhead of lean production in Europe"; in Germany there has been a "rapid introduction of lean-production methods"; in France "lean practices . . . spread rapidly"; in Italy "the unions . . . have embraced the new [lean production] work methods" (Moody 1997, 102–5). Moody concludes:

> [L]ean-production methods . . . are now almost universal across the industrial world. They have modified, though not eliminated, the mass-production techniques that preceded them. Like the mass-production techniques of earlier years, these lean mass production methods have spread from manufacturing to almost every kind of work organized along modern lines. (Ibid., 3)

Or, again,

> Wherever one looks in the developed industrial capitalist world, and in most of the more industrialized countries of the South, lean-production methods are either the norm or rapidly spreading. (Ibid., 106)

Moody also notes that most of the most important labor struggles in the contemporary period have been in response to the diffusion of lean production. Regarding the United States he writes:

> One of the most important confrontations of the mid-1990s was the series of local-level strikes that swept G.M. from 1994 through 1997. The

demands of most of these strikes centered on lean issues, such as staffing levels, subcontracting, and health and safety." (Ibid., 30)

A quick perusal of the important journal *Labor Notes* confirms that the same holds for many other sectors as well.

These two points hardly count as a definitive rejection of neo-Fordism. But they are, I believe, sufficient to motivate the critical examination of lean production in the chapters that follow. It is now time to introduce the issues that will guide the analysis over the course of these chapters.

C. Marxian Theory and the Lean Production Model

According to the proponents of the lean production thesis, the global spread of lean production is the most promising response to the global crisis of Fordism. How does this form of capitalist restructuring address the six dimensions of the crisis of Fordism introduced in the first section of this chapter?

1. Lean production institutionalizes a continuous search for innovations that lower the costs of constant capital. A central intent of the just-in-time production system is to reduce to a minimum the amount of raw materials and partially completed parts shipped by suppliers. This is matched by the commitment to reduce buffers in the production process, and to coordinate relations with distributors in order to minimize stocks of unsold inventories. Another goal is to reduce waste as much as possible in the production process. All these measures lower constant capital requirements.

2. The drive to lower circulation time and circulation costs is also an explicit feature of the model. The just-in-time system is designed to make each stage in the production and distribution process respond rapidly to the demands of the succeeding stage. All of the innovations designed to reduce "slack" and make production and distribution "lean" are also clearly designed to reduce circulation time. So are general purpose machines such as robots, computer-controlled machine tools, and automatic guided vehicles; they all speed up the process of transforming raw materials into finished products. The drive to shorten product cycles through concurrent engineering is another feature of the lean production model aiming at a reduction of circulation time.

The disaggregation of production through outsourcing speeds circulation time as well. If all the stages of a production and distribution chain are traversed within a single vertically integrated company, a considerable amount of capital may tarry for quite a while in the circuit of capital before further accumulation occurs. With subcontracting arrangements, spin-offs, spin-ins, joint ventures, and so on, the different stages of the production and distribution process are assigned to different units of capital, each of which proceeds through its own circuit at a much faster rate than capital invested in the vertically integrated firms of Fordism.[37]

3. The tendency for science to be incorporated within the capital accumulation process is heightened in the "new economy." Kenney and Florida (1993) use the phrase as "innovation mediated production" as a synonym for "lean production." They assert that perpetual innovation has become the main form of value creation in capitalism. A necessary condition of perpetual innovation is an extension of the process whereby science becomes incorporated into the circuit of capital accumulation.

4. Advocates of lean production hold that the medium-to-long-term results of the technical and organizational innovations of lean production will be a multiskilled and "empowered" workforce. Many also speak of a workforce that enjoys employment guarantees. Such a workforce, it is claimed, will be vastly more productive and committed than the mass production workers of Fordism.

5. The defenders of the lean production model also insist that true consumer sovereignty is now being instituted for the first time in history, thanks in part to advances in information technologies. Producing the goods and services that consumers actually want ought to aid the process of restoring growth rates in the global economy to what they were prior to the crisis of Fordism.

6. Lastly, the business press is brimming with statements to the effect that relations among different units of capital are increasingly characterized by trust and cooperation within networks of lean production firms.

These claims can be considered under two headings. All six are intended to substantiate the assertion that lean production can be an essential component of a new stage of expansion in the capitalist global economy. I shall return the theme of lean production and globalization in chapter 6 below. The other main issue concerns the final three claims mentioned above. Advocates of lean production implicitly grant that the capital/wage labor relation, the capital/consumer relation, and the relation among units of capital have all been fundamentally flawed in the history of capitalism. But they vehemently reject the Marxian thesis that the flaws lie in the nature of capitalism itself. In lean production these three social relations are supposedly thoroughly transformed. The profound antagonisms that plagued these relations previously are overcome.

This assertion ought to be of tremendous interest to anyone concerned with social theory and practice, especially normative social theory.[38] Those concerned with the fate of Marxian theory in specific obviously ought to take special notice of this assertion. In the strict sense of the term it is never possible to "falsify" a theory (Smith 1997). Nonetheless, if the lean production thesis can be sustained essential tenets of Marxian theory would have to be abandoned, leaving the theoretical edifice as a whole in utter shambles.[39] The heart of the present work, chapters 3–5, will be devoted to an examination of the assertion that lean production brings about a harmony of social interests where antagonisms had reigned before.

CHAPTER TWO

Lean Production and the Capital/Wage Labor Relation (i): The Deskilling Thesis

Factory work exhausts the nervous system to the uttermost; at the same time, it does away with the many-sided play of the muscles, and confiscates every atom of freedom, both in bodily and in intellectual activity. . . . The separation of the intellectual faculties of the production process from manual labor, and the transformation of those faculties into powers exercised by capital over labour, is, as we have already shown, finally completed by large-scale industry erected on the foundation of machinery. The special skill of each individual machine-operator, who has now been deprived of all significance, vanishes as an infinitesimal quantity. (Marx 1976, 548–49)

If, as this passage suggests, there is an inherent drive to deskill the workforce in capitalism, this would corroborate the thesis that the capital/wage labor relation is inherently antagonistic. In this chapter I shall explore the effects of the technologies and forms of social organization of lean production on the skill level of the labor force. Defenders of the so-called new economy insist that skill levels do not in fact tend to decline in lean production. If this is true, then lean production would appear to provide a compelling counterexample to a central tenet of Marxian theory.

In section A I shall present the argument for the presence of a tendency to deskilling in capitalism and some reasons for thinking that this tendency continues to operate in lean production. In section B three general reasons for rejecting the deskilling thesis will be introduced, followed in section C by four arguments for holding that lean production tends to heighten skill levels. Section D examines the responses defenders of each perspective can make to criticisms. The main conclusion of this reconstruction of the debate between defenders and critics of the deskilling thesis is negative: the question whether there is a fundamental capital/labor antagonism in lean production cannot be conclusively resolved through consideration of skill levels alone. In the final section of the chapter a number of claims regarding other dimensions of the capital/labor relation in lean production will be introduced in order to set the stage for chapter 3.

A. Deskilling and Lean Production

The conclusion of Marx's discussion of the capital/wage labor relation in volume I of *Capital* can be summarized in a single statement: the capitalist mode of production is built upon class conflict between capital and labor. The following argument is often thought to be an important strand of the case for this conclusion:

1. The owners and controllers of capital have a basic interest in deskilling the workforce, and generally tend to introduce technologies and forms of work organization that further this interest.
2. Deskilling goes against the basic interests of the workforce.
3. Therefore, there is a fundamental antagonism of interests between these two groups.

The case for the first premise rests on two closely related suppositions, presented most forcefully in Harry Braverman's seminal *Labor and Monopoly Capital*. First, a reduction in labor costs allows more profits to be retained by capital, and a deskilled labor force reduces labor costs, everything else being equal. Deskilled laborers are easily replaced, so wage costs are lower. So too are training costs (Braverman 1974, 79–82). Second, it is easier for management to maintain control over the labor process when workers are deskilled and know they can be easily replaced.

In volume I of *Capital* Marx discussed deskilling in the context of the transition from the craft labor of early factories to the emergence of "detail labor" in manufacturing and machinofacture. In the twentieth century this process has continued with the rise of scientific management (or "Taylorism" after its founder, F. W. Taylor), in which industrial engineers oversee the fragmentation of the work process into a series of discrete operations, none of which require a high exercise of skill. Management then assigns each of these operations to a separate worker. Once complex jobs have been fragmented into a series of discrete operations performed by different workers, knowledge and control of the work process as a whole lies with management, not the worker.

The case for the second premise in the above argument rests on an appeal to what is self-evident: if deskilling leads to lower wages and less control over the labor process, it obviously goes against the interests of labor. Given these two premises, the conclusion follows that technical change in the workplace generally manifests a fundamental antagonism of interests between capital and labor. Marxists who adhere to this perspective are not committed to the claim that deskilling must occur always and everywhere in capitalism. The nature of a given technology, or the resistance of a particular workforce, may prevent deskilling in specific cases. Nonetheless, they claim, deskilling remains the dominant tendency in capitalism. When it is hampered by the nature of a given technology or by the recalcitrance of a specific labor force, there is a general tendency for those who own and control capital to institute a search for different sorts of technologies and more submissive workers.

How should the lean production model introduced in the previous chapter be evaluated from this perspective?[1] Defenders of the deskilling thesis insist that the drive to lower labor costs and to control the labor process does not suddenly dissipate with the rise of lean production. The owners and controllers of capital retain a strong interest in these matters, and so they retain a strong interest in deskilling. From this perspective the model presented in the last chapter appears to juxtapose descriptions of recent economic developments with a massive ideological distortion of the social significance of these developments. The shift from "just-in-case" production to "just-in-time" production, for example, accurately reflects a tendency in contemporary capitalism. In contrast, the claim that the workforce in lean production facilities is "empowered" and "multiskilled" fundamentally misrepresents the dominant tendency operating in labor relations.

There is no shortage of cases in which the technologies and organizational forms characteristic of lean production were introduced with the conscious intention of deskilling the workforce. Parker and Slaughter document numerous instances in part III of their study, *Choosing Sides* (1988). Other examples of contemporary workplaces where deskilled workers are assigned sequences of simple tasks to perform repeatedly are found both in Howard (1985) and Greenbaum (1995). From this perspective lean production appears as a new form of Taylorism, rather than an alternative. In fact, computer-aided manufacturing and other information technologies now associated with lean production may be said to *extend* the reach of management control. These technologies automate a considerable part of the production process, and as Zuboff writes in her influential book *Work in the Age of Intelligent Machines,*

> Automation shares the same goal of Taylorism—to establish managerial control over a knowledge domain that serves as the basis for a division of labor that is minimally dependent upon the skills or disposition of a (shrinking) workforce. (Zuboff 1988, 303)[2]

Also, as computing power is distributed throughout the "networked economy," more and more workers must maintain high levels of attention and concentration on computer screens and printouts. Yet managers regularly fail to provide operators with access to comprehensive information regarding the enterprise, or to the underlying assumptions and algorithms employed in the computer models used in the workplace. Under these circumstances work with computers is neither more interesting nor more skilled.[3] The result is simply a greater level of mental stress for the worker. In this context it is also worth mentioning that the computer provides management with a tool for enhanced monitoring of the labor process, a temptation that appears to free the manager from many of the hassles of supervision, while greatly adding to the stress of the work process (ibid., 325; Rifkin 1995, 188–89).

Special attention has been paid by defenders of the deskilling thesis to the introduction in factories of numerically controlled machine tools and computer-numerically-controlled (CNC) machine tools, technologies that play a prominent role in contemporary lean production systems (although they predate the adaptation of lean production in the West). David Noble (1984) has argued that numerical control was not selected over available record-playback machining technologies simply because of its technical efficiency. Record-playback machinery was rejected because it left skills in the hands of the machinist, thereby limiting capital's control of the labor process. With numerical control, in contrast, skills that had previously withstood the deskilling process, skills that were once embodied in the laborer, are now objectified in the machine.

Shaiken's study of the introduction of CNC tools echoes Noble's conclusion. This technology was intended to shift control of the labor process from the shop floor to the office, where the machines are programmed. His conclusion is worth quoting at some length:

> In the vast majority of cases, the responsibility for writing instructions for the machines had been removed from the shop floor and given to programmers working in offices, even when this was far from optimal technically. Understanding why requires taking a look at owners' motivations in introducing CNC. They told us they introduced CNC partly to improve the machines' speed and flexibility, but also to tighten control over shop operations. By concentrating planning in the relatively small, white-collar programming department, they believed they could specify more uniform procedures for carrying out jobs. Also, since programmers are not responsible for actually running the machines, they have little incentive to use programming to slow the pace of production, the owners felt. As the officers of the Numerical Control Society, an organization of managers and engineers concerned with comput-

ers in manufacturing, wrote in 1981, CNC has put important decisions "in the hands of managerial and professional personnel rather than machine operators." (Shaiken 1985, 293)

If technologies now associated with lean production further deskilling, and if deskilling reveals an inherent antagonism between labor and capital, then it follows that the rise of lean production does not falsify the argument given at the beginning of this section. Before accepting this conclusion, however, we should examine criticisms that have been proposed against both the deskilling thesis in general and its application to lean production in specific.

B. Three Criticisms of the Deskilling Thesis

In this section I shall put aside the question of lean production and examine three general problems with the deskilling thesis. The first two concern the use of this thesis by Marxists. It can be argued that the derivation of a general tendency to deskilling in capitalism rests upon an inadequate understanding of the logic of capital as Marx understood it, and it also appears to be the case that this line of thought undermines practical concerns of great importance to Marx. The third point concerns the notion of skill implicit in the arguments for deskilling. Replies to these points will be postponed until section D.

1. The Logic of Capital

Everything else being equal, the owners and controllers of capital do indeed desire to limit wage costs, limit training costs, and control labor. Deskilling is often an effective manner of attaining these objectives. There is no reason to think, however, that everything else will be equal, either always or even most of the time.

For Marx, the ultimate goal of capital investment is the accumulation of capital. Other considerations may play various roles as means to that end, but capital accumulation alone provides the ultimate objective. Deskilling labor significantly *lessens* the amount of surplus value that can potentially be produced whenever deskilled labor is significantly less productive than skilled labor. If less surplus value can be produced, then less capital can be accumulated. In such circumstances, the "logic of capital" points away from deskilling, and toward a management strategy of developing workers' skills in the labor process (Adler 1990).

This is not to deny that deskilling regularly occurs in capitalism. But it may not be the dominant tendency in capitalism. From the logic of capital the only thing that can be directly deduced in this context is a general tendency for the owners and controllers of capital to attempt to increase the production of surplus value. Whether this can be better done by lowering or by raising skill levels is a thoroughly contingent matter. On this view, therefore, we cannot assume *a priori* that deskilling will necessarily dominate in the epoch of lean production.

2. Deskilling and Marxian Politics

A second issue of special relevance to Marxists concerns the political implications of the deskilling thesis. If one holds that lean production leads to a significant deskilling of the labor process, then it is plausible to claim that an antagonism between labor and capital remains in place. But this defense of Marxism may come at the cost of having to abandon the heart of Marx's position.

Wage laborers are hardly the first class in history to be exploited. Marx insisted, however, that wage laborers in capitalism—unlike slaves or serfs in previous modes of production—can develop both an awareness of universal social interdependence and the capacity to organize society themselves. In Marx's view these are necessary conditions of the possibility of the working class being able to bring about socialism. The more one holds that the labor force has been thoroughly deskilled by technologies and forms of social organization, the less plausible it is to assert that the working class can develop the awareness and capacity required for it to play this political role (Adler 1990). In brief, the more the working class is subject to deskilling, the less capable it is of self-emancipation.

There are a number of political options at this point. One might follow Marcuse and try to search for other revolutionary agents. The political problem with this option is that the most likely groups to take the place of the working class as a revolutionary agent (oppressed races and nationalities, the so-called underclass, students, those with non-mainstream sexual preferences, etc.) are probably far too marginal to pose a significant threat to the established order. Once this is acknowledged, one is faced with four alternatives: indulging in individual acts of negation that have few positive social consequences (anarchism); abandoning revolutionary politics for reformist politics (social democracy); moving completely to the right; or abandoning politics altogether. If the last path is taken, this can be done in the spirit of tragic defiance exemplified by Adorno, or in Baudrillard's spirit of mindless playfulness. Whichever route is chosen, one ends up far from revolutionary Marxism.

Of course, this in itself does not establish that the deskilling thesis is incorrect. And this reasoning would certainly not be pursued by the new capitalist utopians who defend the lean production model. But it does suggest that the deskilling thesis provides an uncertain basis for a defense against the claim that labor relations in the "new economy" have rendered Marxism obsolete.

The first two objections to the deskilling thesis obviously hold little interest to those not already committed to the Marxian research program. The third general objection to the deskilling thesis is another matter. It is based on a consideration of the meaning of the terms employed in this thesis.

3. The Concept of Skill

The notion of "deskilling" obviously cannot be defined independently from the notion of "skill." Braverman and other defenders of the deskilling thesis appear to employ a notion of skill derived from the craft model of production. In craft labor workers become skilled through years of experience, giving them a tacit knowledge of the production process lacking in both managers and beginning workers. Such embodied knowledge grants them a form of power on the shop floor, a power manifested in the ability to control the sequence of operations they perform and the pace at which they work.

Given this definition of skill, a plausible case can be made that the transition from handicraft production to manufacturing resulted in widespread deskilling. And, given this definition, a case can be made that introduction of the technologies now associated with lean production has extended deskilling even further. With computer-numerically-controlled tools, for instance, the knowledge of how to use the tool is objectified in the program running the machine. It is now the program that dictates the sequence of operations to perform and the pace to which the machinist must conform.

Is it possible to define skill in a different manner? Paul Adler has proposed an alternative conception that goes beyond tacit or embodied knowledge. For Adler, labor is more skilled if it involves more training, higher levels of responsibility, more abstract tasks and goals, and greater functional interdependence (Adler 1988, 2). He argues that his definition accounts better for our shared intuitions regarding the sorts of jobs that are skilled. Airline pilots or surgeons must follow established procedures in every detail. Having little job autonomy, they do not seem to meet the criteria of the Bravermanian definition of skill. And yet the training time and responsibility connected with these occupations are such that most people (correctly) consider pilots and surgeons to be highly skilled. Similarly, manufacturing and office jobs that appear deskilled when measured in terms of craft standards may have to be evaluated quite differently with this more nuanced concept of skill.[4]

Zuboff invokes the same distinction in her analysis of information technologies in the contemporary workplace. She acknowledges that computerizing the workplace tends to devalue the embodied, tacit, skills of the laborer, a process she terms "automating." But information technologies also allow "informating," a quite different transformation. Information technologies generate data bases in which complex and extended relationships in the workplace are represented in symbolic form. Informating occurs when operators are granted access to these data bases. These operators can then develop various skills to replace their now obsolete embodied skills, including:

- the ability to comprehend the referent of abstract data;
- the ability to interpret this data within a conceptual framework, an elaborated language;
- the ability to form inductions and deductions from the given data, and the ability to put those inductions and deductions into practice through operations on the abstract representations of material processes; and
- the ability to revise those inductions and deductions based on feedback from data bases modified by those operations.

Zuboff summarizes the emergence of these new skills as follows:

> The operator must first think about what has to be done. Second, he or she must know how data elements (abstract cues) correspond to actual processes and their systematic relations. Third, the operator must have a conception of the information system itself, in order to know how actions taken at the information interface can result in appropriate outcomes. Fourth, having decided what to do and executed that command, he or she must scan new data and check for results. Each of these processes folds back upon a kind of thinking that can stand independent from the physical context. (Zuboff 1988, 73; see also 192)

In this manner the workplace becomes more transparent to the worker, as the manipulations of abstract symbols allows an understanding of and control over remote relations in the production and distribution process (ibid., 386; Kenney and Florida 1993, 15).

To conclude, defenders of the deskilling thesis rely on a traditional notion of skill based on the practices of craft labor. Both Adler and Zuboff have shown that quite different definitions of skill are possible. In principle, at least, new sorts of skills could arise in lean production that more than compensate for any loss of craft skills.

Even if we assume that deskilling does not follow from the logic of capital, that there is a tension between this thesis and central aspects of Marx's theory, and that there are different notions of skill than the one implicit in the deskilling thesis, the central question of this chapter remains unanswered: does the lean production model involve a net decrease in the skill level of the workforce or not? Defenders of this model must do more than point out general difficulties with the deskilling thesis. They must spell out the concrete mechanisms in lean production that tend to enhance skills.

C. Lean Production and the Enhancement of Skill

Advocates of the "new economy" have proposed four different arguments to support their claim that lean production tends to increase the overall skill level of the labor force in the medium-to-long term. The first two of these can be dismissed fairly quickly, while the third and fourth considerations are far more substantial.

One straightforward defense of the claim that lean production enhances skill levels appeals directly to the nature of the technologies now associated with lean production. Consider, for example, the following passage from an influential article on the computerization of the workplace:

> It is becoming evident that advanced computer technology calls for a radical change in traditional work practices. The old "scientific management" method of dividing work into discrete tasks that require little skill or training becomes obsolete in a computerized workplace. (Hoerr et. al. 1989, 358)

Here we have a fairly strong version of technological determinism: the sorts of technologies employed in lean production simply rule out management attempts to deskill the workforce. This strong version of technological determinism is no more plausible here than elsewhere. No one who has studied part III of Parker and Slaughter's *Choosing Sides* (1988) could deny that the technologies associated with lean production have in fact often been used to deskill the workforce. In Zuboff's terminology, it is indisputable that these technologies can be used as part of an "automating" strategy aiming to take the operator "out of the loop."[5]

A second move found in the lean production literature is to blame the attempts at deskilling that have occurred in lean production on "bad habits" left over from past managerial practices. This second argument is also found in the *Business Week* article just mentioned:

> The old idea that a manager's main function is to control workers is replaced with the concept that a manager should encourage employ-

ees to use initiative. This goes against the grain of everything managers have been taught since the early years of the century. (Hoerr et al. 1989, 359)

This argument immediately runs into an insuperable difficulty: there is no shortage of relatively young managers who have instituted deskilling strategies, managers who were not socialized into the "old way" of doing things. Managers, young or old, have clear interests in maintaining traditional hierarchical organizations, and regularly are able to use their power to further these interests (Appelbaum and Batt 1994, 12, 131; Kochan, Katz, and McKersie 1986, xiv).

The third response by defenders of lean production to the deskilling thesis is far more powerful. This is a contemporary version of Adam Smith's "invisible hand" argument. Smith argued that in market economies we do not need to appeal to the altruism of social agents in order to further the social good. The pursuit of rational self-interest in the market can further common interests whether or not individual social agents intend this result. It is in the rational self-interest of the owners and controllers of capital that their firms flourish in the market. The selection mechanism of the market favors lean production firms that enhance the skill level of their labor force. This will tend to lead the owners and controllers of capital to encourage skill formation in the workforce. Since this is in the interests of labor as well, we may conclude that the interests of labor and capital are ultimately reconciled. We have what management theorists love to term a "win-win" situation, as opposed to a zero-sum game in which the interests of one group are furthered only if losses are inflicted on the other.

This argument stands or falls on the strength of the claim that the market operates as a selection mechanism favoring firms in which skill levels are enhanced. In the literature on lean production five considerations have been introduced to justify this assertion.

(i) The technologies of lean production allow shorter runs of more diverse products, and thus a faster rate of product innovation. Since every shift in products requires adjustments to the process of production, the rate of process innovation tends to increase as well. Continuous innovation can be best furthered when the factory and the office become laboratories where the intellectual labor of shop-floor workers is fused with that of researchers and engineers.

In the factory as laboratory the distinction between intellectual and physical labor that Marx indicated and that Harry Braverman raised to the fundamental contradiction of modern capitalism is at some fundamental level mitigated. . . . [T]he new world of manufacturing will not be an environment of smart machines and automaton-like workers. In fact, this mode of organizing production will surely fail. (Kenney and Florida 1993, 68)

The pursuit of continuous improvement (*kaizen*) by the owners and controllers of capital thus leads them to seek to overcome the split between mental labor and manual labor. Their self-interest leads them to mobilize the intelligence of wage laborers within labor processes where creative challenges must be continually confronted (Imai 1986). This mobilization furthers "learning by doing," which in turn leads to incremental improvements that in the long-term provide greater productivity advances than radically new process technologies (Dertouzos et al. 1991).

(ii) Positions devoted to simple machine repair, housekeeping, materials-ordering, and so on, do not "add value" to the final product. The owners and controllers of capital thus have an incentive to eliminate such positions; this is part of what it means to for production become "lean." The number of these positions can be reduced if production line workers take over these tasks, thereby eliminating the need for separate departments of indirect workers. For this to occur production line workers must become multiskilled (Koike 1988).[6] Lean production thus involves the end of detail labor; no longer is each worker assigned a single task to perform repeatedly.

(iii) As the technologies of lean production lead to a proliferation of products in the social world, product quality becomes ever more important to market success; different quality levels allow consumers to distinguish one commodity from another serving the same purpose. Quality problems are best diagnosed and corrected immediately on the line by workers themselves, rather than left to a specialized quality control departments after the production process has been completed. Quality improvements thus also demand multiskilling. Workers on the shop floor must develop problem-solving skills, such as statistical quality control and other methods of root cause analysis.

(iv) Lean production employs highly complex technology systems. When a number of complex production systems are combined, the result is a system of such hypercomplexity that it is impossible for engineers to foresee all the results that may occur. Under these circumstances it is all but inevitable that emergencies will arise. If workers have been vigilant, curious, and committed, and if they have developed the requisite high level of skill, chances improve that they will be able to respond to emergencies successfully. Otherwise, catastrophes may well occur.[7] And so the owners and controllers of capital have a clear incentive to develop a skilled workforce that can avoid catastrophes (Hirschhorn 1984; Bessant and Chisholm 1989, 314; Schumann et al. 1990–91, 18; Zuboff 1988, 201).

(v) In lean production a consumer order provides the signal for a delivery to be made; a delivery order provides the signal for final assembly; a final assembly order provides the signal for a finished part to be delivered;

and so on, all the way back to the initial stage in the production process. The goals of this "just-in-time" system are to reduce inventory costs to the greatest degree possible, and to allow production to shift rapidly from one product to another (Sayer 1986). The attainment of these goals, however, comes at a cost. If inventories are present, a stoppage in one part of a plant need not result in production ceasing elsewhere. Without the buffer provided by inventories a stoppage in one area may quickly bring the production process as a whole to a halt. This fragility can be reduced considerably if the workforce is skilled and diligent throughout the process as a whole. And so the rational self-interest of the owners and controllers of capital leads them to encourage workers to develop the skills and maintain the degree of diligence necessary for lean production to function smoothly.

These five points underlying the third argument for claiming that there is a tendency in lean production for skill levels to increase can be summarized as follows: Firms operate in a competitive and ever-more rapidly changing economic environment. Enhancing the skill levels of the workforce increases the chances of a firm surviving and flourishing in this environment. And so it is in the rational self-interest of the management of lean production facilities to do all it can to ensure that the skill level of the workforce as a whole rises. This course of action is in the interests of workers as well. And so the "invisible hand" lives.

The fourth and final point introduced by advocates of lean production in this context refers to the empirical evidence on the question at hand. There have been a number of studies investigating whether or not there is a secular trend for the skills of the working class as a whole to be lowered due to technological and organizational changes in the workplace. The consensus view appears to be that the empirical evidence does *not* substantiate such a trend (Adler 1987, 1988; Adler and Borys 1989; Kelley 1986; Spenner 1983; Cappelli 1993; Howell 1994). Summarizing such studies regarding the United States Gordon writes,

> In the aggregate, it does appear that "cognitive" requirements—the need for reasoning ability and specific knowledge on the job—and "interactive" capacities—the ability in particular to coordinate and manage people—have both grown steadily over at least the past thirty years. (Gordon 1996, 183)[8]

D. The Deskilling Debate Continued

How might theorists who defend the deskilling thesis respond to the sorts of objections made in the previous two sections? We can begin with the argument against the claim that a dominant tendency toward deskilling can be derived from the logic of capital. According to this argument, the drive to accumulate leads the owners and controllers of capital to seek to increase the production of surplus value, and a skilled workforce may well produce more surplus value than an unskilled one. Advocates of the deskilling thesis could simply point out in response that what matters for accumulation is not the amount of surplus value that can potentially be *produced,* but the amount of surplus value actually *appropriated* by capital over time. A skilled workforce is often in a position to insist that a significant portion of productivity gains are distributed back to workers in the form of higher wages. If this pattern of distribution continues for an extended period, a portion of what in principle could have been surplus value eventually becomes part of the value of labor power instead. In contrast, measures that deskill the workforce further the ability of the owners and controllers of capital to appropriate surplus value. Since profits, not productivity levels, are their ultimate concern, the "logic of capital" leads managers to rank the retention of control over the production process (and thus over wage rates) higher than increasing efficiency. Since deskilling furthers such control, deskilling measures will tend to be pursued whenever feasible.

What of the claim that the market operates as a selection mechanism favoring lean production firms in which skill levels are enhanced? In the following passage Zuboff lists factors that make it likely that the "informating" strategy of enhancing skills in the workforce will offer advantages to capital. She concludes, however, by noting that deskilling ("automating") strategies may be more advantageous to capital in sectors where these factors are absent:

> [R]apidly changing markets that put a premium on flexibility and responsiveness, competitive conditions that offer opportunities for value-added products or services, substantial variation in customer needs, short production cycles or variability in raw materials, interdependence among production operations or between production and other business functions, the persistence of "unknowns" in the core production process, opportunities for increased quality or decreased costs of production or services, the need to avoid the high levels of cost and risk associated with error when computer systems are broadly integrated, and the perceived need to develop and maintain a motivated and committed workforce—these are factors that contribute to the appropriateness of an informating strategy. Where these factors are *not* present to any significant degree, an automating strategy is likely to be most feasible. (Zuboff 1988, 305; see also 161)

Unfortunately, she does not attempt to estimate what proportion of economic activity falls under each heading. If a higher percentage fits the "automating" paradigm, then there is reason to expect a net loss of skill in the economy as a whole.

There are also stages in the product cycle in almost every sector where high volume production at low cost is more significant than flexibility or innovation. Given Zuboff's reasoning, a strong case can be made that the market operates as a selection mechanism favoring deskilling during these periods.

Another relevant consideration concerns the way past technical choices "lock in" future possibilities. If technologies were employed at some point in time in a way that did not enhance workers' skills, it may be quite difficult to reverse matters later:

> A narrow approach to automation may fail to select or develop a workforce that is prepared for the later challenges of informating. It may also incorporate forms of technological design and implementation that create barriers to further development by "building-out" most requirements for intelligent human participation or failing to develop those aspects of organizational culture that would be resources in an informating approach. . . . (S)uch a limited approach can become an impediment to later efforts to utilize the technology's informating capacity. (ibid., 184–85)

As a result, deskilling may be pervasive throughout the economy as a concrete matter of fact, whatever the force of abstract arguments for enhancing skills might be.

This conclusion is reinforced if we reflect on the reasoning process of the financial officers who must approve investments in new technologies. These managers have been trained to consider expenditures on new technologies justified if and only if they substitute capital for labor or increase output. These sorts of effects can be estimated in dollars and cents, allowing a relatively straightforward quantitative comparison between anticipated benefits and investment costs. It is much more difficult to quantify the benefits that come from using technologies to enhance skills. Arguments appealing to these benefits, therefore, are less likely to be made effectively by the champions of new technologies within the enterprise, and less likely to determine the objectives set by the firm. It thus remains likely that management will continue to look at labor as a cost to be reduced, or as a mere means to pump out increased output. The more often such a perspective is taken, the stronger the case for the deskilling thesis.

All of the responses mentioned thus far count for little if the empirical evidence is overwhelmingly against the deskilling thesis. In the face of this evidence defenders of the thesis make a number of points. One is that some of the empirical studies in question count work as skilled that ought not to be so counted. Consider, for instance, the case of a "multiskilled" operator who performs a variety of tasks in the work process. If each of these tasks taken singly does not involve a high level of skill, does the mere fact that they are combined necessarily result in a more highly skilled worker? An affirmative answer to this question is by no means obvious (Graham 1996; Yanarella 1996).

Another response is to refer to studies that project what the most rapidly growing job categories of the future will be. According to the U.S. Bureau of Labor Statistics, symbolic analysts in knowledge-intensive occupations will account for only 13 percent of projected job growth between 1994 and 2005.

It is now time for the critics of the deskilling thesis to take the floor once again. They would no doubt insist that their opponents continue to ignore the net increase in the substantive complexity, responsibility, abstract reasoning, and complex interdependence of jobs connected with the use of technologies in the "networked economy."[9] They would also point out that their case doesn't rest upon the claim that traditionally knowledge-intensive occupations will grow the fastest in the era of lean production. More crucial is the avowal that other occupations besides those of professional symbolic analysts will become more knowledge-intensive.[10] The projections of the Bureau of Labor Statistics do not undermine this prediction in the least.

Most of all, perhaps, critics of the deskilling thesis would insist that their opponents have failed to comprehend how the market will operate as a selection mechanism in the period we are presently entering. Management recalcitrance and the lingering effects of past practices indeed may prevent enterprises from enhancing the skills of their workforce for an extended period of time. Managers may well introduce new technologies and organizational structures with the intention of deskilling the workforce. But as the Rolling Stones said so eloquently, you can't always get what you want. Over time these enterprises will be at a competitive disadvantage. In the long term, some of them will fall by the wayside. Others will adjust. In the case of computer-numerically-controlled (CNC) machines in specific, Kelley and Harrison (1992) suggest that there has been a reversal of attempts to use these machines to deskill operators. Among recent adopters of this technology, two-thirds involve blue collar programming, which develops a new type of skill.

Similarly, it could be argued that over time there will be fewer and fewer sectors of the economy where continuous innovation is not significant, and this can best be fostered by a skilled workforce. Also, the rise of lean production in sectors previously thought to be "mature" has given the lie to traditional product cycle theory. Flexibility and innovation remain central throughout the life of more and more products; there are fewer and fewer sectors where high volume production at low cost is the only thing that matters for long stretches of time (Ohtani et al. 1997).

Finally, it may be true that the benefits to a firm of a skilled workforce cannot be quantified as easily as lower labor costs or increased output. But sufficient quantitative evidence is available to assert that when firms adopt bundles of related innovative work practices to increase worker participation productivity improves significantly (Jarboe and Yudken 1997; Ichniowski et al. 1996). Quantitative improvements to the bottom line have also been substantiated. Edward Lawler of the University of Southern California recently completed a study in which he examined financial indicators (sales, equity, assets, stockholder investment, etc.) from 216 "Fortune 1000" firms four times at three year intervals. He distinguished firms that focussed on process control to improve performance ("total quality management," TQM), firms that sought to improve performance through downsizing ("reengineering"), and firms that concentrated on upgrading workers' skills to improve efficiency and customer service. He concludes,

> Each of these three strategies produces an effect, but our studies indicate that employee involvement is a stronger driver of financial performance than TQM or reengineering. (Quoted in Ross 1998)

According to Lawler, companies that focussed heavily on TQM had returns on investment that were not essentially different from those that did not, and companies that primarily engaged in reengineering enjoyed a return on investment 2 percent higher than those that did not. In contrast, the returns to companies emphasizing employee involvement exceeded those that didn't by almost 4 percent (ibid.).

Besides this quantitative evidence, advocates of lean production insist that qualitative considerations (the degree of innovativeness of a product or service, its ease of use, its caliber, and so on) are increasing central to success or failure in markets characterized by ever-increasingly product proliferation. Firms that do not take such matters into account when they allocate funds and set policies are sure to be at a competitive disadvantage over time. And these qualitative considerations are furthered when the skills of the workforce are enhanced.

The reconstruction of the debate between advocates and critics of the deskilling thesis has reached a point of diminishing returns. From this point on, I believe, both sides would for the most part repeat variations of the arguments already mentioned.[11] What conclusions ought to be drawn from this debate?

In my view the deskilling thesis has not been definitively falsified, either in general or in its specific applicability to lean production. But neither has it been conclusively established. In chapters 3 and 5 below I shall refer to the distinction in lean production between a "core" workforce employed by major assemblers and a "periphery" workforce laboring for subcontractors (and subcontractors of subcontractors). Generally speaking, the arguments given by advocates of the "new economy" for the reskilling thesis are most plausible for certain groups of workers in the core, while the deskilling thesis appears to hold for many of those working on the periphery of lean production networks.[12] While there are more workers in the latter category than the former, a slight lowering of the skills of many workers could in principle be compensated by a major increase in the skills of a relative few. I do not know of any study that establishes any definitive conclusion here, one way or the other (Lester 1998, 234–40). It follows that any attempt to use the deskilling thesis as a foundation for the Marxian claim that there is a fundamental antagonism between labor and capital is questionable. An ambitious edifice built upon such a weak foundation is bound to be unstable.

At this point I would like to shift the discussion away from the deskilling thesis. The new capitalist utopians do not stop with the claim that the "new economy" reconciles the interests of capital and labor by raising skill levels. They believe that lean production brings about a harmony of interests between capital and labor going far beyond this. Since in my view the Marxian position regarding the capital/labor relation is not tied to the deskilling thesis, the greatest challenges to this position involve these other topics.

E. Beyond the Deskilling Thesis

In section C, I presented a number of "invisible hand" arguments to the effect that the interests of capital in the age of lean production tend to lead to practices that enhance the skills of the workforce. In the present section three other arguments of this sort will be introduced, all of which are meant to further substantiate the conclusion that lean production tends to overcome the antagonism between labor and capital.

(1) If the intelligence of the worker is to be mobilized, if the worker is to develop a variety of distinct skills, and if worker vigilance and curiosity are to be sustained, then the worker cannot be treated as an isolated individual. The best way to attain these goals is to have workers participate in teams in which a variety of tasks are rotated (Aoki 1988). This benefits management by leading to a more productive workforce. Quality improves,[13] it is easier to cover for absences and turnover, and there is a larger available skill base for overtime and emergencies. Most importantly, teams bring about a collective intelligence that furthers the process of innovation and diffusion:

> The team makes the extraction of intellectual (and manual) labor a quintessentially social, intersubjective, and collective process. . . .

Transfer or rotation of workers enhances the process of knowledge acquisition and diffusion. (Kenney and Florida 1993, 39–40)

Workers benefit in a variety of ways as well. Rotation in teams develops more of their capacities, alleviates boredom, and reduces the danger of injuries from repetitive motions.

(2) The team structure has a number of profound indirect effects as well. If teams are to function effectively, they must have access to information regarding the enterprise, including information that has customarily been monopolized by the managerial stratum. Once workers are given access to this information, teams are in a position to take on certain managerial functions themselves. In places where this has occurred, Zuboff writes,

> [T]he degree of organizational integration made possible by the presence of networked real-time systems seemed to obviate the role of the manager as someone who supervised others, gathered information, and controlled communication. (Zuboff 1988, 265)

This allows firms to lower the indirect costs associated with lower-level management and supervisors. But perhaps just as significant is the effect on the organizational dynamic of the enterprise. The traditional claim of management to power and status rested on its privileged access to knowledge. With this gone, workplaces structured in terms of top-down authority tend to give way to sites organized according to principles of dialogue. Once the operations of the workplace have been computerized, they take on objective form in a text, which evokes "the frequent necessity of pooling intellective insight in order to achieve the best possible interpretation of the text" (ibid., 197).[14] Managers are but one voice in this ongoing dialogue, a dialogue that requires truly listening to the voices of others:

> In addition to the quality of skills, the fruitfulness of such collaboration will depend largely upon the grace and enthusiasm that individuals bring to the participative process. Managers who place a premium on control and workers who feel disaffected do not make good colleagues, for the spirit of hypothesis generation and testing is above all a collegial one. (Ibid., 201)[15]

In this manner lean production technologies can lead to a "new covenant" between labor and management, aiming to create "relations of equality" within a "posthierarchical" learning environment at the workplace (ibid., 309, 394, 401). Of course, this does not mean that there are no longer any differentials of knowledge, responsibility, or power. But "they can no longer be assumed. Instead, they shift and flow and develop their character in relation to the situation, the task, and the actors at hand" (ibid., 401–2).

(3) If skilled and attentive workers are absolutely crucial to the successful use of lean production technologies, it follows that those who own and control capital cannot meet their objectives if workers are treated as replaceable parts. Those who own and control capital must incorporate the workforce as a partner, offering guarantees of employment and profit-sharing to keep laborers committed to the firm (Shimada and MacDuffie 1986). Employment guarantees and profit sharing are clearly in the interest of workers, who thereby attain a level of security far beyond the norm in the Fordist period. But the interests of management are furthered as well. When workers are loyal to a firm, shared knowledge does not leak to competitors, and the costs of training are not wasted. The result is a system of "reciprocal obligation" rather than one of mutual antagonism:

> To make this system work, of course, management must offer its full support to the factory workforce and . . . make the sacrifices to ensure job security that have historically been offered only to valued professionals. It truly is a system of reciprocal obligation. (Womack et al. 1990, 102)

This might sound more than a bit hollow in light of the high levels of layoffs that have accompanied the adaptation of lean production practices in the United States and elsewhere. Many advocates of the new system, however, insist that this is a shortsighted strategy that must be reversed if lean production firms wish to be successful in the medium-to-long term (Handy 1994).

If these three arguments capture the essence of work relations in the "new economy," Marx's perspective would be hopelessly irrelevant to contemporary capitalism for reasons that go far beyond the shortcomings of the deskilling thesis. The claim that capitalism necessarily rests upon a fundamental antagonism between labor and capital would be refuted once and for all. In the "new way" of labor relations, declare the advocates of lean production,

> [M]utual interests are emphasized. Management shares information about the business. Labor shares responsibility for making it succeed. (Hoerr et al. 1989, 362)

Before we jump to the conclusion that the Marxian account of the capital/wage labor relation has been superseded, however, we should first recall exactly what that account is. This task will be taken up in the beginning of the following chapter.

CHAPTER THREE

Lean Production and the
Capital/Wage Labor Relation (ii):
Structural Coercion, Exploitation,
and Real Subsumption

As we have seen, much of the discussion regarding the capital/wage labor relation deals with the question of deskilling. Marx's own discussion of this relation, however, focussed more on three different notions: structural coercion, exploitation, and real subsumption. These notions define the social context within which the technologies of the workplace are introduced in Marx's view. The notions of structural coercion, exploitation, and real subsumption have to do with *ownership* of (and *access* to) the technologies used to produce and distribute goods and services, the *ultimate end* to which those technologies are put, and the *means* that are employed in order to attain that end, respectively.

In volume I of *Capital* Marx argued at great length that capitalism rests upon a basic inequality: one class possesses sufficient economic resources to purchase means of production and means of subsistence, while another class lacks such resources. From this asymmetry in property relations Marx went on to derive a necessary tendency for *structural coercion* to arise. Those without access to means of production and means of subsistence are forced by the structure of their situation to sell their labor power to those who own the means of production and subsistence:

> [T]he "free" worker . . . makes a voluntary agreement, i.e. is compelled by social conditions to sell the whole of his active life, his very capacity for labour, in return for the price of his customary means of subsistence, to sell his birthrate for a mess of pottage. (Marx 1976, 382)[1]

For Marx, there is a direct link between the concept of structural coercion and the notion of *exploitation:* those who own and control capital are generally able to impose a wage contract whose terms allow them to appropriate an economic surplus created by wage laborers:

> Capital developed into a coercive relation, and this compels the work-
> ing class to do more work than would be required by the narrow cir-
> cle of its own needs. As an agent in producing the activity of others, as
> an extractor of surplus labour and an exploiter of labour-power, it sur-
> passes all earlier systems of production . . . in its energy and its quality
> of unbounded and ruthless activity. (Ibid., 424–25)

The owners and controllers of capital also necessarily tend to transform the
labor process, in order to increase the amount of surplus produced by the
workers. Marx termed this transformation the *real subsumption* of labor under the alien power of capital, as opposed to the merely formal subsumption that occurs with the purchase of wage labor:

> With the real subsumption of labour under capital a complete (and
> constantly repeated) revolution takes place in the mode of produc-
> tion, in the productivity of the workers and in the relations between
> workers and capitalists. (Ibid., 1035)[2]

An economic system based upon structural coercion, exploitation,
and the real subsumption of labor under capital, is one in which the goal of
economic life is capital accumulation, with wage laborers serving as means
to the end of accumulation. This arrangement, Marx thought, systematically
furthers the interests of those who own and control capital, while it systematically hampers the interests of working men and women. The claim that
there is a fundamental conflict of interests between capital and labor thus
does not stand or fall with the deskilling thesis. Marx derived this claim from
the persistence of structural coercion, exploitation, and real subsumption
in capitalism. The question of deskilling is but one issue falling under the
third category.

Marx's criticism of the capital/wage labor relation would be refuted
if it could be shown that structural coercion, exploitation, and the real subsumption of labor under an alien power no longer hold in the "new economy." Many arguments formulated by the defenders of lean production imply precisely this.

A. Structural Coercion

Marx held that the owners and controllers of capital, on the one hand,
and working men and women, on the other, do not meet as equals in the labor market. Workers' lack of access to means of production and means of
subsistence subjects them to a form of coercion that is not inflicted on the
representatives of capital. Job guarantees, however, secure access to means

of production and means of consumption. An investigation of structural coercion in the "new economy" thus should begin with a consideration of lean production and employment guarantees. In the literature on the "new economy" three perspectives are articulated on this issue, the third of which provides a serious challenge to the Marxian perspective.

Many advocates of the "new economy" believe both that contemporary economic restructuring will not result in guarantees of employment, and that this is to be applauded. In their view the ability to shift jobs repeatedly over the course of a lifetime manifests the positive capacity to redefine yourself as contexts change (Kelly 1998). This position is the business school version of the postmodern affirmation of fragmented and multiple identities. The idea that lifetime employment is not on the agenda has great empirical plausibility.[3] But proponents of this first view appear unable to distinguish between forms of subjectivity flexible enough to renegotiate definitions of self in the course of free interactions with others, and forms of subjectivity where external market pressures result in "the corrosion of character" and generalized anxiety (Sennett 1998; Elliott and Atkinson 1998). The rhetoric of freedom here masks the continued coercive powers of capital (See Smith 1993a, chapter 8).

A second strand of thought in the lean production literature shifts from talk of guarantees of employment to guarantees of "employability" (Kantor 1995). The thesis here is that in the "new economy" successful employers will be those who guarantee their workers access to state-of-the-art skills, so that they will be employable elsewhere even if economic conditions lead to layoffs. Such a vague and unenforceable promise does not seem to me to count as a fundamental transformation of the capital/wage labor relation. It certainly does not remove the structural coercion of which Marx spoke (Lester 1998, 276).

This leaves a third view, from which it is possible to extract an argument justifying the assertion that structural coercion does not hold in the "new economy." The argument rests on the claim that lean production will mark a radical rupture with the way labor markets have functioned previously in the history of capitalism. Labor costs have usually been categorized as variable costs to be kept as low as possible by management. This tends to change with lean production, although management shortsightedness may obscure this for an extended period of time in certain firms and regions.[4] High levels of training, a deep commitment to the process of continuous improvement, and the willing cooperation of the workforce when new technologies are introduced, are all required if lean production is to function most effectively. These demands can best be met if workers are granted lifetime employment. Laborers are more forthcoming with suggestions to improve productivity when they are assured that they will not design themselves out of a job. In the view favored by Kochan and colleagues,

[I]mplementing the practices of lean production per se does not determine success. What is required is an organization characterized by flexibility, problem solving, and motivation, which lean practices are designed to encourage. In some plants, however, lean production practices have been accompanied by considerable downsizing and/or layoffs that served to counteract the behavioral and motivational benefits of these practices. (Kochan et al. 1997, 309)

This suggests that the selection mechanism of the market will tend to favor companies that combine lean production with employment guarantees. Such companies would enjoy the added benefit of being able to fully recoup their training costs, unlike enterprises in which workers leave the firm that trained them. Lean production, in short, works best when labor costs are treated as fixed rather than as variable costs (Womack et al. 1990; Tapscott and Caston 1993; Tapscott 1996).

Workers enjoying guaranteed employment would seem to escape the structural coercion discussed by Marx. They do not have the threat of unemployment hanging over their heads day in and day out. If this were indeed a long-term tendency in the "new economy," one of the three considerations underlying the claim that there is an inherent antagonism between labor and capital would appear to be no longer valid.

I believe that there are good reasons to reject this perspective. In the remainder of the present section five counterarguments will be presented against this line of thought.

(1) In the cases used by defenders of lean production themselves to illustrate their argument, only a relatively small proportion of workers are offered lifetime employment. These are workers in larger "core" plants, primarily manufacturing assembly plants and office headquarters. A much larger "periphery" of workers employed by smaller subcontractors are not granted this benefit.[5] In Japan, for instance, lifetime job security is offered to less than one third of the workforce according to Parker and Slaughter, while Price puts the figure at 20–25 percent (Parker and Slaughter 1988, 60; Price 1992, J5; Lester 1998, 67).

Whatever the precise figure, there is nothing in the lean production model to prevent the relatively small percentage of workers enjoying lifetime employment from declining over time. Even without layoffs, jobs will still be eliminated in core firms by attrition whenever productivity advances outstrip growth in market demand (Aronowitz and DiFazio 1994, 25, 49–50). When this occurs, a growing percentage of workers may find themselves working in part-time or temporary employment, where employers have the "flexibility" to hire or fire them at will. In other words, the de facto job security of the labor force as a whole may well decline in lean production, even if certain individual workers continue to enjoy job guarantees.[6]

For the labor force as a whole, structural coercion may thus be increased, not alleviated, by lean production.

(2) Lean production has proven more productive than "Fordist" production. The firms that initially mastered the technologies and organizational structures associated with it have won considerable surplus profits as a result. Guarantees of employment are relatively painless to provide when a firm is among the first to shift to more profitable technologies and modes of organization. As innovations are diffused, however, early innovators face the threat of losing surplus profits. As lean production spreads and profits come under increasing pressure, job losses may soon follow, job guarantees or no job guarantees. In other words, the job guarantees proclaimed by some to be intrinsically tied to lean production may represent temporary benefits stemming from the competitive advantage of initial innovators. If so, we cannot say that a basic transformation in the dynamic of the capital/wage labor relation has occurred.[7]

(3) In lean production firms today employment "guarantees" are management policies, not formally guaranteed rights. It is true, for example, that in Japan many lean production firms have resorted to cuts in executive salaries, the temporary elimination of stock dividends, and investment in retraining, in order to avoid layoffs. Despite this, however, management retains the ultimate "right" to fire. This right is extremely important to those who own and control capital. Again and again they have refused to allow employment guarantees to be written into contracts on the grounds that this would limit their "flexibility" (Kenney and Florida 1993, 281). Needless to say, workers lack a symmetrical ability to depose of management.[8]

(4) The owners and controllers of capital retain the ultimate power to shut down plants and invest elsewhere. Even in the absence of an explicit threat to take this course of action, those who sell their labor power are forced to take this possibility into account. And even if presently employed workers are assured that they would be offered positions at a new site, the disruption this would impose on them and their communities is generally quite severe. The implicit threat of capital flight thus may coerce wage laborers to accept contracts they would not accept in the absence of this threat, whether or not they enjoy "job guarantees." With developments in communication and transportation technologies, the implicit threat of capital flight to overseas plants and offices weighs more heavily upon all categories of workers with each passing day—job guarantees or no job guarantees.

It is true that capital mobility is never absolute. If an enterprise has made a significant investment in fixed capital in a particular region, threats to shut down production and move elsewhere may not be credible. This remains true in lean production. Yet as the pace of innovation quickens, fixed capital investments become obsolete more rapidly. This implies that the period in which threats to walk away lack plausibility tends to shorten.

A second factor limiting capital mobility arises whenever a workforce in a particular region enjoys a monopoly (or near monopoly) on essential technical skills. In lean production there are certainly some design, engineering, and marketing skills that are not widely dispersed. "Symbolic analysts" possessing these skills do not have to fear capital flight, at least not to the same degree as other categories of workers (Reich 1991). But only a subset of symbolic analysts can be justifiably confident that they are protected from globalization in this way (Brouwer 1998, 75–76). And as we have seen in the previous chapter, for the average factory or office worker lean production involves a shift from (monopolizable) tacit skills developed over an extended period of time to "intellective" skills. Many of these intellective skills are broad rather than deep, requiring general mathematical knowledge and the capacity for abstract reasoning and symbol manipulation, neither of which is job specific. Also, process innovations occur at a faster rate as a result of *kaizen* ("continuous improvement") practices. This means that "learning how to learn" becomes more important in the "new economy" than the perfection of any specific skill, since any specific skill may be made obsolete in the course of process innovations. And this in turn tends to make workers who have successfully monopolized specific skills more susceptible to credible threats of capital flight.

Empirical evidence of a declining monopolization of skills is found in Shaiken's studies of the introduction of lean production plants in Mexico. He has documented how plants there attained quality and productivity levels rivalling the best facilities in Japan within eighteen months to three years of start-up, employing young workers with basic education and little industrial experience. No doubt there are many aspects of this situation that cannot be generalized to other lean production facilities. But Shaiken's work does suggest that capital mobility may now be less restricted by skill differences (Shaiken 1990).[9]

(5) Let us now return to the (relatively few) instances of lean production where binding lifetime job guarantees are in place. Up until now we have assumed that structural coercion is necessarily lessened in such circumstances. Is this a correct assumption? Or could a case be made that this arrangement simply transforms how the coercion operates? Instead of being forced to seek employment from some unit of capital or other, the worker may now be forced by the logic of the situation to continue in employment with a particular unit of capital (Kumazawa and Yamada 1989). In general, there is no reason to think that the latter is necessarily less coercive than the former.

The possibility of working for another employer can be removed as a viable option in two ways. Womack and his co-authors, who surely count among the strongest defenders of lean production, mention one: "[B]rilliant team play qualifies workers for more and better play on the same team but makes it progressively harder to leave. So a danger exists that employees (may) feel trapped in lean organizations." They do not propose a solution to this problem beyond the vague (if not vacuous) statement that, "Western companies, if they are to become lean, will need to think far more carefully about personnel systems and career paths than we believe any have to date" (Womack et al. 1990, 251; see also Adler 1988, 28; Parker and Slaughter 1988, 79).

The other way in which employment guarantees can coerce workers to remain at a given place of employment has to do with the organization of wages and pensions. In Japan the familiar rhetoric of class harmony and job satisfaction disguises a quite different basis for the "loyalty" of the worker to a firm. Workers leaving firms automatically start at the very bottom of the pay scale in their new place of employment, so that "jumping ship would be quite pointless" (Womack et al. 1990, 251). Also, almost all Japanese workers receive a lump-sum payment at time of retirement rather than a pension. Any worker who resigns prematurely receives either a mere fraction of this sum or nothing at all. Does not the structure of this situation in effect coerce the worker to remain at his or her place of employment?

These five points, I believe, are sufficient to establish that the basic condition of the working class as a whole in lean production continues to be defined by a lack of access to the means of production and means of subsistence. This remains the case despite the (limited) lifetime employment guarantees associated with at least some variants of this system. The first of the three considerations introduced by Marx to justify the assertion that there is a fundamental class antagonism in capitalism thus remains quite relevant in lean production even regarding these variants, let alone the many other variants of lean production where no job guarantees whatsoever are provided.

B. Exploitation

Turning to the question of exploitation, Marx's general definition of this concept has two components. The first refers to a division in the working day. During the initial period workers engage in necessary labor, that is, labor necessary to obtain the goods and services required if they and their dependents are to survive at the standard of living established in the given social context. During the remainder of the day they engage in surplus labor, producing a surplus product that is not distributed back to them. The second component of the concept of exploitation refers to the process whereby this surplus product is appropriated by another class. In capitalism, where the surplus product takes the form of commodities with exchange value, exploitation is a matter of producing surplus value, that is, economic value exceeding the value received back by workers in the form of wages. This surplus value is then appropriated by the capitalist class in the form of profits.

The whole point of "lean" production is to produce more with less, that is, to increase economic output per unit of labor power purchased. Various technical innovations contribute to this, of course. No less significant, however, is the attempt to eliminate the "pores" in the working day. In traditional Fordist automobile plants workers actively labored forty-five seconds each minute. In the typical lean production auto plant, in stark contrast, workers are engaged in productive activity around fifty-seven seconds a minute. If we assume a ten second per minute differential applied to a plant of 2,000 workers, then 2,667 extra work hours are performed over the course of an eight-hour shift as a result of this speed-up. Some 13,335 extra work hours are added over a five-day week. This is equivalent to hiring an extra 333 workers to work a forty hour week. Or, to put it another way, this is equivalent to each worker performing the equivalent of more than an extra day's labor every five-day week (Fucini and Fucini 1990, 37, 148).

More labor may also be performed as a result of an extension of the labor process. Workers in lean production plants typically are required to submit to forced overtime, serving as a buffer against the firm having to hire more workers or hold larger inventories (Moody 1997, 95–96). They also receive fewer vacation days.[10]

Does this intensive and extensive increase in labor count as an increase in the economic surplus produced? The answer would be no if the collective workforce received back the fruits of this increased labor, either in the form of higher wages or in public goods. They do not; neither wage levels nor public goods tied to working-class communities increase proportionally to the intensive and extensive increase in labor. The latter is well known, and so I shall just comment briefly on the former.

In Japan, the first nation to introduce lean production practices, even core workers failed to win wage increases matching the rate of productivity gains (Kawanishi 1992; see also Preo 1994). Between 1990 and 1997—that is, during a period when lean production practices rapidly spread through the economy—productivity in the U.S. economy grew by 7 percent, while wages and benefits grew by a mere 1 percent (Bernstein 1997). Faced with such data, some writers in the business press have wondered whether productivity gains are still correlated with increased wages. A 1995 *Business Week* cover story on wages posed the question as follows:

> [H]ow long must we wait for productivity gains to boost living standards? At this point in previous business cycles, gains from increased efficiencies would already have started to wind their way through the economy. But after closely tracking each other for decades, wage gains

now are lagging behind productivity growth. The unnerving question that is starting to creep into the discussion: Are we simply in the midst of an especially long and wrenching transition, or have structural changes in the economy severed the link between productivity improvements and income growth? (Bernstein 1995, 56)

In 1997 real wages did begin to grow, and very recently they have even outpaced productivity gains, thanks to two increases in the minimum wage and historically low unemployment rates. But this development must be kept in perspective. These wage gains have not offset the losses between 1989 and 1993, and the U.S. distribution of income in 1997 was the most unequal since the Census Bureau began collecting figures in 1947 (Henwood 1998).[11] Also, these gains are likely to be reversed by the next recession, the next round of layoffs,[12] and the flooding of the labor market due to the dismantling of welfare programs.

While this last point is a matter of speculation, the following one is not. In economic cycles in capitalism wages tend to fall relative to price hikes in recessionary periods, and rise during periods of recovery. In the cycles of the U.S. economy since 1973, the wage gains during recovery periods have failed to match the losses during recessions; the purchasing power of paychecks at the height of each recovery was lower than at the height of the previous recovery. The introduction of lean production practices has been correlated with a worsening of this pattern. Real wages declined during the recession of the early years of the decade, and then continued to stagnate as the recovery spread. It took six years of economic recovery for real wage increases to even begin to reverse the losses from the recession of the early 1990s (Bernstein 1997). As a result, in the United States between 1991 and 1997—which is, once again, a period in which lean production spread rapidly in the economy—the share of national income going to profits rose to the highest level since 1968, while the share appropriated by workers fell to its lowest since that year (Bernstein 1998a). This provides strong empirical evidence that the rise of the "new economy" is correlated with a tendency for the rate of exploitation to increase.

What of the profit sharing agreements that are part of the social organization of many lean production enterprises? They are not designed to return to workers the fruits of their extra labor. They are explicitly designed instead to encourage workers to identify their fate with the fate of the companies for which they work, and to give management considerable "flexibility" in outlays for labor. Suppose wage levels at some company are fixed at some amount x. Then suppose that the company moves to an arrangement where fixed wage levels are set at $\frac{2}{3} x$, with the remainder of the compensation packet based on bonuses that are a function of the firm's profits in a given period.[13] Under this new arrangement, if the firm's earnings lag below management targets, labor expenses can be cut by up to a third immediately while the same amount of labor continues to be performed. From this perspective profit sharing arrangements not only fail to eliminate surplus labor; they provide a mechanism that can *increase* the amount of surplus labor performed with relative ease.

The mere existence of an economic surplus does not in itself establish that there is exploitation in the Marxist sense; this is a necessary, but not sufficient, condition for the applicability of the concept. After all, socialist societies will also not distribute the entire surplus product back to the workforce, as Marx emphasized in "The Critique of the Gotha Programme" (Marx 1977, 567). The decisive issue is who controls the surplus that is produced. If the surplus is controlled by the workforce or its elected representatives, exploitation is not present.[14] If it is not so controlled, then the category is applicable.

How do things stand with lean production? Who is in control of the surplus? Defenders of lean production talk at considerable length about getting rid of the "boundaries" between labor and management, about shifting management functions to the shop floor, and about moving away from authoritarian hierarchies. Any claim that lean production removes the relevance of Marx's category of exploitation rests on these sorts of considerations. It is certainly true that in lean production facilities a number of matters that previously were the sole prerogative of management have been delegated to work teams, or made the topic of joint management/labor discussion. But for all the talk of worker participation in the team model, for all the homilies in praise of blurring the lines between management and labor, a chasm remains between the decisions in which workers participate and the decisions management retains for itself.

The goal of team participation is to extract ideas from the workforce regarding how to improve productivity. In order to encourage this, management may make some concessions regarding issues of status. Separate lunchrooms for management and labor can be done away with; reserved parking for management can be abolished; and so on. In some cases decisions regarding matters such as hiring, pay and progression, training, profit sharing, safety, process control, scheduling, and the like, may even be left to worker-run teams (Kenney and Florida 1993, 173). But this is all a world away from allowing workers (or representatives accountable to them) to determine democratically the allocation of the economic surplus. When this is kept in mind, arguments that Marx's category of exploitation has no place in the new epoch of lean production lose their force at once.[15]

In the previous chapter Zuboff's notion of a "new covenant" between labor and management was introduced, a covenant that supposedly replaced hierarchical authority with dialogue. We are now in a position to see the limits of this dialogical model. There is a world of difference between a dialogue confined within pregiven parameters and a dialogue with the openness to call given parameters into question. The lean production model establishes a dialogue within the following parameters: the private ownership of enterprises; a management appointed by—and ultimately accountable to—representatives of those private owners; an economic system that makes accumulation of capital the ultimate goal, reducing all else to mere means; and a management retaining the ultimate power to dictate the basic strategies to be employed in the pursuit of that goal. Whatever dialogue occurs in lean production is carefully structured to not call any of these parameters into question.[16]

This point is consistently overlooked by the new capitalist utopians. In Zuboff's view the management of lean production ("informated") enterprises is a self-selecting meritocracy, whose authority is self-legitimating as a result:

> While some degree of hierarchy is inevitable in any social group, the values and beliefs that animate these distinctions can operate very differently from the traditional assumptions of imperative control. In the informated organization there is no reason why these individuals could not elect to align themselves with the jobs best suited to their sensibilities or talents. The difference here lies in the voluntary, nonarbitrary, and reversible nature of their decisions. (Zuboff 1988, 411)

Yet top management is not self-selecting. It is appointed by boards who are accountable to shareholders. Granting labor a seat on the board of directors, or even a number of seats, does not reverse this situation.[17]

Even within the established parameters, there is an asymmetry of power between the two partners in speech. The management of lean production firms retains rights to certain one-way forms of communication. These include company newspapers, internal TV stations to communicate company messages, and the use of "visual management," for example, signs encouraging workers to devote themselves to the company.[18] Management also has the power to use the dialogue for ends quite different from those of the participating workers. The management of lean production firms in the United States, for example, has used dialogue to identify workers who are potential sources of "trouble" (Kenney and Florida 1993, 277). And management has the power to shift at will from the search for a true consensus to the imposition of a pseudo-consensus; often the results of "dialogue" are pre-ordained unilaterally, with only the pretense that worker input can affect the final decisions (Delbridge 1998, chapter 7).

If the workforce produces an economic surplus, and if those who determine the allocation of this surplus are not accountable to the workforce, then Marx's category of exploitation is applicable. Both conditions hold in the lean production model. Therefore this dimension of Marx's theory has not been made outdated by the rise of lean production technologies and forms of organization.

Before turning to real subsumption, the third and final topic of this chapter, I wish to consider two other matters relevant to the issue of exploitation: social divisions in the workforce and the effects of these divisions on the distribution of the total social product.

C. Social Divisions and Exploitation in Lean Production

Defenders of lean production typically dismiss questions regarding the balance of class power in the workplace by insisting that the model they advocate institutionalizes unity and harmony. Certain forms of collective identity and shared sense of purpose are indeed systematically encouraged by lean production. The relation between top management at corporate headquarters and the local managers of plants is an obvious example. The desire of local plant managers to receive rewards allocated by those at the top of the corporate chain of command ensures that members of the two groups will tend to share a collective identity over time. There is nothing new about this, of course. What is new, according to the defenders of lean production, is the shared sense of purpose between management and the workforce. This unity is maintained over time by both external and internal factors.

Externally, market competition works to create an "us against them" mentality, in which the fate of management and the workforce together depend upon the "competitiveness" of the enterprise. Market competition, of course, is a general feature of capitalism, and not anything unique to lean production. But advanced technologies associated with the "new economy" allow the globalization of production and a faster rate of innovation, which intensify competition and thereby intensify the sense that management and labor share a common fate.

Internally, work teams provide an institutional mechanism that may lead individual workers to internalize management decrees regarding absenteeism, the work pace, and so on. In lean production there are no surplus workers ready to help out on an as-needed basis, as was generally the case in the Fordist workplace. And so if an individual worker is absent or especially slow, the burden is felt first and foremost by his or her fellow team members. The team arrangement thus tends to lead these team members to enforce norms of attendance and work pace themselves through peer pressure, thereby defusing labor/management conflicts in a plant (Delbridge 1998, chapters 5, 9; Dassbach 1996; Graham 1996).

The talk of unity and harmony by defenders of lean production thus has a material basis. But the structure of the lean production model also encourages a number of social divisions, a point usually not emphasized by advocates of this variant of capitalism. Any attempt to consider the former while ignoring the latter results in a thoroughly distorted picture of the model. The following are among the social divisions that tend to arise due to organizational structures:

- Peer pressure can generate a potential division between an individual worker and the team of which he or she is a part (Graham 1994).
- There is a division in lean production between the workforce of one plant and the workforce of other plants producing products for the same market. This division can hold even if the two plants are both owned by the same corporation.
- There is a division between the workforce of a "core" firm and that of the "periphery" firms engaged in subcontracting from the core firm.
- There is a division between the permanent workforce of an enterprise and those who are hired only temporarily or part-time.
- There is a division between those who have found waged work and those who have not.

There is nothing "natural" about the unities that are created within lean production. And neither is there anything "natural" about the divisions it fosters. Here as elsewhere, both group identities and divisions among groups are constituted by social processes arising within given social structures. Different sorts of social structures would tend to result in the formation of different group identities and different social divisions. It is possible to imagine, for example, institutional structures encouraging a sense of shared identity and common purpose uniting all those who either labor for a wage or would if they could find employment. *This* common purpose is not encouraged by lean production firms, which "are opposed to forms of alternative worker identification . . . which create a separate sphere of identity for workers and disrupt the alignment between worker and company" (Kenney and Florida 1993, 285; see Graham 1996).[19]

The question of the unities and the divisions furthered within the lean production model is relevant to the issue of exploitation. If the model is structured so as to encourage a unity among the owners and controllers of capital, and a unity between management and the workforce, while it simultaneously encourages divisions among various segments of the workforce, then the balance of power between labor and capital tend to shift in favor of capital, everything else remaining equal. The rate of exploitation can be expected to tend to rise over time as a direct result of this "divide and conquer" dynamic, at least as long as the present balance of class forces remains in place.

There are a number of specific mechanisms underlying this tendency. Divisions among the various workforces on the global level tend to set off a global competition regarding which one can work harder for less. Divisions among the workers of various plants within the same corporation tends to lead to whipsawing, in which different plants are forced to bid against each other to see which can offer the largest work increases and cuts in pay and benefits. The pervasive use of temporaries and part-time labor provides a source of cheap and often submissive labor that can be hired and fired at will. Temporaries and part-time workers also form a labor pool that may work at extraordinary levels in order to have a shot at more secure and full-time employment within the firm, thereby pressuring established workers to increase their work pace. And temporary and part-time laborers provide a constant reminder to the permanent workforce that there is no shortage of potential replacements if they are not satisfied with their work conditions and levels of remuneration.[20] Similar points hold regarding the relation between workers in core firms and those employed by subcontractors. The wages of those in the former camp are significantly lower, putting downward pressure on the wages of all.[21] Most obviously, the division between those who are engaged in waged work and those who have not been successful in finding employment puts downward pressure on wages.[22] All of these social divisions make it more difficult for labor to retain or expand its share in the distribution of the total social product.

The phrase "divisions in the workforce" has been used thus far to refer to the different roles defined by the structure of the lean production model, such as the distinction between working for a "core" firm and working for a supplier. The discussion until now has abstracted from gender, ethnic, racial, and age differences among those who labor. Does the lean production model foster divisions within the working class along these lines? In the following passage Kenney and Florida suggest that just the opposite holds, that lean production functions most smoothly when these sorts of difference do not divide one part of the workforce from another:

> [T]here is no reason to believe that the Japanese model of innovation-mediated production is premised upon racial and/or ethnic division or that it should be *a priori* biased against minorities. In fact, it is likely that racial and ethnic divisions in the labor force, if transferred into the workplace, will impede the transfer and effective functioning of the Japanese model of innovation-mediated production. Such divisions are problematic since they divide workers and decrease information transfer and cooperation. (Kenney and Florida 1993, 283)

The interesting thing about this passage is that it refers only to the workforce of a single plant, and not to the relation between workers in core firms and those employed by the smaller subcontracting firms that form rings around core enterprises. When we examine instances of core/ring lean production networks, there is a clear pattern for women to be separated from men (Murray 1983, 1987; Sayer 1986; Jenson 1989; Sassen 1998; Delbridge 1998, 207),[23] for people of color to be separated from whites,[24] for older workers to be separated from younger ones.[25] Young white males have a disproportionate number of the better paid and more secure jobs in the "core," while women, people of color, and older workers are disproportionately found working for smaller firms where pay is low and employment more precarious. Kenney and Florida themselves admit that access to jobs and benefits is "structurally unequal" in countries where the lean production model has been institutionalized, such as Japan:

> Divisions among workers are integral components of the labor market and production in the Japanese political economy. Small firm/large firm relations and patterns of gender-based divisions provide clear evidence of structurally unequal access to jobs and benefits. These relationships are important supports for the "core" of the Japanese economy and help to create the institutional topography upon which the Japanese organization of production rests (Kenney and Florida 1993, 36)

This is not to say that the lean production model creates racism, sexism, or ageism. But lean production does consist of a set of material practices that encourage these phenomena to persist. There is extensive historical evidence that the persistence of such phenomena encourages the rate of exploitation in the economy as a whole to be significantly higher than it would otherwise be (Davis 1986). The persistence of racism, sexism, and ageism thus further substantiates the claim that the category of exploitation remains relevant to the lean production model.

D. Real Subsumption

The third basis for Marx's conclusion that there is a fundamental antagonism between capital and labor has to do with the labor process and the question of alienation. Marx developed this point by means of a historical typology of the labor process in capitalism.

In the initial phase of capitalist labor relations, the "putting-out" system, merchant capitalists hired independent artisans to produce commodities for them. In this arrangement workers retained full control over the labor process. In the following stage, producer capitalists hired ex-artisans and ex-peasants to engage in labor activity as wage laborers in factories.

These arrangements left control of the labor process in the hands of the workforce, although they were now subjected to external supervision. Marx refers to such arrangements as instances of the "formal subsumption" of labor under capital; the social form of the labor process had changed, while the content of the process remained what it had been.

With the rise of manufacturing this changed. The owners and controllers of capital insisted that the labor process be transformed in order to increase the amount of surplus value produced in a given period of time. The result was the rise of the detail laborer, condemned to perform simple tasks repeatedly. With this transformation, which Marx termed the "real subsumption" of labor by capital, the worker is alienated from his or her own labor process in a qualitatively new way. For Marxist theorists this form of alienated labor endured through the Fordist epoch.

Contemporary defenders of capitalism do something quite rare in the history of capitalist apologetics. They freely concede that the labor process in capitalism has been alienating in precisely the pernicious way Marx described (Tapscott 1996, 48). They deny, however, that this alienation condemns the capital/wage labor relation per se. Some lean production theorists hold that alienation in the process of laboring has been overcome. Others concede that alienation in the labor process may continue, but insist that it is no longer pernicious. There are three arguments to consider here, the first defending the former claim, the other two articulating the latter position.

1. The "Good Taylorism" Argument

In Fordism, industrial engineers undertook time/motion studies and imposed standardized procedures on the workforce as a result of the studies, thereby raising the real subsumption of labor to a "scientific" level. Defenders of lean production now agree that the resulting work practices were alienating. How do things stand with the model they advocate?

The rhetoric of teamwork, multiskilling, and worker empowerment might seem to suggest that in the "new economy" the members of the workforce decide for themselves how production should be structured from day to day. This is not at all the case. Teams often do have some say in who gets to rotate into what job when. But once a worker has been assigned a task, he or she must typically adhere to a rigid set of procedures governing each detail of the labor process, procedures determined by time/motion studies (Moody 1997, 88–89; Delbridge 1998, chapter 7; Babson 1996). Paul Adler insists that the alienation of the Fordist labor process has been overcome despite this. In his view alienation results only when standards are imposed on the workforce externally. This is the "bad" form of Taylorism. In lean production plants, in contrast, time/motion studies are undertaken by work teams. Adherence to a set of standardized procedures thereby loses its alienating character. This is a "good" form of Taylorism (Adler 1993, 98). This distinction between a bad form of Taylorism and a nonalienating form has a number of serious difficulties. For one thing, there are a great number of cases where we would all agree that arguments of this general form are not convincing. Consider two different ways of organizing slave plantations. In the first the slave masters themselves impose order on the camp down to the tiniest detail. In the second they leave the task of keeping order to the slaves themselves, intervening only when things get excessively unruly. From the standpoint of the slave, perhaps, there is something to be said for the second form of organization. However, no one would conclude that in this arrangement the activities of the slaves are no longer shaped by an alien power above them. As Foucault has reminded us, having those subject to an alien power participate in their own subjugation is one of the oldest and most effective tactics of power. Any general claim that this tactic removes alienation must surely be rejected.

In the specific case at hand another problem has to do with the fact that the "good" form of Taylorism addresses at best the situation of only some members of the workforce. Not all workers in lean production plants participate in the setting of work standards. In many cases work standards are set by industrial engineers and team leaders before a plant opens. In North American transplants, they are usually simply taken over from Japan (Robertson 1993).

Further, even if it is unclear whether lean production leads to an overall decline in skill levels, it certainly is compatible with the deskilling of numerous categories of workers. Workers in these categories typically did not participate in the work design that deskilled them. For them the transformation of the labor process obviously continues to be imposed by capital as an alien force standing over and above them (Mann 1994).

Even workers who do participate in time/motion studies and the formulation of work standards are subjected to an alien power whenever the general parameters of the labor process are removed from discussion. Despite the rhetoric of cooperation, the long-term strategic objectives of lean production enterprises are imposed by managers appointed by those who own and control the capital invested in these enterprises. They are then imposed on workers by an external power.[26]

The "good Taylorism" argument also neglects the fact that worker participation in lean production results in the objectification of the tacit knowledge of the workforce, allowing this knowledge to then be appropriated by management. As the authors of a study of the leading lean production plant in Canada write,

> CAMI does encourage workers to use their brains and knowledge to reduce costs and raise productivity, but workers have always possessed such production wisdom or "trade secrets." What distinguishes CAMI from traditional auto plants is not the intelligence of its workforce but its systematic efforts to appropriate this knowledge to realize the company's objectives. (Rinehart et al. 1994, 170–71)

The balance of power between capital and labor shifts to the advantage of the former with this appropriation of knowledge previously monopolized by the workforce. The more tacit knowledge is objectified and appropriated, for example, the easier it is for managers to train replacements in the event of a strike, thereby making it more difficult for the members of the workforce to defend their interests effectively.

Another relevant matter here is that lean production systems making use of teams and rotations significantly reduce work rules, job classifications, and the importance of the seniority system. This leaves management free to impose job assignments at will. Those identified by management as having "an attitude problem" (those, for example, who insist that safety regulations be rigorously followed) can be transferred to the most arduous jobs in the plant until they are forced to quit. The elimination of classifications and the security system also rules out older workers transferring to less physically and psychologically demanding jobs.[27] In these dimensions too the labor process is defined by forces alien to the workers themselves.

A related point is that the lean production system is structured so as to subject individual workers to considerable peer pressure. I have already noted that teams are set up so that when a worker is absent or has a bad day this places an immediate and severe burden on his or her co-workers. In this manner a tremendous amount of peer pressure is created to not miss work and to submit to the established work pace. This pressure retains its force even when a worker is ill, or should be home taking care of an ill family member. This arrangement defuses labor/management conflicts at the cost of aggravating conflicts among workers. The real subsumption of labor under the alien force of capital may be more disguised here than in Fordism, but it is no less present:

> Managers at Toyota, Nissan, and numerous transplant suppliers suggested that teams provide the peer pressure required to keep most workers in line. (Kenney and Florida 1993, 279)

Finally, the commodity form, the money form, and the capital form all operate as alien forces operating behind the backs of economic agents in capitalism. They impose the imperative to reduce socially necessary labor time, regardless of the social costs of doing so. Time/motion studies determining standardized procedures are an expression of this imperative, whether or not workers participate in these studies. In either case, the members of the workforce are still forced to submit to the power of alien social forms, to the force of the law of value.

I conclude from all that has been said that the first attempt to argue that lean production overcomes alienation in the labor process fails. Some forms of Taylorism might be preferable to others, but this is not sufficient to show that the category of real subsumption is irrelevant to lean production.

2. The Fragility of Production Argument

A second argument rests on the "fragility" of production in lean production plants. Suppose, the argument goes, we grant that in lean production the potential for the owners and controllers of capital to impose their will upon workers increases. It cannot be denied, after all, that microelectronics technologies provide opportunities to monitor the workforce, to reduce the workforce, to increase work loads, to institute speed-ups, and so on. Still, potentials are not always actualized. The lean production system demands the cooperation of the workforce to succeed. If management were to exercise its power in a manner the workforce found alien, laborers could simply refrain from contributing suggestions, or act in a manner that throws off the delicate balance of the just-in-time delivery system. As a result of this fragility, "it is in management's own interest that any abuse of management prerogatives should meet with swift and certain penalties" (Adler 1993, 108). In this manner alienation in the labor process is overcome.

This is a very striking argument, but it too is questionable. First of all, are arguments of this general type always convincing? The following example suggests not. For much of the post–World War II period the doctrine of mutually assured destruction underlay nuclear strategy in the United States and the Soviet Union. Each side possessed the weapons to attack the other. Yet each refrained, at least partially out of fear of retaliation. It was certainly in the interest of each party to have the other refrain from nuclear attack. But would anyone seriously suggest that the alienation between the two countries was removed as a result of this sort of strategic thinking? The fragility argument is the industrial equivalent of the mutually assured destruction doctrine of nuclear strategy; management refrains from a first strike because it fears the retaliation labor can muster. Does not the rhetoric of harmony and the overcoming of alienation sound similarly hollow in this context?

A more basic question is whether the lean production system is in fact as fragile as the above argument supposes. It is true that just-in-time production systems cannot work unless laborers are committed and diligent. However it is quite a jump to conclude that management must therefore completely accommodate the interests of labor. There are a great number of other strategies for motivating commitment and diligence, strategies that are especially likely to be successful in the absence of strong independent unions and high levels of class consciousness. Besides peer pressure, failure to keep up with the line can also result in pressure from management, reduced perks, undesirable new assignments, and disciplinary actions, with the fear of unemployment always lurking in the background (Parker and Slaughter 1988, 18; Gee et al. 1996, 124; Kochan et al. 1997, 307; Delbridge 1998, chapter 5). Ideology may play a role here too. The ideology that management has a "right" to impose its will on the labor process retains its force among many workers; to the extent this is the case, this too makes the system less fragile. The owners and controllers of capital can also rely on many workers having a strong psychological desire to find meaning in their work lives, even when central aspects of the labor process are imposed upon them externally. Lastly, fragility can be overcome to a considerable extent if problems in the workplace are personalized, that is, blamed on particular managers rather than on the general dynamics of lean production.

This is not to say that the just-in-time system does not have any weak points. There are indeed many points at which it is potentially vulnerable, points at which organized workers can apply pressure.[28] But this fragility is not extensive enough to abolish magically the need to struggle. Fear for the fragility of the system among managers is not so great that they automatically will seek to harmonize their interests with those of labor in the absence of such struggles.

3. The Compensation Argument

This brings us to the final argument for the irrelevance of the concept of real subsumption. Unlike the two just considered, this argument grants that aspects of the labor process in lean production are indeed imposed upon the workforce externally. The labor process in lean production plants is characterized by hyperintensive work; once again, in traditional Fordist plants the labor process took up approximately forty-five seconds every minute, while in lean production plants the figure is fifty-seven seconds. This unrelenting pace is inflicted on labor by capital. Many of the strongest advocates of lean production freely admit that this increases worker stress. This increase in stress is not an unintended by-product of lean production; the entire point of just-in-time production is to optimize the stress level, since anything less represents an "excess" that could be made "lean" (Tomaney 1990). Defenders of the "new economy," however, insist that the process of continuous improvement presents never-ending challenges to workers, mobilizing their intelligence and creativity. This, it is alleged, fully compensates for any increase in stress they may experience (Womack et al. 1990, 101).

There are two major difficulties with this argument. First, it is not so much an argument as a dogmatic assertion. Where is the evidence substantiating the conclusion? Production workers on Toyota's assembly lines in Japan are reported to make twenty motions every eighteen seconds, or a total of 20,600 motions in a working day. This leads to a level of stress that threatens both physical and psychological health. In the extreme case it can lead to *karoshi*, "sudden death from overwork." According to the citizen's volunteer group Karoshi Dial 110, some 1,500 cases of *karoshi* have been reported as of June 1990 (Watanabe 1992, J4). Where is the proof that the challenges faced by the workforce are sufficiently high to compensate for such a level of suffering and risk?

Second, is this the sort of issue that management consultants are able to adjudicate, even in principle? Surely only those who have experienced both the stress and the challenges of the lean production workplace are in a position to weigh the extent to which the latter compensate for the former. Perhaps from the workers' perspective it would be better to have a somewhat smaller number of chances to exercise their creativity in return for a lower level of stress. A work process designed to evoke the same degree of creativity in a less stressful environment would be better yet. The lean production system rules out the workforce making decisions based on these sorts of evaluations. The management of lean production firms have consistently emphasized that the 57-second-a-minute pace is not a subject for negotiation (Fucini and Fucini 1990, 217). None of the new capitalist utopians has criticized them for this. And so a crucial aspect of the labor process is not decided by the group that bears the burdens of this decision, the laborers. This central dimension of the labor process is instead imposed upon them. Here too the conclusion seems to be that capital operates as an alien power over these laborers at the point of production in a manner captured by Marx's concept of the "real subsumption" of labor under capital.

E. Conclusion

The defenders of lean production assert that in this new version of capitalism the fundamental antagonism between labor and capital is overcome. For this claim to count as a refutation of Marx it would have to be shown that structural coercion, alienation, and the real subsumption of labor under capital are overcome. I have examined the arguments that could be used to make this case. These arguments are unconvincing.

CHAPTER FOUR

The Capital/Consumer Relation
in Lean Production

For Marx, the formation of new consumer desires in capitalism extends human capacities and emancipates individuals from the confines of traditional societies, where rigid customs trapped human development within a relatively narrow set of roles:

> [A condition of production founded on capital is] the discovery, creation and satisfaction of new needs arising from society itself; the cultivation of all the qualities of the social human being, production of the same in a form as rich as possible in needs, because rich in qualities and relations. . . . [Capitalism involves] the developing of a constantly expanding and more comprehensive system of different kinds of labour, different kinds of production, to which a constantly enriched system of needs corresponds. (Marx 1973, 409)

To concentrate solely on the negative side of consumption in capitalism would be one-sided, and hence undialectical and mistaken, from the Marxian perspective (see Marx 1976, 1032–33).[1] Nonetheless, it is also true that for Marx the circuit of capital accumulation provides the overarching framework within which consumer activity is subsumed as a subsidiary moment:

> The volume of the mass of commodities brought into being by capitalist production is determined by the scale of this production and its needs for constant expansion, and not by a predestined ambit of supply and demand, of needs to be satisfied. (Marx 1978, 156)

Marxists, of course, have always regarded the notion of consumer sovereignty with hostility, considering it a legitimating ideology masking the essential social forms of capitalism. The Marxian position is that the realm of consumption, no less than the realm of production, is one in which the rhetoric of liberty prevents an adequate comprehension of basic social relations. The sphere of consumption, no less than the sphere of production, is one of fundamental social antagonisms. In contrast, perhaps the single most important element of the "hard core" of neoclassical economics is the proposition that the final purpose of economic activity in capitalism is the satisfaction of consumer demand. From this perspective the accumulation of capital is simply a means toward that end. If the neoclassical view is correct, Marx's assertion that capital accumulation has become the ultimate end of economic life, subsuming all other aspects of the social world to its imperatives, gets everything topsy-turvy.

As we shall see, the advocates of the "new economy" agree with Marx that consumers have not reigned as sovereigns in the history of capitalism. They deny, however, that capital/consumer relations are inherently antagonistic. In their view lean production practices will inaugurate a period in which the interests of capital and the interests of consumers are reconciled at last. In its own way this position threatens the foundations of Marxism as profoundly as the claim that the interests of capital and the interests of labor will be reconciled. The goal of the present chapter is to examine this thesis. But first the viewpoint of the defenders of the "new economy" must be presented in more detail.

A. From Fordist Consumption to Flexible Consumption

In volume I of *Capital* Marx traced the path from the putting-out system to the early factory, manufacturing, and machinofacturing ("big industry"). Marx's own attention was directed primarily to modifications in the labor process occurring in the course of this development. But this was not the only significant dimension of the historical change. The increasing ability to mass produce uniform commodities was another. In the putting-out system many goods were produced to the specifications of individual customers. And even when this was not the case, merchant capitalists could only enforce relatively loose standards of uniformity on the various instances of a product made in workshops. By the time we get to machinofacture, however, the vast armies of wage laborers brought together in factories were expected to produce mass numbers of nearly identical products.

Fordism can be seen as a continuation of this progression. The assembly line, the calculations of scientific management, the scientization of production, the use of interchangeable parts, the employment of dedicated machinery, and other characteristic features of Fordism, all extended the technical ability to mass produce nearly identical goods (Hounshell 1984). The desire to attain economies of scale in order to lower unit costs then provided firms with a powerful economic incentive to undertake extended runs of these standardized products. As purchasing power became more widely dispersed—thanks in part to successful union struggles and various forms of state intervention in the economy—mass consumer markets for these commodities expanded. This did not mean that the production of customized goods disappeared. Domestic labor, labor producing goods for luxury markets, artisan labor for local markets, and labor in various industries where the recalcitrance of raw materials and other factors prevented the introduction of Fordist procedures, all continued to produce nonstandardized goods in the Fordist epoch (Walker 1989, 77). These forms of production, however, were not hegemonic. Economic power shifted more and more to enterprises that were successful in the mass production of standardized goods. And so the capital/consumer relation in Fordism was defined by the drive to mass production and mass consumption.

How should the social relation between capital and consumers be evaluated in this context? Adherents of the "new economy" insist that there was an unbridgeable gulf in Fordism between unique individuals, on the one hand, and the mass produced standardized commodities that confronted them in the market, on the other. So long as this gulf persisted, commodities necessarily remained alien to consumers, things that didn't quite "fit" their specific needs and desires.

It is true, of course, that in Fordism different commodities were produced for different segments of the market. For example, soon after Henry Ford proclaimed that consumers could have the Model T in any color they wanted so long as it was black, General Motors proceeded to develop different products for different niches of the automobile market, thereby winning market share from Ford. But these segments were defined in relatively broad terms, based on group categories such as class, geography, age, sex, race, and so on. There was nothing in mass production that approached an affirmation of the individual uniqueness of consumers. This affirmation was lost with the move away from the craft labor of artisan workshops.

As a result of the unbridgeable gulf between unique consumers and mass-produced commodities the satisfaction of the wants of individual consumers could not be said to be the ultimate goal of economic life in Fordism. The leading ideologues of contemporary capitalism, the advocates of the "new economy, thus implicitly agree with Marx that "consumer sovereignty" has been a legitimating myth of capitalism rather than an institutionalized reality. These theorists, however, insist that this alienation of consumers from commodities is not an inherent feature of capitalist economies. As a result of the technical and organizational changes associated with lean production, the commodity is now no longer a standardized product, but something that closely reflects the unique tastes of individual consumers or very narrowly defined consumer segments. With the establishment of a continuous feedback loop between consumers and the product design process, the alienation of the consumer from the object of consumption approaches the vanishing point:

> Defining businesses from the producers' point of view, as was done in the industrial [that is, Fordist T.S.] economy, is simply no longer workable. One hallmark of the ambiguous, new economy is the need to define business in terms of customers' changing needs. (Davis 1987, 195)[2]

On this view the consumer is the sun around which the "new economy" turns; consumer sovereignty is now being instituted on a mass scale for the first time in human history. If this thesis is correct, then economic evolution in capitalism has accomplished something that all of neoclassical economics with its vast mathematical sophistication could not do: provide a convincing empirical refutation of the core Marxian belief that consumer needs are a secondary matter in capitalism. It is thus worth examining the continuous feedback loop connecting capital and consumers in more detail, based on descriptions found in the lean production literature.

The first step in this loop is the gathering and processing of information regarding patterns in consumer behavior. Various types of information technology are employed to this end, including scanners that instantaneously record consumer purchases at the point of sale, cable or multimedia technologies that enable home shopping, networked computers capable of transmitting consumer preferences directly from distributors to producers, computer memory sufficient to store extensive data bases on individual customers, software allowing these data bases to be manipulated and updated in real time, toll-free numbers for consumers' questions and complaints, interactive voice mail, computer bulletin boards that let firms monitor product user groups, and so on. Firms can also choose to purchase relevant data regarding consumers from information providers (Tapscott and Caston 1993, 108; McWilliams 1998, 172).

Greater information gathering and processing capacity allows much more nuanced information regarding consumer desires, information that can be continuously updated. In principle, this information allows lean production enterprises to define the limit point of a "segment of one," as they discover the product features desired by each individual consumer (Winger and Edelman 1990).

The next stage is to provide a good or service that has the specific product features desired by individual consumers. When this occurs on a mass scale, the result differs from both the customization of artisan labor and the mass production of the traditional factory. This new phenomenon has been termed "micromass consumption" or "mass customization" (Davidow and Malone 1992, 5; Davis 1987, passim.). Production occurs on an extensive

scale as with the mass production of Fordism, but this production is now customized to meet the unique needs of individual consumers or very narrowly defined groups of consumers.[3]
Mass customization can occur in a variety of fashions. In certain sectors computer screens tied to customer data bases instantaneously provide sellers with extensive information regarding special needs of individual customers. Hotels, airlines, and financial services are examples of industries customizing the products or services they sell to the unique needs of their individual clients (Womack et al. 1990, 169–93; Tapscott and Caston 1993, 67, 158). In other sectors mass customization can be attained through the design of open-ended products. These are multipurpose consumer goods that can fulfill a variety of different consumer needs depending upon how they are programmed. When the programming is left in the hands of customers, consumers are no longer merely passive recipients of commodities. They now are integrated into the design process as "prosumers," helping to produce what they consume (Toffler 1983; Tapscott 1996, 62–63). Examples of prosumer activities include printing out your own airline tickets or news, undertaking home banking, performing diagnostics and repair on electronic machines, using camcorders to produce your own movies, and so on.

Other technologies of mass customization provide manufacturers with the ability to produce a diverse product range, to deliver their products to consumers quickly, and to respond rapidly to sudden shifts in consumer demand. The replacement of single-purpose ("dedicated") machinery with general purpose machinery is of great significance in this context. Computer-aided-design (CAD) and computer-aided-manufacture (CAM) programs allow new products to be introduced without having to replace the machinery controlled by the computers running these programs. This means that the imperative to extend product runs in order to recoup the costs of the machines loses much of its force.[4]

Once designs have been specified, they can be transmitted instantaneously to computers operating on the shop floor, setting in motion the production of products embodying that design. In this manner the time between the commencement of the initial design phase and the delivery of a new product line to consumers is shortened considerably. In Japan, the goal is to have a car roll off the assembly line with the specifications ordered by an individual consumer and deliver it to that consumer within seventy-two hours of when the order was made. Japanese auto manufacturers also cut the period between the beginning of a new design process and the bringing of the new car to market to forty-six months, as opposed to the sixty months taken by Fordist firms in the United States. This time advantage means that lean production enterprises can design cars taking into account more recent shifts in consumer preferences.[5] With shorter life spans, Japanese firms produced fewer units of every model than U.S. or European manufacturers did prior to adapting lean production practices, five hundred thousand vehicles versus almost two million (Womack et al. 1990, 111, 124). Also essential here are advances in transportation technology that deliver the manufactured item in a timely fashion.[6]

Mass customization requires organizational innovations as well as technical innovations. The just-in-time production system abolishes large stocks of unsold inventory and partially finished products, removing one reason for the reluctance of Fordist firms to make quick changes in product lines (Tapscott and Caston 1993, 85, 98). The decentralization of decision making, sometimes referred to as the move to the "horizontal corporation" (Byrne 1993) allows a more rapid response to shifts in consumer demand than the bureaucratic hierarchies of the typical Fordist firm. Replacing detail laborers with teams of multiskilled workers removes another barrier. Product design teams including service and marketing representatives alongside product engineers warrant special mention.[7] These teams enable product designers to take into account up-to-date knowledge of consumer trends. They also provide a site where customer complaints and questions can be transformed into ideas for product innovations. The move to concurrent engineering is another organizational change enabling corporations to adjust to shifts in consumer preferences more rapidly. This term refers to the process whereby the different parts going into a final product are designed simultaneously, including parts produced by subcontractors (Clark and Fujimoto 1989).

The feedback process connecting consumers and manufacturers is completed with the monitoring of consumer responses to the introduction of the new product or service. Information-gathering technologies enable capitalist enterprises to measure levels of customer satisfaction, to determine whether the complexity of the product design matches the competence levels of consumers, and so on. Lean production technologies and organizational forms allow a close-to-instantaneous shift in product mix and product design in response to this feedback, thus beginning the cycle anew (Gross 1998, 142).

None of the above implies that the low-overhead, low-cost mass commodities typical of Fordism will no longer be produced in the "new economy." Scale and volume have hardly become irrelevant. For that matter, there will still be markets where artisans customize a product for individual buyers. But neither mass consumption nor customization by artisans will define the characteristic form of the capital/consumer relation in the coming period. In lean production the greatest profits are won from tailoring goods or services to the specific needs of particular customers in a way that cannot be easily duplicated by others. The highest rates of growth will be located in sectors where the individual consumer confronts a product that targets a relatively narrow band of consumers, or where he or she actively participates in commodity design.

How ought we to evaluate Marxian theory in the light of all this? From one perspective the features of lean production just discussed simply confirm Marx's emphasis on the importance of reducing the time capital is tied up in the various stages of the capital circuit.[8] The circuit of capital examined by Marx culminates in the C′-M′ stage, the selling of commodities for money. Marx believed that there was a general imperative in capitalism for the owners and controllers of capital to search for innovations that shorten the time it takes to get commodities to the market, lessen the inventory costs prior to final sale,[9] quicken the process of sale,[10] encourage consumers to increase their rate of consumption, and so on. The technologies and forms of social organization associated with lean production provide a striking confirmation of this thesis.

The challenge to Marxian theory lies elsewhere. The crucial issue is the proper categorization of a key social relation underlying this stage of the circuit, the capital/consumer relation.[11] The advocates of the "new economy" claim that this relation is now qualitatively different from what it was in earlier stages of capitalism. The very logic of the capitalist system has been transformed in a way Marxian theory is incapable of grasping. Defenders of lean production assert that with "mass customization" the alienation of the consumer from the object of consumption, an alienation characteristic of Fordist consumption, approaches the vanishing point. For the first time in the history of capitalism consumer sovereignty is truly instituted. Enterprises and consumers are now connected in a long-term relationship where the satisfaction of consumer desires has become the goal of economic activity:

> The goal of . . . corporations is to maximize the binding energy between themselves and their customers. This is done by maximizing customers satisfaction and by enlisting the customer into a co-destiny relation. (Davidow and Malone 1992, 222)

In this "co-destiny relation" consumers invest the money required to purchase the commodity and the time necessary to educate themselves regarding the company's product line. In return they receive up-to-date information regarding available products, a higher level of service, the opportunity to provide feedback affecting future product development, special discounts, and perhaps permission to tap into a company's data base to track their orders and shipments. Consumers develop a stake in the company's future as a result of this expenditure of time and money.[12] This is a long-term commitment; it may take years for an enterprise to become credible, to build a service infrastructure, to establish deep relationships with customers. But when it does, it can enjoy customer loyalty through a number of product generations. This is an extremely important accomplishment. In the "new economy" start-up costs tend to be high and product life-spans short. Many manufacturers may not see a return on new product lines until the third or fourth generation. This means that the rewards of retaining customers are quite significant. It costs five times more to create new customers than to keep old ones, and retaining two percent more customers is equivalent to cutting costs by ten percent (Davidow and Malone 1992, 222, 153).

With so many resources going into the maintenance of this co-destiny relation, the customer is said to be *in* the lean production firm, not outside it. In fact, for advocates of the "new economy" customers are "inside" the firm in as deep a sense as the firm's stockholders:

> Ultimately, the customer . . . will most resemble the shareholders of that corporation. Both will share a common commitment to the company's long-term success. . . . [T]he consumer of expensive goods such as cars or appliances, may have an even greater stake than the shareholder, in that he or she will be less likely to jump to a competitor for only a marginal gain. (Davidow and Malone 1992, 229)

Most of the critical attention on the lean production model has been directed toward the capital/wage labor relation and the relations among different units of capital in networks. Just as central to the analysis of this model, however, is the capital/consumer relation.[13] If the claim that lean production truly institutes consumer sovereignty could be redeemed, then the Marxian analysis of capitalism would be significantly undermined. Can this claim be redeemed?

B. A Critical Look at the Capital/Consumer Relation in Lean Production

I shall grant for the sake of the argument that in lean production consumer demand is incorporated into design and production in qualitatively new ways. Even under this assumption, however, the language of consumer sovereignty continues to mystify and distort the true state of affairs. The argument can be divided into two parts. The first concerns the limits of consumer power in lean production, the second the subordination of consumer activity within the circuit of capital.

1. The Subservience of the Consumer in the Age of Mass Customization

Under this heading three issues will be examined: the asymmetry of power between capital and consumers in lean production, the effects of consumption on the subjectivity of consumers, and the limits to the knowledge conveyed to consumers by the price mechanism. All three points suggest that the claim that consumer sovereignty has been institutionalized in lean production cannot be sustained.

The first point to note is that the role of consumers in the design process can increase without undermining the asymmetry of power between capital and consumers. Four questions ought to be examined in this context. Which of the two parties had the power to institute the changes in the capital/consumer relation? What was its motivation for doing so? Which of the two has more power to ensure that its interests will be met as the transformation continues? And finally, does one of the two attempt to manipulate the psychic dispositions of the other on a massive scale?

With regards to the first question, whatever transformations in consumer relations are occurring in the "new economy" are being initiated by the representatives of capital. Kenney and Florida's remarks regarding Japan can be generalized to other instances of the lean production model:

> Japan is also witnessing the fragmentation of mass consumption in line with the rise of innovation-mediated production. This is not the illusory, democratic fragmentation championed by U.S. marketers, economists, and post-modern theorists, but rather a structured, rational, and almost planned fragmentation which is informed by the production capabilities of innovation-mediated production. (Kenney and Florida 1993, 320)[14]

The motivation for making this transition is straightforward. The integration of consumers into the design process in lean production is not an ultimate end in itself, but merely a means to expand capital accumulation. This integration is a strategy undertaken by capital in the hope that it will increase the rate of consumption, a point acknowledged by one of the most vociferous advocates of this version of capitalism:

> Shifting the determination of a product's final configuration downstream, into the space of the consumer, has very practical consequences. Consumers who create and control the manufacture of their goods and services are likely to consume more than people who do not. (Davis 1987, 55)

Next, which of the two parties has more power to ensure that the transformation of capital/consumer relations furthers its interests? The notion that the consumer in lean production is as much of a stakeholder in the lean production enterprise as stockholders is a classic instance of ideological nonsense. The managers of enterprises remain agents of capital investors, and there are numerous social mechanisms in place to ensure that they generally act in a manner that furthers the interests of those investors. This "principal/agent" relation does not extend to consumers. There are no representatives of consumer interests serving on boards of directors, overseeing the actions of management.

Finally, how can the consumer be the sun around which the capitalist system now turns if there are pervasive attempts by capitalist firms to manipulate the psychic dispositions of consumers? Inflated if not fraudulent claims intrude into more and more nooks and crannies of everyday life in the "new economy." They are hammered home through the repetition of images and music, bypassing the conscious reasoning process and appealing directly to subconscious desires. Can any more graphic manifestation of the asymmetry of power between capital and consumers be required?

Some advocates of lean production have responded to this last point. They claim that the integration of the consumer into lean production implies that there will be significantly fewer "free-floating" consumers out there to be reached by mass advertising. As we have seen, more and more consumers are participating in the design of products. For advocates of the networked economy, this participation is just one part of an ongoing dialogue between enterprises and consumers, a dialogue enabled by contemporary information technologies. Consumers make use of these technologies to supply personal data to the company, fill out consumer surveys, learn about new products, participate in users' groups to educate themselves about a product and its features, monitor the information presented in computer bulletin boards by the company, read the custom magazines and industry newsletters, study point-of-purchase communications from the manufacturer, customize the product for their own use, and so on (Winger and Edelman 1990; Neuborne and Hof 1998). Such activities involve a significant commitment of time and money to the product line of a given enterprise. As this commitment increases, it becomes less and less likely that customers will switch over to competing product line when they hear an advertising jingle, no matter how catchy it might be. And so these champions of the "new economy" expect the pool of people potentially reachable through mass advertising to shrink considerably.

With so many resources going into the maintenance of a co-destiny relation between enterprise and consumer, these theorists conclude, mass advertising will not retain the central role it had in Fordist mass marketing.

And much of the advertising that does remain will lose its manipulative features, since excessive hype undermines the long-term trust necessary to maintain "long cycles of satisfaction maintenance" (Davidow and Malone 1992, 227; Tapscott 1996, 232). Advertising will stress instead the credibility of a corporation, the quality and service it provides, and the level of past customer satisfaction.

Unfortunately there is not the slightest evidence that the introduction of lean production practices is correlated with a decline in advertising. Ad expenditures in the United States jumped from $61 billion in 1981 to over $130 billion in 1994 (Rank 1994). People in the United States are exposed to 3,000 marketing messages a day. By the time of high school graduation the average eigtheen-year-old in the United States has had 350,000 commercials inflicted upon him or her (Matsu 1994). This surely must count as the most extensive and sophisticated propaganda system ever seen on the face of the planet.[15] And ever-new technologies for distributing advertisements and testing their effectiveness are being devised, including color printers installed in homes that periodically produce coupons and color brochures, TV sets in airports and supermarkets that play ads continuously, and heat sensors installed in home television sets that feel when a viewer from a particular demographic category is watching the ad.

Most manipulative of all, of course, are ads targeting the young, who are less cognizant of the techniques of persuasion (Kline 1993). There is every reason to believe that such ads will increase with the move to the so-called "new economy." Lean production firms hope to provide consumers with a continuous product growth path, from cradle to grave. Ads aimed at children play a crucial role in integrating them into the vaunted "co-destiny" relation, extending the asymmetry of power between capital and consumers yet deeper into the social world.

Defenders of lean production would no doubt respond to the above by insisting that the "empowerment" of the consumer must still be acknowledged. In lean production the desires of consumers directly shape processes of production in a way that is qualitatively new. This last point must be granted. Information technologies in the networked economy have linked consumers and producers together in new ways. But talk of consumer "empowerment" in lean production runs into some of the same difficulties as talk of worker empowerment. I would like to develop this point by drawing out an analogy between formal and real subsumption in the capital/wage labor relation and in the capital/consumer relation.

As we have seen in chapter 3, wage labor is formally subsumed under capital when contractual agreements between capital and labor bring the labor force under the supervision of capital in factories. The real subsumption of labor occurs when the representatives of capital go beyond mere supervision, transforming the details of the labor process in the furtherance of their interests. The real subsumption of labor is rather obvious when management dictates decrees unilaterally from above, as in Fordism. In lean production things are more subtle. Management mobilizes the intelligence and creativity of the work force, trying to objectify the insights of workers in a form that can then be appropriated. Once appropriated, these insights can then be used against the interests of labor, as they are when workers' suggestions lead to speed-ups and higher stress levels. However different this may be from previous arrangements at the workplace, this too counts as a real subsumption of labor under capital (Smith 1994a, 1994b).

The distinction between formal and real subsumption can also be drawn in the realm of consumption. Consumers can be said to be formally subsumed under capital when they are tied to capital by contractual arrangements of purchase alone. A process of real subsumption is set off whenever manufacturers and distributors attempt to go beyond this and actively mould consumer demand. The real subsumption of consumers is rather obvious where the manipulations of mass advertising are concerned. But more subtle forms of real subsumption are also possible in the realm of consumption.

In lean production, firms attempt to mobilize consumers' self-definition of their needs. The use of information technology to track individual consumer's responses instantaneously and continuously can be seen as an objectification of the consumer's subjectivity and self-understanding. Once this information has been objectified, it can then be appropriated by manufacturers and distributors. Information technologies often allow enterprises to know the name and address of each person who buys a product, and to maintain files on their purchase history (Hapoienu 1990; Davis 1989; McDonough 1988; Browning and Reiss 1988, 113; McWilliams and Stepanek 1998).[16] Once this information has been appropriated in this manner, it can then be used against the consumers who were its source. With this data they can then engage in "micromarketing," that is, the transmission of individual messages for each customer (Mayer 1990; Gross and Sager 1998). Messages addressed to an anonymous mass are less effective than those directed to you personally; the more one knows about you, the more open to manipulation you are.[17] This is surely a form of the real subsumption of the consumer under capital.[18]

Thus far we have examined the structural balance of power between capital and consumers. The general effects of consumption on the subjectivity of consumers in the "new economy" is also of great relevance here. Some of these effects will be noted now, all of which argue against the claim that lean production institutes true consumer sovereignty.

For the circuit of capital accumulation to proceed smoothly, it is not enough that commodities be produced and purchased within a given time period; the objects purchased must be consumed within a given period as well, so that the consumer can return to the market ready to make the next round of purchases. The shorter the extension of "socially necessary consumption time," the quicker capital passes through its circuit, and so the more capital can be accumulated in a given period, everything else being equal. In the "new economy" a reduction in socially necessary consumption time is accomplished through shorter product cycles, more frequent design changes, and increasing emphasis on fashion (Harvey 1989). Now the more lean production successfully increases the rate of consumption, the greater the pressure for consumers to define themselves in terms of consumption activity ("you are what you buy"). Tremendous psychic energy must be expended in order to negotiate the proliferation of symbolic values taken on by various commodities. This intensification of consumption profoundly shapes human subjectivity in a way that encourages it to fragment and dissolve, that is, to be less "sovereign." There is thus a fundamental incoherence in the position of the advocates of lean production: they defend a system that tends to lead to a "postmodern" fragmentation of subjectivity by means of an appeal to the traditional notion of an integrated ("sovereign") subject. This point can be made from another angle. Commodities promise a fulfillment they cannot provide (Lane 1993; Scitovsky 1992); if they did, there would be less reason to return to the market for other commodity purchases. Consumerism, as Adorno and Benjamin noted, has the same structure as drug addiction. Purchasing the commodity brings about a temporary high; then you crash and have to make another purchase to get another fix. As the pace of consumption increases, lean production tends to leave the consumer is a state of perpetually unsatisfied desire and anxiety, interrupted by the fleeting rush of a purchase. An addict does not suddenly become "sovereign" simply because he or she participates in drug design.

Of course, the drug metaphor captures only a tendency in lean production; there will be many consumers for whom the metaphor is not applicable. It might seem that for noncompulsive consumers, at least, measures to incorporate customer desires in design and production do remove the gulf between consumers and commodities, thus making the case for consumer sovereignty more plausible. Even here, however, the situation is far more complex than this.

One difficulty stems from the limits of the commodity form. Capitalism certainly possesses an astonishing ability to incorporate diverse forms of experience into the commodification process. Sexuality and its signifiers are offered for sale everywhere, evoking desires and anxieties in equal measure. Art works become objects of commercial speculation. Political activism is replaced by the purchase of T-shirts or compact disks that proclaim support for some cause or other. Commodity exchange can even assimilate rebellions against commodity society; surrealism becomes just another technique employed to get the consumer's attention, and punk sets off a new round of clothing fashions.

Commodification comes at a cost. Something in human life is impoverished when sexuality, aesthetic experience, political activism, and rebellion are reduced to the commodity form.[19] This impoverishment is not removed simply because in lean production many commodities are customized to specifications defined by individual consumers or small groups of consumers. Immersion in those commodities continues to cut the consumer off from possibilities opened up by noncommodifiable experiences. Lean production, no less than other variants of capitalism, leads to the systematic neglect of consumer wants and needs that do not fit the commodity form. In this sense a gulf remains between the consumer and commodities, regardless of whether those commodities have been customized to the specifications desired by individual consumers.

One last point remains. Even when consumers purchase commodities customized to their specifications there can still be a gulf between consumers and products consumed. Such a gulf arises when consumers make purchases that undermine the fulfillment of collective interests with which they identify. The limitations of the price mechanism as a means for transmitting information regularly have this result. Market prices convey relatively accurate information regarding the effective demand for a commodity, the internal costs of its production (that is, costs the producing firm itself must pay), and prevailing profits rates. Prices, however, are not an efficient manner of transmitting relevant knowledge regarding the external costs of production imposed on workers and their communities. Examples of such "externalities" include the physical and psychological stress inflicted on the workforce and environmental damages.

Let us suppose that a given set of consumers does not wish to inflict avoidable harm on either the workforce or the environment. The prices of the commodities they are considering purchasing do not reveal whether the firms producing these commodities impose such harm. The information on these matters available to consumers outside of the price mechanism is often unreliable and conflicting, demanding considerable amount of time and training to sort out. And so consumers who wish to limit environmental degradation and to promote safe work conditions may make purchases furthering precisely what they wish to avoid. In these sorts of cases it makes sense to say that consumers are alienated from the commodities they have purchased, even if these commodities have been customized with them in mind (Smith 1995a).

This completes the first part of the critique of the claim that the "new economy" institutionalizes consumer sovereignty. The next task is to shift the focus to the circuit of capital accumulation and the place of consumer activity within it.

2. Consumption and the Reproduction of Capital

If we exclude the portion of surplus value devoted to capitalists' consumption, the capital/consumer relation takes the form of a circuit in which wage laborers exchange their labor power for money (L-M), and then use that money to purchase commodities for their personal consumption (M-C). In volume II of *Capital* Marx explored how this L-M-C circuit of consumption remains but a secondary moment in the general process of circulation in capitalism, subordinate to the circuit of capital accumulation:

- The circuit of consumption for wage laborers produces the commodity, labor power, which when sold takes on the reified form of variable capital. Engaging in acts of consumption by no means enables wage laborers to escape this reification:

  > The worker spends the money he receives on maintaining his labour-power, and thus—if we consider the capitalist class and the working class as a whole—on maintaining for the capitalist the only instrument by means of which he can remain a capitalist. (Marx 1978, 457)[20]

- The purchase of commodities, that is, the M-C stage of the L-M-C circuit, is simultaneously the C'-M' stage of the capital circuit of a firm in Division II, the division devoted to the production of means of consumption (Marx 1978, 138, 369–70, 384–85, 408; 517–18). In other words, the commodity purchases of wage laborers allow units of capital in Division II to realize surplus value, to accumulate capital. With this capital they can then turn around and invest in variable capital, continuing the reification and exploitation of their wage laborers.

- The variable capital invested in the purchase of labor power ultimately stems from the activity of wage laborers themselves:

  > The money that is here advanced to the worker is only the transformed equivalent form of a portion of the commodity value that he himself produces. (Marx 1978, 151)

Again,

> [T]he constant purchase and sale of labour-power perpetuates the position of labour-power as an element of capital, and in this

way capital appears as the creator of commodities, articles of use that have a value; this is also how the portion of capital that buys labour-power is regularly restored by the product of labour-power itself, so that the worker himself constantly creates the capital fund out of which he is paid. (Marx 1978, 457)

These passages take us to the heart of the Marxian claim that capital accumulation, not consumer sovereignty, is the alpha and omega point of the capitalist mode of production. When we turn to the lean production literature, are any concrete phenomena described that might lead us to question this part of Marx's general theory of capitalism? As far as I can tell, the answer must be no. Not even the most rabid advocate of the "new economy" has ever claimed that one can escape one's class position in the accumulation process through consumer spending on commodities! At this crucial point in the argument the defenders of lean production are silent.

The more closely one considers the way consumer relations in lean production are shaped by class dynamics, the less plausible the claim that consumers are at the center of this version of capitalism. Under the capital form only those needs and wants that have sufficient purchasing power behind them are socially acknowledged. What counts is not "demand" per se, but *effective* demand. And the first and foremost factor determining the level of a social agent's effective demand remains his or her place in the circuit of capital accumulation. Those who own and control capital necessarily tend to enjoy high levels of effective demand, while the consumption opportunities of those who do not necessarily tend to be much more precarious. Lean production does nothing to reverse this; if anything it exacerbates the differences in consumption opportunities of the two groups. In the "new economy" there is a significant amount of involuntary unemployment.[21] There are also growing numbers of part-time and temporary workers, especially among subcontractors. Involuntary unemployment, part-time work, and temporary work all significantly squeeze the purchasing power of these (potential) consumers, restricting their ability to enjoy the wonders of mass customization. Lean production is also correlated with a global fragmentation of the workforce, as capital successfully searches for regions where it can combine high levels of productivity with low wages (Shaiken 1990). The resulting pressure on real wages ensures that the gulf between consumers and consumable commodities will be exacerbated for wage laborers, even for many of those fortunate enough to retain full-time employment.

C. Conclusion

We must conclude that the arguments asserting that lean production inaugurates a golden age of consumer sovereignty ring hollow indeed. The asymmetry in economic power between units of capital and consumers is if anything yet more pronounced in the "new economy"; the effects of consumption on the subjectivity of consumers are ever-more pernicious; relevant knowledge conveyed to consumers by the price form remains limited. And talk of consumer sovereignty mystifies an economic system where the imperatives of capital accumulation continue to be the alpha and omega of social life. As long as this is so, Marxian theory will remain the starting point for any serious attempt to comprehend the social world in which we live.

CHAPTER FIVE
Intercapital Relations in Lean Production

Besides the capital/labor relation, and the capital/consumer relation there is a third social relation that defines capitalism, the relation among different units of capital. Marx considered a variety of intercapital connections in volume III of *Capital,* including relations among units of industrial capital; relations among units of merchant capital, finance capital and industrial capital; and relations between units of capital based on the appropriation of rent and other sorts of capital. All of these social relations are affected by the rise of the "new economy."[1] Here, however, I shall concentrate on relations among units of industrial capital, especially on the lean production networks connecting suppliers, assemblers, and distributors.[2]

In the first section of this chapter I shall discuss how relations among units of capital in Fordism were based on a particular trade-off between the advantages for capital of vertical integration and the benefits of market transactions. In section B I shall examine interenterprise networks, the characteristic form taken by relations of different units of capital in lean production. These networks both depend on certain technical advances and themselves advance technical innovation and diffusion in certain directions. According to their advocates, these networks combine the strengths of both organizational hierarchies and pure markets, while avoiding the weaknesses of these two social forms. Most of all, these theorists argue, lean production networks overcome many of the social antagonisms that characterized relations among different units of capital in Fordism. In the final section of the chapter I shall subject the network model to critical examination.

A. Markets and Hierarchies in Fordism

The production of almost all goods and services requires a variety of inputs. Every firm faces a basic choice regarding each input: should the enterprise itself produce it, or should the input be purchased in the market? Any answer to this question necessarily involves a trade-off (Harvey 1982). If an enterprise purchases an input in the market, the time it takes its capital to complete its circuit from initial investment to final accumulation is reduced from what it otherwise would be, since it itself does not have to expend time to produce the input. Everything else being equal, a reduction in circulation time allows more capital to be accumulated over time. But other things are rarely equal. Purchasing the input on the market generally increases the firm's constant capital costs. This is because the price of the input now includes the profits of the company that produced it, a cost that would not be incurred if the original enterprise had made the input itself. Everything else being equal, an increase in constant capital costs results in less capital being accumulated over time.

Capitalist enterprises are continually seeking the most favorable balance between vertical integration and reliance on the market for inputs. There is no reason to suppose that the most advantageous balance will be fixed once and for all. In certain circumstances, the savings resulting from reduced circulation time may outweigh increases in constant capital costs; in other circumstances, they may not. If an enterprise wishes to produce a given input itself it must have sufficient capital for start-up costs, it must be confident that it can develop sufficient managerial expertise in the area, and it must trust that laborers with the required skills can be found in the available labor pool. Conversely, if the firm wishes to purchase the input on the market, it must be confident the input will be easily available for purchase when required at an affordable price and in the necessary quantities and quality. These matters are, of course, all contingent.

The sort of trade-off in place in a given historical context provides another criteria for a rough division of different variants of capitalism. Just as "Fordism" can be defined in terms of mass production and mass consumption, so too it can be characterized in terms of a specific trade-off between vertical integration and markets. Fordism was a complex contradictory unity of oligopoly and competition. Central (or "core") sectors were dominated by a handful of giant firms with high levels of vertical integration culminating in final assembly. To manage this vertical integration the core firms were organized into bureaucratic hierarchies. Surrounding these firms were a variety of suppliers and distributors, typically much smaller than the core firms. Finding the right balance between vertical integration and the use of suppliers in the market was tricky; Henry Ford's dream of integrating all aspects of the automobile production process within a single organization did not prove feasible. Nonetheless, the benefits of vertical integration were thought to be considerable, extending beyond the lower constant capital costs that have been the focus of discussion thus far.

These bureaucratic organizations were able to reduce transaction and coordination costs for complex and capital-intensive tasks better than smaller firms (Williamson 1975). Put in less neutral terms, a chief benefit for capital of vertical integration was control. The more aspects of production were concentrated under a single roof, or within a single organizational flow chart, the more calculable and predicable production could be, at least in principle (Beniger 1986). This allowed product cycles and innovations to be planned, at least to a certain extent ("planned obsolescence"). Another advantage of size, economies of scale, has been noted earlier. As different sections of the production process were centralized within the same organization, administrative costs, energy costs, warehouse costs, and so on, all tended to be smaller per unit of output.

Regarding relations between assemblers and their suppliers and distributors, the former kept an "arm's length" distance from the latter, approximating a pure market relation. The larger assembly firms attempted to play off various suppliers and distributors against each other in price competition. If a new supplier came along who offered a lower price, or if a distributor offered a higher price, assembly firms would often drop the companies they had been associated with. This relative lack of loyalty held in the reverse direction as well. A supplier or distributor who gained privileged information from one assembler would often use that knowledge to win subcontracting work from a competing assembler.

A series of problems eventually emerged that challenged the stability of the Fordist trade-off between oligopoly (vertical integration) and competition (markets). Evidence accumulated that the giant oligopolies had extended vertical integration too far in certain respects. They pushed into areas where they lacked expertise. Their labor costs were often as high (or higher) in relatively secondary areas as they were in areas of strategic importance to their operations. In many sectors economies of scale stagnated or even reversed once firms grew past a certain size (Womack et al. 1990; Davidow and Malone 1992; Dertouzos et al. 1991).

The hands-off relations between assemblers and their suppliers also generated difficulties. In order to win contracts assemblers had to cut prices. An exclusive concern with price tended to lead to a neglect of quality, as price pressures forced suppliers to cut corners. Suppliers, having no special loyalty to the core firms, often refused to devote themselves religiously to meeting delivery schedules. The resulting fear of disruption in supplies led core firms to stockpile parts, leading to high inventory costs. Distributors resisted attempts by assemblers to intervene in the selling process, resulting in regular breakdowns in feedback regarding customers.

The hands-off relations between supplier and assembler, and between assembler and distributor, also affected the innovation process. Subcontractors and distributors were generally too small to engage in significant research and development themselves. From the assembler's perspective, it made little sense to share technical innovations with suppliers, since in the medium term these suppliers might well be working for competitors. And when suppliers or distributors did discover technical improvements on their own, from their standpoint it made little sense to share these innovations with assemblers, since these assemblers could turn around and transmit them to competing supplier firms. The short-term nature of the relation between suppliers and assemblers thus lessened cooperation on medium-to-long-term research projects, and significantly increased the time it took for innovations to diffuse. Also, suppliers would be given the information they required to design a part only after the design engineers of the assembly firm had completed their work, further extending the time it took to bring product innovations to market.[3]

In the view of the defenders of the lean production model, the arrangements just described added up to a considerable degree of social antagonism in intercapital relations. In the long wave of expansion after World War II, growth rates were high enough to mask many of these problems. But as an extended period of economic decline began in the early seventies, and as relatively protected national markets gave way to globalization, all that changed. Pressure increased to restructure relations among different units of production, just as there was increasing pressure to restructure capital/labor and capital/consumer relations. Here too the lean production model can be seen as the most significant result of this restructuring to have emerged thus far.

B. Markets, Hierarchies, and Networks in Lean Production

From the standpoint of lean production, market relations in Fordism were at one and the same time too restricted and too extensive. They were too restricted in that the limits of vertical integration seemed to have been reached in a number of sectors. The solution to this problem was clear: partially dismantle the hierarchy ("downsize"), and rely more on market relations. Inputs that in Fordism would have been produced within the organization can be purchased from subcontractors; new products that would have been developed within the firm can be handed over to spin-offs, joint ventures, or independent profit centers.[4] From another point of view, however, market relations in Fordism were too extensive. As we have seen, the "hands-off"—that is, pure market—relations between core firms and their suppliers and distributors had severe disadvantages, especially regarding technical change. As a result, lean production networks can be seen as an attempt to find a third way between bureaucratic hierarchy and pure market relations, rather than simply as a shift from the former to the latter.

Kenney and Florida term this third way "quasi-integration," referring to the way suppliers, distributors, and assemblers are united in networks that transcend pure market relations (Kenney and Florida 1993, 78). Aoki (1988) refers to the same model as "quasi-disintegration," stressing instead the transformation from vertical integration to increased reliance on subcontractors. Gerlach's description of "intercorporate alliances" is helpful as well:

> Intercorporate alliances, as defined here are institutionalized relationships among firms based on localized networks of dense transactions, a stable framework of exchange, and patterns of periodic collective action. (Gerlach 1992, 3)

Perhaps the best term is Harrison's "core/ring networks"; a lean production network consists of a (downsized) core firm surrounded by a ring of subcontractors and distributors with which it is connected. For Harrison, it would be difficult to overestimate the significance of this new form of relations among units of capital:

> Of all the reactions [to the crisis of Fordism, T.S.], all the experiments, the most far-reaching may well turn out to be the creation by managers of boundary-spanning networks of firms, linking together big and small companies operating in different industries, regions, and even countries. *This* development—not an explosion of individual entrepreneurship or a proliferation of geographically concentrated industrial districts, per se—is the signal economic experience of our era. (Harrison 1994, 127)

In lean production networks a core assembly firm may have up to ten tiers of suppliers. The core company, usually a final assembler, structures linkages and coordinates flows among the first-tier suppliers.[5] Each subsequent tier then coordinates the tier directly beneath it. One measure of the growth of this arrangement is that between 1966 and 1981 the percentage of manufacturing workers employed by subcontractors in Japan increased from 53 to 66 percent (Kenney and Florida 1993, 45).[6] Over half of medium and small firm manufacturing enterprises there engage in subcontracting for larger companies (Aoki 1988).

There are a number of preconditions for the formation of networks of lean production enterprises. Geographical proximity is one factor, although advances in transportation and communications technologies make this factor somewhat less significant.[7] A variety of formal and informal organizational innovations are also important. Formally, networks can be bound together through equity holdings. Core companies typically hold considerable equity in their spin-offs, as do the two or more core firms contributing to a joint venture. Debt holdings, dispatched directors, equipment leases, and trade associations are other formal arrangements designed to ensure that particular firms fit the needs of the network as a whole. This goal is also furthered when a top executive for one firm within a network holds a seat on the board of directors of another enterprise in the same network. Or a multicompany presidents' council can be formed, bringing together the top executives of affiliated crossheld companies. When such a council is in place, there is less need for companies to hold seats on each other's boards (Gerlach 1992, 61). These various institutional bonds enable the members of a network to undertake industry and public relations projects as a group (ibid., chapter 4). In the course of such projects numerous informal bonds arise as well, personally connecting the managers and employees of different firms in the network.

The development of information technologies is surely one of the most crucial preconditions for the formation of lean production networks. In the industrial districts of Italy and elsewhere, manufactures have insisted that suppliers use identical capital equipment with identical software programs and tooling. Their goal is to guarantee that outputs will be compatible throughout the network (Davidow and Malone, 1992). Quality Function Deployment software furthers this same goal. This software allows an assembly firm to determine whether its suppliers' output fulfills the specifications set for them (Stefanides 1989, 82). Perhaps most pivotal technical change in this context has been the development of Electronic Data Interchange (EDI) and the internet. These technologies allow direct computer-to-computer information exchange of various business documents. They affect invoicing, data control, engineering data exchange, warehouse and transport planning, delivery notification and acknowledgement, electronic funds transfer, and contract progress between firms (Beckett et al. 1990, 62; Hof et al. 1998). They both significantly reduce the paperwork involved in intercapital trade, lessen clerical errors, shorten the order cycle, and cut administrative costs.

> The greatest benefit that EDI offers, however, is that it enables the integration of interenterprise business operations and eliminates manual business transactions. This results in an improved metabolism between enterprises—for example, shortening turnaround time from weeks or days to seconds. (Tapscott and Caston 1993, 97)

The Internet allows firms that could not afford expensive and complex EDI software to enjoy this same benefit as well (Reinhardt 1998).

Once core/ring networks of lean production enterprises are established, they provide a variety of advantages to core firms according to writers in the business press. Spin-offs provide new career paths for employees whose entrepreneurial drive would otherwise be stifled. They help firms avoid difficulties associated with a lack of management expertise in a specific area. It becomes easier for them to monitor the quality of components shipped by subcontractors, and to correct potential quality problems before they occur; previously the firms would have had to manufacture the components themselves to have the same level of quality control. In brief, networks allow core firms to combine the governance and coordination advantages of vertical integration with the flexibility, internal cohesion, and entrepreneurial focus of smaller companies (Gerlach 1992, 202). Suppliers benefit as well. For instance, they do not have to deal with sudden emergency orders, or with unexpected cancellations.

For both sorts of firms the move to networks has positive effects on the innovation and diffusion process. Regarding innovation, some of the advantages of networks over both bureaucratic hierarchies and pure market relations include the following:

- No single company is able to maintain a position on the frontier of all technical developments. Networks allow firms to exploit complementarities of technical expertise (Porter and Fuller 1986; Powell 1990; Kerwin 1998).[8]
- When a number of different firms cooperate in the innovation process, the risks and the costs associated with innovation can be spread out. As a result, a more extensive search for innovations can be undertaken (Reinhardt 1998).[9]
- With flatter hierarchies, the flow of information and decision making can be sped up, allowing the rate of innovation to increase (Ohtani et al. 1997, chapter 4).
- Close cooperation with supplier firms allows just-in-time delivery. This keeps inventory levels low (Hof et al. 1998, 126). As a direct result firms do not need to work off high levels of inventory prior to introducing product innovations. And so the pace of product innovation can quicken. Costs come down as well. Besides lower inventory costs, with just-in-time delivery there is no need for incoming inspection, or expensive billing procedures. All this means that more revenues are available for innovation.
- As we have noted already in the previous chapter, when dealers transmit orders directly to factories manufacturers receive continuous feedback on product quality and market developments. This also spurs product innovation.
- Feedback from firms using products made by other firms in the network can hasten innovation. In Japan, 47 percent of the firms listed technology users as a source of ideas for new technologies. Only 37 percent cited their own research laboratories (Gerlach 1992, 216).
- Suppliers tied to a single core firm in a network develop "relation-specific skills" that enhance their basic technological capability (Aoki 1988; Lester 1998, 66–67; 315–16).

- When patent protection is weak, the unity of innovators and users in an alliance allows the innovator to capture more of the benefits of the innovation, thus encouraging more innovative activity (Teece 1986).
- Parent companies often provide bank loans, trade credit, and loans or sales of production equipment at low prices to small firms in their networks. This enables these smaller firms to undertake technological upgrades that would not otherwise be possible (Gerlach 1992, 218).[10]
- Cross equity holdings within networks lessen worries about hostile takeovers. This enables enterprises to take a long-term perspective, allowing greater investment in long-term innovation projects (Gerlach 1992, 33).

A similar list can be drawn of the benefits of networks regarding the diffusion of innovations:

- "Concurrent engineering" is one of the most significant manifestations of intercapital cooperation within networks. When engineers in an assembly company cooperate closely with engineers working for suppliers, the final product and the parts for that product can be designed simultaneously. Innovations in design can be instantaneously diffused in a multidimensional flow of information from assembler to supplier and back again. This joint participation in product development allows a significant reduction in the time it takes to ship new products to market.[11]
- The last point can be seen as a special case of a more general feature of the relations of firms within lean production networks. As subcontractors and distributors maintain long-term relationships with core companies, the stability in the relationship encourages sharing of other forms of technical information besides product design plans, such as advances in materials, machinery, workplace organization, and so on (Goto 1982).
- Cooperation among supplier, assembler, and distributor firms within a network may also involve personnel sharing. This too allows innovations to diffuse within the network at a more rapid rate than would otherwise be the case.

Lifson summarizes the role of networks in fostering innovation and diffusion as follows:

> Knowledge is not only what economists call a public good—it is not diminished by consumption—but is what Adler calls a *super-public*

good—the more it is used, the more it expands. Neither markets nor hierarchies nor any mix of the two can optimize the production of public goods. Market forms that lock up property rights to knowledge create incentives to make the risky investments needed to create new knowledge, but then society loses by the lack of general availability of the resulting knowledge. . . . The spontaneous sharing and commitment to a higher purpose characteristic of the network form is far better adapted to knowledge growth than either the exchange characteristic of markets or the authority characteristic of hierarchy. (Lifson 1992, 296)

These considerations suggest that the restructuring of the relations among different units of capital is just as significant a part of the lean production model as the restructuring of labor and consumer relations documented in previous chapters. I thus cannot accept Kenney and Florida's attempt to downplay its significance. They contrast their approach, which emphasizes restructuring at the point of production, with the flexible specialization perspective that stresses the rise of new forms of interfirm networks. They refer to the latter as an "important but nonetheless second-order phenomenon" (Kenney and Florida 1993, 13). There are indeed reasons to reject the flexible specialization perspective, as we saw in chapter 1. And the importance of the sphere of production is not in dispute. Nonetheless, Kenney and Florida's remark is misleading. They themselves insist that the enhanced diffusion of innovations is an absolutely central element of lean production, and that "the transcendence of traditional industrial boundaries" contributes to this (ibid., 17). If it is true that networks "can capture advantages of market efficiency while retaining some of control and coordination advantages of integration," this is hardly a secondary matter (ibid., 127).

How do the new capitalist utopians assess lean production networks? Their general claim is a familiar one. They hold that the intercapital relations described above are not plagued by the intercapital antagonisms that characterized Fordism. As production and distribution is more and more tightly linked in networks, that is, as the suppliers, assemblers, and distributors become ever more functionally integrated, conflict and suspicion give way to cooperation, trust, and harmony:

It has become obvious to many manufacturers that their ability to become world-class competitors is based to a great degree on their ability to establish high levels of trust and cooperation with suppliers. (Spekman 1984, 77)

Another typical expression of this claim reads as follows:

> The road to world-class supply chain management meanders through a series of cultural changes—to a new plateau of trust. To achieve true partnership, customers and suppliers must share information—on new product designs, internal business plans, and long-term strategy—that once would have been closely guarded. (Sheridan 1990, 13)

Or, again,

> The nature of the new business relationship will result in stronger and more enduring ties based on a mutual destiny, one shared by groups of both suppliers and customers. (Davidow and Malone 1992, 142)

This "mutual destiny" is manifested in "unprecedented levels of trust . . . between the company and its suppliers" (ibid., 183; see also Sabel 1992; Powell 1990).

The general form of the argument here ought to be very familiar by now. We have already seen that the proponents of the "new economy" assert that few attempts were made in Fordism to mobilize the creativity of labor, or to incorporate consumers into the design process. In their view this explains why Fordism has proven to be a less productive mode of organization than lean production, in which the intelligence of the workforce and consumers is tapped. Their analysis of intercapital relations is analogous. The "hands-off" relations of Fordism have proven restrictive. Suppliers are sources of insight into the production process, and distributors are sources of insight into the most efficient manner of getting commodities to end users. It is in the interests of core firms to form organizational networks in order to tap these insights. As these core firms flourish, firms on the ring of the network prosper as well. Once again, it is claimed, we have a "win-win" situation.

There is a clear parallel between the claims made by the defenders of lean production regarding labor relations, consumer relations, and the relations among different units of capital: in all three cases it is asserted that social antagonisms associated with Fordism are overcome. Past a certain point, however, the analogy quickly breaks down. The new capitalist utopians proclaim that conflicts between labor and capital, and between capital and consumers, are all but entirely removed in lean production. No one would ever assert this regarding intercapital relations. After all, firms must still compete against other units of capital in the market. And so the claim is not that antagonisms will be removed altogether, but that *excessive* antagonisms will be eliminated, that is, antagonisms that hamper rather than further the social good. The emphatic rhapsodies to harmony and trust in intercapital relations thus imply that a fundamental change has taken place in capitalism.

Marx did not anticipate this change. And so here too the Marxian perspective is called into question by the emergence of the "new economy."

C. A Critical Look at Intercapital Networks in Lean Production

The talk of greater cooperation among units of capital is not a sham. Joint endeavors do indeed often occur that go far beyond the standard intercapital relations of Fordism. Nonetheless, I shall argue that the rise of lean production networks does not necessarily lessen intercapital antagonisms, let alone reduce the amount of antagonism in the social system as a whole. There are four social contexts to consider here: intercapital relations within networks; intercapital relations among different networks; relations between networks of capital and alternative forms of social networks; and relations between capital networks and the state. I shall attempt to argue that the very reasoning used to legitimate intercapital networks by the advocates of the "new economy" can ground a critique of the inevitable limits of these networks.

1. Relations within Networks

In this section the interconnection between small subcontractors on the ring of networks and larger core (assembly) firms will be considered.[12] The first point to emphasize is that the increase in the number of small firms in the rings of various networks has not undermined the relative position of large firms in the core:

> We are constantly being told that technological change now systematically favors (or is mainly the product of) small companies. The idea is pervasive, but it is simply not correct. Take that quintessential high-tech activity: the design and manufacture of computers. It is no secret that in Japan, the computer industry has from the beginning been dominated by the NECs, the Toshibas, and the Fujitsus. But dominance by major firms is also true in America. In 1987 . . . 85 percent of all the individual enterprises in the computer industry in the United State did indeed employ fewer than 100 workers. Only about 5 percent of all computer makers had as many as 500 employees. Yet that comparative handful of firms—that 5 percent at the top—accounted for fully 91 percent of all employment and of all sales in the computer industry in that year. (Harrison 1994, 5)

The use of the term "dominance" in this passage is no accident. Where the new capitalist utopians see harmony and trust, Harrison and other theorists see a power relation. Even Kenney and Florida, two of the most sympathetic scholars of lean production, bluntly state, "Of course, in actuality, it is the assemblers who have the real power" (Kenney and Florida 1993, 146). There are three dimensions of this power relation that warrant mention here. They concern (a) the control of production, (b) the flow of information, and (c) the capacity to affect pricing and profits.

(a) In comparison to Fordism, production activities in lean production networks are relatively decentralized, that is, spread out among the various firms in the network. But this does not at all imply that *control* over the production process is decentralized. As Kumazawa and Yamada write,

> The Toyota-style production control based on the "no-buffer principle" or the "just-in-time system," for example, would not work efficiently without the parent firm's power also to control the production of parts-suppliers, and the parts-delivery service of forwarding firms. Giant firms distinctly benefit from the large-scale industrial gradation of firms. (Kumazawa and Yamada 1989, 109)

The scope of decision-making power of core firms may actually increase, even as more productive activities are shifted to ring firms:

> [T]he vertical groups that comprise upstream supplier firms and downstream distributors introduce at the interfirm level some of the characteristics one associates with standard hierarchical organization (notably a degree of centralization of product-related decision making, which is managed by the parent firm . . .). (Gerlach 1992, xviii)

Harrison puts the point even more forcefully:

> *Production* may be decentralized into a wider and more geographically far-flung number of work sites, but *power, finance,* and *control* remain concentrated in the hands of the managers of the largest companies in the global economy. (Harrison 1994, 47)

The effects of strategic decisions made by the core firm ripple throughout the network of subcontractors and distributors, but those making the decisions are not accountable to these smaller firms. This should make us wary of the claim that these decisions will automatically tend to reflect the interests of all firms within the network. The new capitalist utopians, for example, point to the way the risks associated with innovation are shared within networks of lean production firms. But in many cases, at least, it would be more accurate to say that core assembly firms aim to shift the risks of innovations onto smaller enterprises:

> As they expand, first-tier suppliers are being forced by auto makers to assume complicated new responsibilities, such as systems design, without being compensated for the extra risk and cost. . . . In their efforts to cut costs the Big Three auto makers have shifted design and engineering work to their top suppliers, even requiring them to supervise smaller suppliers as well. Chrysler Corp., for example, entrusted the auto-parts unit of Textron Inc. with the co-ordination of the work of other suppliers on the interior of its new minivans—yet didn't pay Textron any extra cash for the service. (Vlasic 1996, 60)

The power of core firms within the network is a function of the extent to which the subcontractor is dependent upon the core assembly firm for its survival. Most core firms have an explicit policy of dealing with suppliers who are dependent on them. Honda, for instance, likes its suppliers to be dependent on it for 33 to 100 percent of their total volume. Of course there are other cases where suppliers within a given network are not as dependent on sales to one customer, especially if they possess firm-specific knowledge desired by many core enterprises. The defenders of lean production cannot make such cases central to their defense of core/ring networks, however. The more subcontractors escape the sway of a particular core firm, the less likely it is that the positive phenomena these theorists emphasize will be found, such as the free sharing of information within networks. Also, the more successful small independent firms are, the more likely it is that they will either be bought out by multinational firms (Harrison 1994, 87, 114), or themselves become core firms exercising asymmetrical power over subcontractors on *their* ring (ibid., 91–92).

(b) The defenders of the "new economy" insist that the flow of information among suppliers, assemblers, and distributors within lean production networks counts as a significant difference from intercapital relations in Fordism. This may be granted. But these analysts fail to note an asymmetry in this information flow, one that mirrors the asymmetry of power within lean production networks. Subcontractors dependent upon a core assembly firm can be coerced to share proprietary data and technology. They can also be forced to let the assembler make inspections regularly, tap into their computers, and pick the brains of their work force. And they can be made to set aside board seats for representatives of the main assembler.[13] These measures all ensure a flow of information from the subcontractors to the assemblers. *But the subcontractors are not in a position to force core firms to reciprocate.* The flow of information from core firms to those on the ring of lean production networks is thus likely to be much more restricted than in the reverse direction.

> In return for comfy, long-term contract, suppliers have to jump when they're told to. "We won't do business with them otherwise," declare Cummins Engine President James A. Henderson. And, increasingly, suppliers are being asked to open their books to ensure that profits aren't too fat. Excel does this for Ford. "They know every cost we incur," says Excel CEO Lohman." (Kelly et al. 1992, 59)

Another consideration reinforces this conclusion. In capitalism, proprietary knowledge is a potential source of profits. As long as this is the case, we can expect there to be limits on the willingness of assemblers to share information with suppliers. No network is entirely stable. There is always the possibility that a supplier will later become a competitor in a given market, using information derived from the core firm.[14] Core firms (unlike smaller enterprises on the ring of lean production networks) are in a position to chose between maintaining secrecy or risking the leakage of proprietary information. There will surely be many cases where the former option appears preferable. In fact, the transition to the "new economy" has been accompanied by an *extension* of intellectual property rights in the economy.[15] All the talk of free flow of information within lean production networks must be balanced against this development. Intellectual property rights can hamper innovation and diffusion, and waste social resources in legal disputes. They disproportionately aid the largest firms, which are best positioned to wage extensive court battles. And they help maintain unequal development on the international plane, since the more affluent societies possess both a greater base of scientists and technicians and a more extensive scientific-technical-legal infrastructure (Kloppenberg 1988). None of this fits easily with the talk of how information technologies lead to "unprecedented levels of trust" in intercapital relations.[16]

(c) The last passage quoted above points to a third way in which the asymmetry of power within networks is manifested, one having to do with prices and profits. As noted in section A, the vertical integration of Fordism lowered capital costs associated with inputs, while it increased circulation time. Lean production involves a different trade-off. Production is decentralized as levels of outsourcing increase, thereby reducing the turnover time of the capital invested in core firms, which in turn tends to further the accumulation process of these firms. But this arrangement simultaneously tends to increase constant capital costs, hindering the accumulation process. It follows that core assembly firms have a powerful incentive to keep the prices they pay to their subcontractors as low as possible. Since these input prices include the profits of their subcontractors, another way of making the same point would be to say that core assembly firms have a powerful incentive to monitor and squeeze the profits of their subcontractors. This can be done in a variety of ways. I have already mentioned the shifting of risks connected with innovation to subcontractors. Other measures include the following:

- Core firms can force smaller firms on the ring of the network to purchase machinery (raw materials, etc.) from the assembler (or from another business owned by that assembler). If the costs are higher than the market norm, economic surplus is transferred from the suppliers to the core firms.
- Core firms can retain the most significant "value added" parts of the production process for themselves, shifting the least profitable activities to their suppliers (Tapscott and Caston 1993, 8).
- Multiyear contracts with suppliers are often based on rapidly falling delivery prices (Womack et al. 1990, 168). If rapid productivity advances are not forthcoming, these contracts force subcontractors to cut wages or accept lower profit levels.
- In periods of economic downturn, core firms can unilaterally insist that payment contracts be renegotiated to allow cuts in the prices paid to suppliers. In this manner they can displace the burden of the downturn onto their subcontractors.[17]
- Core firms in lean production networks can play different suppliers within the same network against one another in price competition, just as Fordist firms did with independent suppliers. The very Internet technologies that aid the formation of networks in the "new economy" also further this price competition (Florida and Kenney 1993).[18]
- Core firms can monitor their subcontractors for cost savings, and then insist that these cost savings be passed on to them. This has led some suppliers to conceal savings from the core firm (Morgan 1993). So much for relationships of trust!
- Core assembly firms have used the transition to just-in-time production as a way of shifting inventory costs to their suppliers.[19]

How would the promoters of the "new economy" reply to this critique? Two responses could be made. First, the fact that core firms often hold equity in their key suppliers and distributors must be taken into account. Squeezing the margins of suppliers would hardly be in the interest of the core assemblers in such cases. Another possible response would be to insist that intercapital relations within networks may still allow a rough symmetry of power, even among units of capital of quite different size. Assemblers are dependent upon the flexibility and specialized skills of small firms on the ring of lean production networks, granting the latter firms considerable leverage:

> Obviously, suppliers will become very dependent upon their down-stream customers; but by the same token the customers will be equally trapped by their suppliers. (Davidow and Malone 1992, 7)

Given this rough symmetry of power, it would seem to be in the interests of core firms to respect the interests of smaller firms in the network.

These replies appear to have considerable force. But they are both fundamentally flawed. One obvious limit of the first argument is that it only concerns those ring firms in the "first tier" of lean production networks. Core firms do not typically have equity as we proceed further down the chain of subcontractors, so that this argument for trust and harmony within networks as a whole loses its plausibility. As *Business Week* notes regarding bailouts within *keiretsu* in response to the recession in Japan in the early '90s,

> [T]he problem with this safety net is that it only works for Japan's largest corporations. The small and mid-size companies, which almost entirely account for the rise in bankruptcies, have no such recourse. (Neff 1992, 49)

Further, the first argument is flawed even if we restrict our attention to network relations that do include equity holdings. A core firm finding itself facing strong competitive pressures may find itself confronting a choice between accepting lower profit margins itself or squeezing the profit margins of its suppliers. Suppose that the core assembly firm itself owns a considerable amount of equity in a subcontractor. If it takes the latter path at least the other equity holders in the subcontractor firms are forced to share the burden as well.

But core firms that squeeze ring firms in which they hold equity are not primarily motivated by a desire to force their fellow investors to absorb greater losses. The main problem with the first argument is that it completely overlooks the way the capital/labor relation affects these intercapital relations. Labor organizations are generally stronger in core firms than in firms on the rings of networks. If core firms are able to put increasing economic pressure on firms in their ring, this pressure is likely to be passed on to the workers in the latter enterprises in the form of lower wages, lower benefits, greater intensity of work, forced overtime, and so on, leading to a "super-exploitation" of this sector of the workforce (Harrison 1994; Brown et al. 1990; Gee et al. 1993, 78–80). To the extent this strategy is successful, the profits of the ring firms are not adversely affected, and thus the returns on equity held by core firms are not adversely affected. When this elementary aspect of intercapital relations is noted, the force of the first argument dissipates completely.[20] Turning to the second response, two points must be kept in mind. First, whenever the core firm has a number of different suppliers, while the ring firm relies on the core firm for most of its business, then the structure of the situation systematically favors the core firm, even if the ring enterprises have expertise the latter needs. And that is a typical situation in lean production networks.

Second, for any given product, generation of product, or generation of technically related products, core firms may well be dependent on the specialized knowledge of their subcontractors. With radically new innovations, however, the expertise of previous suppliers may not be as needed; it may, in fact, become irrelevant. Interfirm networks established for one generation of technology may not be appropriate for another; networks of lean production firms are thus in continual flux. The core assembly firm may be in a position to anticipate this sort of technical change due to proprietary strategic knowledge not shared with subcontractors. In this case it could well be in the long-term interests of the assembler to squeeze its present suppliers. In brief, the more rapidly innovation occurs, the less likely it is that long-term intercapital relations will be stable and harmonious. And, as proponents of the "new economy" continually insist, the lean production model is explicitly designed to increase the rate of innovation.[21] There is a parallel here with an argument discussed previously in the context of the capital/wage labor relation. Supporters of lean production argue that the owners and controllers of capital need to show loyalty to their workforce, since they are dependent on the skills of its members. But if the skills required for one generation of technology are significantly different from those needed for the next, why should the enterprise care about a long-term relation with a given labor force? The identical point holds for intercapital relations.

It is worth noting that there is a significant internal tension in the thought of the new capitalist utopians on this matter. In some contexts they stress how information technologies allow much closer cooperation among the firms in lean production networks. But on other occasions these same writers discuss how these technologies enable lean production firms to become "virtual corporations," rapidly arising in one configuration only to dissolve and take on another form. Davidow and Malone, for instance, write,

> To the outside observer, it [the virtual corporation] will appear almost edgeless, with permeable and continuously changing interfaces between company, supplier, and customers. (Davidow and Malone 1992, 5–6)

The obvious problem here is that this constant flux tends to undermine the very long-term relationships of trust that Davidow and Malone themselves claim characterize intercapital relations within lean production networks. Trust demands much more continuity than virtual corporations are ever likely to provide.

The conclusion of this discussion must be that the relations among the different units of capital within a network continue to be characterized by a fundamental antagonism:

> Interviews with auto parts suppliers reveal that the typical manager of a supplier firm in this country continues to be wary of being blindsided by his large business customers, whether by being forced to take a sudden large price cut or by being expected to upgrade his technology without the financial wherewithal to do so. (Harrison 1994, 182)

The advocates of lean production present a quite misleading picture when they downplay this. They fail to consider intercapital relations within networks over time; arrangements that are of mutual benefit at some time T1 can swiftly turn to aggressive attacks in the market at a later T2. If all cooperation is provisional and apt to be removed when economic pressures appear, and if the eventual appearance of economic pressure is inevitable in the game of capitalism, then it does not seem out of line to suggest that intercapital antagonisms remain fundamental within lean production networks.[22]

The claim that there is an increase in harmony and trust in intercapital relations cannot be justified simply by examining networks of assemblers, suppliers, and distributors. There are other forms of intercapital relations that need to be considered as well, to which we now turn.

2. Limits of Harmony and Trust between Networks

Suppose we assume, contrary to fact, that trust and harmony reign within networks of lean production firms. Even then it is possible that intercapital relations, taken as a whole, are just as antagonistic as ever. An increase in conflicts among various networks might counterbalance any lessening in antagonism along the supplier/assembler/distributor axis. Note, for instance, the initial phrase in the following hymn to harmony within networks:

> *Because competition is intense,* [assembly firm] A and its suppliers are conscious of the need to cut costs, improve quality, design, performance, or otherwise add value. They also see themselves as sharing a common source of prosperity in the sales of their widgets to end users. This sense

of a collective fate provides them with a basic goal congruity. (Lifson 1992, 304; emphasis added)

The "basic goal congruity" within networks is thus but part of a bigger story, and a relatively secondary part at that. First and foremost in the account is the intensification of competition among the networks of capital; the sense that firms within a particular network share a "collective fate" is externally imposed by this conflict.

For Marx, the root source of intercapital antagonisms stems from the value form itself. The category of value holds when production is privately undertaken by economic units that then must take their product to the market in order to discover whether their production was socially necessary. Assuming there is sufficient effective demand for the commodity in question, the best way to ensure that labor is not socially wasted is through technical change that increases labor productivity relative to competitors. Producers with higher levels of productivity are generally able to amass surplus profits, encouraging imitation (Marx 1981, 373; Smith 1999).[23] As technical advances are imitated, there is a necessary tendency for an overproduction of capital to result. Extended overproduction eventually demands the devaluation of certain units of capital. Each individual unit of capital has a fundamental interest in shifting the burdens of devaluation onto other units.

The value form is not put out of play with the move to lean production networks, even if we suppose for the sake of the argument that firms within these networks are united in harmony and trust. The fear of socially wasted investment and the drive to appropriate surplus profits do not disappear in the "new economy." The tendency to overproduction crises remains, as does the fact that the only ultimate solution to overproduction is devaluation. To the extent that conflicts within networks are overcome, this simply means that the relevant unit of intercapital conflict has shifted. Antagonisms among different firms would now be displaced to antagonisms among different networks of firms, with each network attempting to transfer the burdens of devaluation onto its competitors.

I have referred throughout this work to the fact that the rate of innovation increases (or, equivalently for our purposes here, product cycle time decreases) in lean production. The faster the rate of innovation, the greater the danger that previous investments will be devalued prior to a full return on the investments. Therefore in lean production the law of value comes to hold with more force, not less. More and more aspects of social life are determined by the pressure to lower socially necessary labor time; taking demand as given, this is the best strategy for displacing the costs of devaluation onto other units of capital. As competitive battles increase in intensity in the "new economy" there is less and less margin for error, and fewer and fewer guarantees that success in one round of innovation will continue in the following one. In brief, any extension of trust and harmony *within* networks of capital is completely consistent with an increase in antagonisms *across* networks. The new capitalist utopians are so fixated on the potential for information technologies to strengthen ties within networks that they downplay this wider context.

It would be possible to consider the various alleged manifestations of trust and harmony within networks in turn, and show that each one ultimately involves antagonisms among various networks of capital. A single example should suffice here, taken from a feature of networks especially praised by the new capitalist utopians, the sharing of information within networks. Consider the following passage:

> Instead of hoarding information as proprietary, suppliers seek to enhance their relative bargaining position with [other firms in the network] by offering information as a source of potential value to the collectivity. *They want to enhance the collectivity's competitiveness with rival product systems.* (Lifson 1992, 304; emphasis added)

In other words, any increased flow of information within networks confirms, rather than contradicts, Marx's emphasis on antagonisms in intercapital relations. If there is an overall rise in intercapital competitiveness and insecurity, why should any isolated pockets of increased "harmony" and "trust" among units of capital be taken as a defining characteristic of lean production?

3. The Limits on Information Flow within Networks

If we are to evaluate the flow of information within intercapital networks in the "new economy," other things are relevant besides the question of the *quantity* of information exchanged. There is also the issue of the *types* of information that flows within networks. The initial development of information technologies was funded with public monies.[24] But the subsequent use of these technologies in the economy is generally directed by private resources. This means that the advantages of information technologies have been predominantly enjoyed by private companies with the resources to set up expensive private communications systems. And this in turn implies that the sort of information that flows through lean production networks is information that furthers the economic interests of those who own and control these private companies, that is, information that furthers capital accumulation. Other sorts of information are systematically neglected, even when they are intimately connected with the activities of firms within lean production networks.

Where in the lean production networks is information regarding workers' health and safety transmitted? Where are the hiring and promotion practices of the various divisions of a firm and its subcontractors tracked? What corporate networks share information on discrimination on the basis of gender, race, ethnic identity, or sexual preference? Which intercapital networks in the "new economy" have opened their computers to local environmental groups attempting to monitor pollution resulting from the activities of firms within the networks? When have firms used information technologies to connect the geographically dispersed homeworkers in their employ with each other? What linkages have been set up to unite all workers employed by subcontractors (and subcontractors of the subcontractors, and so on) of the same company over the globe? In these sorts of cases there are systematic (that is, non-contingent) restrictions placed on the flow of information within lean production networks. The full potential of information technologies thus remains unrealized, a point that should be of interest to the new capitalist utopians. Worse still, the extension of intellectual property "rights" in lean production makes it increasingly more difficult to gain access to relevant information regarding the activities of the firms within a lean production network.

We may conclude that the extension of information technologies does not automatically lead to an extension of information flow in the society as a whole; here as elsewhere the ultimate consequences of technical change depend on the social context within which that technology is used. Information technologies are used in lean production networks to foster the private control of decisions affecting economic life. In this manner they ultimately contribute to the restriction of public discourse, not its expansion. They can help shield the owners and controllers of capital from accountability for their decisions:

> Private businessmen . . . are involved in discreet networking rather than public industrial policies with their risks of democracy, publicity and raised expectations among the workforce. Strict albeit unwritten codes of secrecy and limited entry are the characteristics of networking of the ruling economic elite. (Wainwright 1994, 169)

In the business press intercapital networks in the lean production system are applauded for furthering the flow of information, as if that were an ultimate goal of the system. But the true goal of the system remains capital accumulation, despite the use of rhetoric suggesting otherwise. Social innovations that further the flow of information are assimilated with great fanfare when they are compatible with capital accumulation, and ignored or suppressed otherwise. When ends and means are confused like this, it is a sure sign that ideologies are at work. This confusion also provides a precondition for an immanent critique of the new capitalist utopians' position.[25] Proponents of the "new economy" rest their case here upon an appeal to the claim that the free flow of information furthers the social good. The very argument that is used by them to legitimate lean production networks can thus also be used to critique the restrictions on information flow that those networks institute.

4. The State and Lean Production Networks

Marxian social theorists have viewed the capitalist state in various ways: as an instrument used by a particular faction of capital to further its interests; as a structure that furthers the interests of the capitalist class as a whole; as an institution that reflects the interests of a dominant bloc, including factions of both ruling and nonruling classes; or as a subsystem forced by the need for legitimation to consider the common interests of the society as a whole, however limited and contradictory this consideration may be due to the simultaneous need to further capital accumulation (see Ollman 1993, chapters 3, 4). I suspect that at some time or other each of these perspectives has captured aspects of particular capitalist states, while none has held always and everywhere. Rather than explore these themes here, however, I shall simply assume for the moment the last perspective, perhaps most closely associated today with Jürgen Habermas (Smith 1992). Given this view, the following thesis can be formulated: any increase in cooperation among units of capital within lean production networks comes at the cost of hampering the state's ability to institute policies in the common interest. Therefore, any increase in trust within lean production networks is bought at the cost of a lessening of harmony within the social order as a whole.

This thesis can be defended by reference to three points, the first two of which have been made by Robert Reich. Although he ultimately falls into the camp of the new capitalist utopians, Reich has recognized some of the pressures on the capitalist state in the epoch of lean production.[26] The first has to do with the state's ability to collect taxes. More and more international trade takes place among divisions of the same corporation and through "complex employment contracts, profit-sharing agreements, and long-term supply arrangements." As a result,

> [I]t is becoming impossible to tell with any precision how much of a given product is made where. National governments seeking to levy taxes on parts of global webs are often baffled. . . . As more and more enterprises become parts of global webs whose internal accounting systems record the transfers of intermediate goods and related services, earnings and revenues can appear in all sorts of places (often, not coincidentally, where taxes are lowest). (Reich 1991, 114–15)

Reich does not explore how this feature of networks—made possible by advances in transportation and communication technologies—tends to exacerbate the fiscal crisis of the state. This omission is all the more striking when we note that Reich foresees that states will have to provide significant tax breaks and subsidies if they hope to attract investment (ibid., 163). He does acknowledge elsewhere that these tax breaks and subsidies can threaten the financing of public hospitals, schools, and other public goods. But he does not draw the obvious conclusion that the state in the age of lean production will be increasingly hard pressed to provide such public goods.

A second issue concerns the ability of the state to regulate capitalist enterprises. Reich correctly notes that in many respects this capacity may significantly decline in the age of interenterprise networks. In order to avoid restrictions against investments in South Africa in the 1980s, for example, U.S. corporations simply adjusted exchanges within their intra- and interfirm networks. General Motors sold its South African subsidiary to its South African executives, while continuing to supply the enterprise with components, designs, and spare parts from its European subsidiary. The example can be generalized:

> As global corporations are transformed into ever more decentralized webs, moreover, the capacity of governments to assert such control is greatly diminished. A subsidiary that markets or distributes what its parent company produces is clearly dependent on headquarters, and thus susceptible to [government] control; a more independent firm, working within an enterprise web and contracting with strategic brokers at the center, is far less so. (ibid., 157)

The third point concerns the fact that the information technologies that enable lean production networks are not restricted to industrial capital. The biggest market for these technologies has been in the financial sector, where they have played an indirect role in the erosion of popular sovereignty. *Wired* magazine recently published an extremely interesting interview with Walter Wriston, who reigned for seventeen years as chair and CEO of Citicorp/Citibank. Referring to sites where financial capital is transferred electronically across the globe—such as the Clearing House Interbank Payments System in New York, which handles over a trillion dollars a day—Wriston remarked:

> What annoys governments about stateless money is that it functions as a plebiscite on your policy. There are 300,000 screens out there, lit up with all the news traders need to make value judgements on how well you're running your economy. Before the Euromarket and floating ex-

change rates, the president could go into the Rose Garden and make a statement about the dollar, and the world would quietly listen. Today, if the president goes into the Rose Garden and says something dumb, the cross rate of the dollar will change within 60 seconds. . . . The huge volume and speed of the international financial markets has put a break on the ability of sovereign governments to do a lot of things they used to do. (quoted in Bass 1996, 201–02)

The problem here, of course, is that these 300,000 financial speculators get to decide what counts as "dumb," and this will surely include whatever goes against their private self-interest. Information technologies combined with the power of capital have in effect given them something approaching a veto power over state legislation in a manner that has nothing whatsoever to do with the processes of democratic debate and decision making.

Many theorists have concluded from these sorts of considerations that in the "new economy" capital has cut itself off from all forms of social control, a view captured well in the following passage:

The new informational mode of development allows capitalism to restructure itself in the dream of a free movement of endless circulation, unlimited by the rigidity of societies and political institutions. To be sure, business corporations do have to relate to national political systems, and dominant classes are still socially specific. Yet, their organizational logic can now follow a pattern of variable geometry, in which specific interests are fulfilled in different spaces and different times, in a dynamic whose logic is only found in the structure of flows of information and power. Such structure dramatically undermines the process of social control over economic development. . . . Cities, regions, localities, become powerless in their efforts to seize the power impulses upon which their daily life depend. (Castells 1993, 203)

I believe that this perspective goes too far. The "death of the state" has been greatly exaggerated (see Weiss [1998] and chapter 6 below). Social movements still have a potential to force public authorities to exert social control over economic development. The point I wish to make here is different. Mass social movements and widespread social struggles are not part of the lean production model. In their absence lean production will lead to a social world where taxes become ever more regressive, where more and more public revenues are devoted to tax breaks and subsidies for corporations, where fewer and fewer revenues remain for public transportation, public education, public health care, and other types of public goods, where there is less ability to regulate enterprises for the sake of the social good, and where more and more people retreat into cynicism and indifference toward the political process. This would add up to a significant loss in the capitalist state's ability to harmonize the common interests of society as a whole, an ability that is severely restricted under the best of circumstances. It follows from this that even if pockets of increased harmony, trust, and cooperation were to grow within lean production networks, the "new economy" in itself involves an erosion in these qualities within society as a whole.

D. Conclusion

Advances in information technologies have enabled enterprises to communicate more closely and to coordinate production and distribution activities more intimately. This communication and coordination is occurring within the institutional form of networks of lean production firms. These networks provide a clear contrast to the intercapital relations of Fordism. The new capitalist utopians claim that the "new economy" will inaugurate an era in which trust, cooperation, and the sharing of information within networks increasingly replace the excessive antagonism among units of capital characteristic of Fordism and earlier periods. In this chapter I have argued that this claim provides at best a partial and misleading picture. It overlooks various shortcomings of intercapital relations in lean production, including:

1. The asymmetry of economic power within core/ring networks, which allows core firms to control production and the flow of information, and to shift economic burdens onto ring firms, thereby leading to the superexploitation of workers in those ring firms;
2. the heightened competition among networks, which increases the economic pressure to force the pain of devaluations onto other networks;
3. the institutional restrictions on the kinds of information that flow within networks, along with restrictions on who has access to that information; and
4. the long-term shift in the balance of power between the state and private capital, which makes it increasingly difficult for the state to address common interests.

In the light of these problems, talk of harmony and trust is ultimately as hollow here as in discussion of the capital/labor relation and the capital/consumer relation in lean production. Here too the Marxian thesis that capitalism is beset by fundamental social antagonisms has been corroborated, not refuted, by the rise of the so-called new economy.

CHAPTER SIX

Globalization and the "New Economy"

At the conclusion of chapter 1 six fundamental ways in which lean production has been seen by its proponents as a response to the "crisis of Fordism" were presented. According to these theorists lean production aims to lower constant capital costs, reduce circulation time and circulation costs, further the incorporation of science in the circuit of capital, transform the capital/wage labor relation, transform the capital/consumer relation, and closely unite different units of capital within networks. Two questions were then posed. First, can the normative claims made by advocates of lean production regarding social relations in the "new economy" be sustained? This question has been addressed in chapters 2 through 5, and has been answered negatively. Lean production does not reconcile class interests in the workplace. Nor does it institute true consumer sovereignty, or bring about a net increase in trust and harmony among units of capital, let alone in the social order as a whole. In the following chapter I ask what a socioeconomic system would have to look like in order to sustain the normative claims mistakenly made for lean production. Prior to this, however, we must return to the second question posed at the conclusion of chapter 1: how likely is it that the spread of lean production will inaugurate a new period of extended economic dynamism in the capitalist global system?

The discussion of the "new economy" in the previous chapters has been at the level of individual firms and their relationships to employees, customers, and other firms. But the crisis of Fordism discussed in chapter 1 was not limited to individual firms. While this crisis affected different regions in different ways at different times (Webber and Rigby 1996, chapter 8), it must nonetheless be considered as a crisis of capitalism as a global economic system. If lean production is to resolve the crisis, it therefore must do so on the level of capitalism as a global economic system. Proponents of the "new economy" insist that changes in technology and social organization associated with lean production do indeed have the potential to inaugurate a "long boom" in the twenty-first-century global economy (Schwartz and Leyden 1997).

Not even the most adamant advocate of the "new economy" holds that extended global prosperity follows automatically with the introduction of flattened corporations with knowledge workers producing short runs of diverse product lines in cooperation with other enterprises within core/ring networks. Political policies leading to extensive wars or protectionism, economic and political corruption ("crony capitalism"), natural catastrophes (global epidemics, etc.), cultural movements (e.g., a global triumph of fundamentalism), and a host of other contingent factors, could very well derail the global economy. But such matters are all *external* to lean production. The claim is that in and of itself the global diffusion of lean production intrinsically holds the promise of a new "golden age" of economic growth. How ought we evaluate this claim?

I shall consider this question in the following steps. In section A the two leading mainstream perspectives on globalization will be briefly sketched. While these views differ in significant ways, supporters of both hold that the global diffusion of the lean production model is intrinsically capable of initiating an extended economic upturn in the global economy. In section B I shall present a view that is critical of this contention for reasons having to do with the balance of supply and demand in the global economy. Then in the third section I shall present a critique of globalization and the "new economy" based on Marx's notion of the law of value.

A. Two Perspectives on Globalization

The literature on globalization is vast. For our purposes mainstream views on the global economic may be grouped under two main headings, which may be termed "neoliberalism" and "competitive regionalism." Both perspectives hold that the global diffusion of the lean production model is an essential part of the regeneration of the global economy.

1. Neoliberalism

The neoliberal view of globalization can be summarized in three statements. First, technological developments in the "new economy" have granted both finance capital and productive capital an unprecedented ability to escape national boundaries. Second, this historical development has the potential to benefit all groups in the world economy ultimately, whatever the short-to-medium-term costs of adjustment might be. Third, governments, which are powerless to stop this development in any case, ought to enforce property rights, maintain the value of their currencies, and then get out of the way.

Perhaps the most important factor behind the first assertion is the information technology revolution. Firms in the financial sector are by far the biggest private-sector purchasers of information technologies. These technologies allow investments in currencies, bonds, equities, futures, derivatives, and other financial instruments to flow across borders with a magnitude, speed, and complexity that no government could hope to monitor accurately, let alone regulate effectively. In the realm of industrial capital, global computer networks enable engineers from across the globe to cooperate simultaneously in product design ("concurrent engineering").

Computer-aided-design and computer-aided-manufacturing (CAD/CAM) software allow engineers working in one region to program computerized numerically controlled machine tools on the other side of the planet. Electronic Data Interface (EDI) and Internet software allow managers in corporate headquarters to track processes of production and distribution spread out across the globe involving hundreds of subsidiaries and subcontractors. All of this, the story goes, profoundly extends the geographical range in which profitable investments in production can be made, enabling the rise of networks of lean production firms extending across national borders.

The arguments for the second assertion are no less familiar from our earlier discussion of the "new economy" (Tapscott 1996). Those who own and control corporations benefit from globalization, as the pressures of global competition force firms to become flexible learning organizations, capable of taking advantage of opportunities that arise anywhere, any time. Workers for these corporations benefit as well; as their knowledge becomes the most important productive resource in the new economy, they gain the power to negotiate favorable contractual agreements (stock options, profit sharing, etc). Workers also benefit from workplaces where creativity and multiskilling are encouraged and rewarded. Consumers benefit as global competition ensures that prices of commodities decline while their quality and diversity improves. Countries in the so-called Third World benefit by having access to state-of-the-art technologies and products that were previously unavailable due to trade barriers. Third World countries also have the opportunity to attract foreign capital investment, allowing them to industrialize (and enjoy the resulting rise in living standards) rapidly.

Last, but certainly not least in the eyes of neoliberals, globalization furthers the social good by subjecting the policies of particular nation-states to a continuous referendum by finance capital. Governments that maintain a stable value of currency and encourage a high rate of savings are rewarded in international finance markets; those do not are punished in these markets. The currencies overseen by the former enjoy favorable exchange rates, and investors are willing to purchase government bonds at relatively low interest rates. In the latter case, in contrast, currencies are forcibly devalued and the interest rates governments must offer in order to sell their bonds must be raised. Stable currencies and high rates of saving are certainly in the private interests of finance capital. But they are in the general social interest as well, according to neoliberal theory, since a stable currency and a high rate of savings encourage the productive investments that generate economic growth and higher standards of living.

If technical change grants capital unprecedented mobility, and if this development can be expected to further the public good, then the general policy prescription we ought to adopt follows at once. Free trade agreements ought to be established that move us closer to a global economy of free capital flows, unhampered by irrational restrictions on investment. Market-distorting subsidies and trade restrictions ought to be phased out. When this occurs the benefits of the "new economy" will spread throughout the world.

2. Competitive Regionalism

Defenders of the position I shall term "competitive regionalism" (see Cox 1997) agree with neoclassical theorists that the technologies associated with the "new economy" have enabled a "deterritorialization" of production. From a technological standpoint there is no special reason why certain stages in production processes should be located in one region rather than another. The ties that once bound capital investment to specific localities are indeed loosened.

In contrast to neoliberals, advocates of competitive regionalism are generally sympathetic to populist concerns regarding this development. Increasing capital mobility may undermine the extent to which workers and local communities can appropriate a fair share of the benefits of economic activity. Despite this sympathy, however, competitive regionalists reject the protectionism advocated by many populists (see Mander and Goldsmith 1996). They do so for two main reasons. First, whatever one's normative commitments might be, the "ought implies can" principle commands our respect. Short of some unforeseen calamity, the rise of the global economy simply cannot be reversed. Second, populists (and the defenders of neoliberal orthodoxy) have made one crucial mistake in their empirical analysis of globalization. Deterritorialization is but one trend holding in the global economy. The rise of the global economy has simultaneously resulted in a new importance of local spaces, a "reterritorization" (Storper 1997). This implies that globalization offers new opportunities to workers and local communities.

In many sectors success in global markets depends upon access to an extensive labor pool with specific sorts of skills. This pool is most likely to arise when a number of firms in a given sector locate in the same region, where their workers can undergo qualitatively similar forms of "learning by doing." Enterprises also benefit in global markets if their managers and technicians are able to engage in informal exchanges of information within face-to-face networks. This too is most likely to occur when a number of firms in the same (or closely related) sectors locate in the same region. Further, there is evidence that enterprises in which engineers and line workers cooperate together in cross-functional teams are in the long term more likely to flourish than those in which engineering work and production work are spatially separated. The geographical proximity of the former arrangement allows design engineers access to the insights and creativity of those who actually produce the product in question. The result can be a series of incremental advances in productivity that in the aggregate are often immensely significant (Florida and Kenney 1990). It is also the case that in some industries proximity to world-class universities and research labs is a tremendous strategic advantage. Similarly, global marketers need access to localities with exceptional transportation facilities. And for profitable "just-in-time" systems to be introduced, final producers and their suppliers must be in reasonably close proximity.

All of the above considerations suggest that geographical "clusters" of firms and the construction of "technology milieus" are significant factors in the global economy (Storpor and Walker 1989). It is thus quite misleading to assert that the technical and organizational changes associated with the spread of lean production now make space irrelevant, as most neoliberals and their populist opponents hold. The concept "reterritorialization" is meant to capture the great many respects in which the globalization of economic activity is dialectically united with an increased importance of local spaces. This implies that workers and their communities are not necessarily doomed in the new economy. Relatively high wages can be won if regions develop strengths in the areas mentioned in the previous paragraph.

This account of globalization leads to a more nuanced view of the state than that proposed by neoliberals, who applaud the erosion of state capacities. Competitive regionalists concede that global markets have put inescapable pressures on governments to cut back the traditional redistributive programs of the social state (that is, the "Fordist" or "Keynesian" state). This, however, hardly counts as the death of the state. Regional governments can help create the conditions for regional success through support for education and training, funding for infrastructure and research, the formation of formal and informal networks of government, business, and labor leaders, the institution of government/business partnerships for specific projects of essential importance to regional growth, and so on (Kantor 1995).[1] If the shift from "the redistributive state" to "the enabling state" is successful, the lean production model can be instituted in a way that allows all groups within the community to share the benefits of economic growth. From the perspective of competitive regionalists, those who share populist values thus ought to embrace the global economy, not flee from it.

The differences between the neoliberal and the competitive regionalist perspectives are thus quite substantial, especially regarding the proper role of governments in the global diffusion of the "new economy." For our purposes, however, it is more important to stress what the two viewpoints have in common rather than the points of divergence. Adherents of both positions insist that moving to flattened corporations, knowledge workers, mass customization, and intercapital networks tends to reduce significantly the turnover time of the circuit of capital. The "new economy" involves a significant compression of the time spent in product design, a reduction in the time of deliveries of inputs from subcontractors, a speed-up of production, a faster delivery of finished commodities to distributors and final consumers, and so on. Everything else being equal, a faster turnover time allows more capital to be accumulated over time. Neoliberals and competitive regionalists thus both hold that an extended upswing in the global capitalist economy can result from the global diffusion of the technologies and forms of social organization associated with lean production, everything else being equal. Their disagreement simply regards the most effective means for attaining this common goal.

B. Globalization and Global Justice

There are a number of straightforward and fairly obvious points that can be made in criticism of the neoliberal and competitive regionalist perspectives. Regarding the former, there is sufficient evidence of the horribly uneven nature of capitalist development to warrant extreme skepticism regarding the claim that unrestricted global trade and capital mobility tend to bring about prosperity for all. For one thing, capital investment tends to remain in the most prosperous regions. Most foreign direct investment in production has been made in countries of the First World; only about 20 percent of overseas investment from the North flows South. For another, global inequality has significantly increased with the expansion of global trade. In 1960 the ratio between the income of the 20 percent of the world's population living in the richest countries and the income of the 20 percent in the poorest was 30 to 1. Today, after four decades of increasing global trade and a fivefold increase in foreign direct investment, the ratio is well over 60 to 1. Between 1960 and 1991 the share of global income claimed by the richest 20 percent rose from 70 to 85 percent, while the poorest 20 percent's share of global income declined from 2.3 percent to 1.4 percent. And the richest 358 individuals in the world today have a net worth that matches the total held by the 2.3 billion who make up the poorest 45 percent of the world's population (Moody 1997, chapter 3).

The shift of power from governments to financial speculators is also profoundly troubling. As already noted in the previous chapter, their decisions regarding which government actions are "dumb" and which are not—

decisions that can directly and indirectly affect all of the world's six billion people—are based primarily on the private interest in accumulating capital shared by these speculators and the investors whose interests they represent. From this perspective there is no reason whatsoever to assume that globalization will tend to maximize the social good. Further, all social agents sharing a normative commitment to democratic values ought to deplore the rise of international agencies and speculators shielded from accountability to those over whom they exercise power (Nader and Wallach 1996).[2] Finally, all those who embrace a plausible environmental ethics ought to condemn international agencies willing to sacrifice environmental concerns for the sake of easing capital flows (Harvey 1996).

Regarding the competitive regionalist position, three critical remarks can be made initially. First, to my knowledge no defender of this perspective has ever attempted to estimate the relative weights of "deterritorialization" and "reterritorialization" in the "new economy." How many sectors have or have not been freed from spatial constraints in how many of their operations? Competitive regionalists provide an *a priori* reason to consider reterritorialization the more important tendency in the medium-to-long term: as customer satisfaction increases and product cycle times shorten, the development of highly skilled knowledge workers in specific regions grows in economic importance. But is there empirical evidence that this is indeed the dominant tendency in the global economy? Shaiken's (1990) study of skills, productivity, training costs, and training time in Mexican automobile plants suggests that many of the productivity advantages of lean production can be transferred to Third World contexts of low wages and high labor turnover. The idea that capital is perfectly mobile, that capital flight is always and everywhere a real possibility, is indeed a social myth, an ideological weapon used by capital in its struggles against workers and local communities. But the number of cases in which the threat of capital strike is not a mere bluff may be far higher than competitive regionalists appear willing to grant.

A second difficulty concerns the competitive dimension of competitive regionalism. This perspective embraces the logic of global competition in the hope that regions with which the given theorist identifies might win in this competition. But competitive regionalists accept a game whose rules assure that not all can win; for every successful region there are always a multitude of other areas that do not enjoy the fruits of the global economy. Further, this is a game whose rules favor the already advantaged. If, for example, there is an unequal concentration of scientific-technical labor, there will tend to be an unequal global distribution of intellectual property rights (Kloppenberg 1988). As intellectual property rights become more crucial to the process of economic accumulation, global inequality is heightened. And this is a game where even the winners must constantly press ahead, diverting ever more public resources to maintaining their competitive advantages. The world of lean production is a world of ever-compressed product cycles and rapid technological jumps. In such a world the set of skills and infrastructure that allows a region to compete successfully in the global economy at one point of time may rapidly be rendered all but useless. Competitive regionalism is a recipe for continued uneven growth, unrelenting economic insecurity for the vast majority of the world's population, and the sacrifice of social goods that do not contribute to local competitiveness. Competitive regionalism is, in brief, but another variant of social Darwinism.

However relevant the above points might be to issues of global justice, they are not sufficient to answer the question at hand. There has never been an expansionary period in the history of global capitalism characterized by even regional growth or shared prosperity! Capitalism has *always* been a system in which capital accumulation in "core" regions has been inseparably united with oppressive processes in the "periphery," such as slavery, colonialism, extreme environmental degradation, the dumping of excess commodities in captive markets, and so on. The fact that the diffusion of lean production fails to result in an equitable sharing of social wealth may be very relevant to a normative assessment of contemporary forms of globalization. But by itself this does not count against the thesis that the diffusion of lean production may inaugurate a new period of global expansion. Or, rather, this fact may count against the above thesis in one respect only, to which we now turn.

Both neoliberalism and competitive regionalism are "supply side" theories, focused on the conditions that supposedly must be in place for entrepreneurial energies to be unleashed in the "new economy." Neoliberals are confident that the absence of burdensome governmental regulations is all but sufficient in itself, while competitive regionalists stress the positive tasks governments must fulfill. Despite this disagreement, both positions share one significant feature. They both devote next to no attention to problems on the demand side of the global economy. Can it be assumed that global consumer markets will grow at a rate sufficient to absorb exports produced within the various lean production networks scattered across the globe? This question brings us to a third perspective on the global economy, which may be termed "global underconsumptionism."

C. Global Underconsumptionism

Theorists whose work fits under this heading agree with many of the points raised by competitive regionalists against neoliberals regarding the continued significance of the nation-state. What sets global underconsumptionists apart is their attention to the demand side of the global economy.

In their view, the condition of the global economy today eerily parallels the industrialized national economies in the period from the late 1800s through the early 1920s. Technical advances in that era led to a level of productive capacity far exceeding what national markets could absorb. This led to mergers and cartels that restricted production and allocated market shares among a handful of national oligopolies. In the global underconsumptionist story, neither the vast concentrations of economic power resulting from these agreements, nor the fundamental imbalance between supply and demand, were in the public interest. The nation-state had to develop a countervailing power to the cartels and oligarchies in order to regulate their behavior effectively. And the nation-state had to institute policies that raised the level of effective demand significantly above what the market would attain left to itself.

Global underconsumptionists hold that precisely the same structural problems are now recurring on a much vaster scale (Greider 1997). Revolutions in the technologies of production have led to an expansion of productive capacity in segment after segment of the global economy. Real wages in the so-called First World have simultaneously stagnated or declined, while political repression, massive unemployment, and the threat of capital flight have constrained the rise of real wages elsewhere. The result is a structural imbalance between supply and demand that threatens to erupt in a global underconsumption crisis. In response to this state of affairs the pace and scope of corporate mergers continues to increase, reaching two and a half trillion dollars in 1998. Strategic alliances have formed in most major market segments, alliances that in many instances have included agreements to restrict production and divide up markets (Garland and Thornton 1998). Once again, according to the global underconsumptionists, such vast concentrations of economic power, and such a dangerous imbalance between supply and demand, cannot be said to be in the public interest.

If this diagnosis of the structural flaws in the global economy is accepted, and if nation-states continue to have significant capacities to act, the solution follows at once: nation-states must use the full range of their powers to raise levels of demand in the global economy. This will include the reinstatement of national controls on the flow of capital investment and trade. Nations in the so-called First World, for example, should refuse to allow imports from countries where basic labor rights, especially the right to organize collectively, are not respected *de facto* as well as *de jure*. If such a public policy were rigorously implemented, this would counteract tendencies to underconsumption crises. Wages of "First World" workers would stabilize, as the threat of shifting production to areas where labor is superexploited became less credible. And if labor reforms were a necessary condition for exporting to the world's largest domestic markets, it would be in the self-interest of the rulers of exporting countries in the so-called

Third World to install such reforms, allowing wages to rise there as well (Greider 1997).

The global underconsumptionist position enjoys many advantages over its rivals. The empirical assessment of state capacities in the global economy proposed by its defenders appears far more accurate than the assessments associated with neoliberal orthodoxy. The recognition that the very public policies enabling high growth in particular regions generate problems in the world economy as a whole gives global underconsumptionism a breadth missing from the writings of the competitive regionalists. And the level of compassion for the countless victims of global capitalism sets this perspective apart from those who blindly trust in Adam Smith's invisible hand, or those who devote their concern exclusively to the well-being of this or that particular community. Nonetheless, the global underconsumptionism perspective is fundamentally flawed.

Money squeezed out of wages does not simply disappear; managers and investors appropriate it. The money may then be spent on luxury consumption, invested, or saved, in which case the banks in which those savings are held can themselves throw the money into circulation again. This means that on the aggregate level no net loss of effective demand in the economy necessarily results due to pressure on wages. There may instead simply be a shift in the sorts of commodities demanded away from the consumption goods purchased by workers and their families toward luxury consumption items, or from working-class consumption toward investment. There may be compelling ethical reasons to lament such shifts. But in themselves they do not appear to constitute a fatal internal flaw in the functioning of the global economy. Of course, once a downswing threatens, wealthy individuals and banks may choose to hold onto their money rather than spend or reinvest it. But this behavior is a more a response to crisis than its cause. The root of crisis tendencies lies elsewhere.

D. Globalization and the "Law of Value"

The heart of Marx's crisis theory is found in the famous slogan, "Accumulate, accumulate, that is Moses and the prophets!" Once the capital form has been established as dominant, the ceaseless thirst for surplus value, defined as the difference between M' (the money funds held at the end of a circuit of capital) and M (the initial money M invested), becomes the driving force of social life. This imperative to accumulate underlies both the capital/wage labor relation and the ceaseless competition among units of capital. For *any* given level of the value of labor power, there is an inexorable drive to accumulate more capital through increasing the exploitation of wage laborers, *even if their labor power is paid its full value*. For *any* given level of success in market competition, there is an inexorable drive to expand production in order to capture market share and increase accumulation. The drive to expand production leads to an increasing mass of capital. If the drive to increase exploitation does not increase in tandem—and sooner or later it will fail to do so—then the rate of profit falls:

> The capitalist crisis is an overproduction of capital only with respect to a given degree of exploitation. . . . [Accumulation is] halted only because the accumulated capital proved too large in relation to the rate of profit it was able to bring forth. (Mattick 1969, 67)[3]

The all but inexhaustible creativity of the best and the brightest minds of finance capital will then develop ever more complex forms of fictitious capital to provide outlets for the accumulated capital, all of which simply displace the overaccumulation crisis in time to a greater or lesser degree (Harvey 1982). Ultimately, the only solution to the overaccumulation of capital is the devaluation of capital, which then allows the cycle to begin again. Ultimately, the only solution is extended economic crisis.

It is true that overaccumulation crises always appear as underconsumption crises, that is, as a lack of sufficient demand in the economy to purchase all the available commodities.[4] But attempts to increase levels of consumption in the economy of the sort proposed by global underconsumptionists can never remove the underlying tendency to overaccumulation crises. That tendency—an expression of the so-called "law of value"—kicks in at artificially high levels of consumer demand with not a bit less force than at lower levels of overall consumer demand. The recurrent need to suffer massive devaluations of capital could only be removed by eliminating the law of value. Needless to say, this goes far beyond global underconsumptionist proposals to use the power of the state to increase consumer demand among workers and other disadvantaged groups. The global underconsumptionist position cannot deliver on its promises because it has misdiagnosed the root causes of the problems it is supposed to resolve.

This analysis suggests that the discussion of both the causes and the solution to the crisis of Fordism found in the "new economy" literature are flawed. In chapter 1 I presented a list of the various factors introduced in this literature to explain the emergence of the extended economic slowdown beginning in the late 1960s/early 1970s. The one factor absent from this list is the one that matters most, the overaccumulation of capital in the world economy. Robert Brenner summarizes his magisterial analysis of the crisis as follows:

> In this view, the fall in *aggregate* profitability that was responsible for the long downturn was the result . . . of the over-capacity and over-pro-

duction which resulted from intensified, horizontal inter-capitalist competition. The intensification of inter-capitalist competition was itself the manifestation of the introduction of lower-cost, lower price goods into the world market, especially in manufacturing, at the expense of already existing higher-cost, higher price producers, their profitability and their productive capacity. (Brenner 1998, 8–9)

In the standard textbooks of neoclassical economics, when lower-cost competitors arise, market share is immediately ceded to them. The capital that would otherwise have been invested in older enterprises in the sector then flows to other sectors. However, when the position of U.S. manufacturers began to erode in the face of competition from West Germany and, especially, Japan, this path was not taken. Nor was this path chosen later when imports from the so-called newly industrializing countries began to grow significantly. U.S. manufacturers did not want to abandon the sector-specific expertise of their managers and workers. As long as the rate of profit they could expect from returns on circulating capital exceeded what they could anticipate from shifting to other sectors, making use of their massive investment in fixed capital seemed preferable to writing it all off. And manufacturers could rely on regional and national governments to introduce labor, monetary, and fiscal policies that would put their private interests before all other social concerns. And so they chose to respond to increased global competition by undertaking a massive class offensive against labor, while appropriating many of the innovations of Japanese lean production systems. Combined with favorable currency revaluations, this strategy eventually improved the competitive position of many U.S. firms. But the underlying problem of global overcapacity has not been overcome.[5]

This same point can be made in slightly different terms. From the standpoint of any individual firm, it is rational to respond to global competition by increasing productivity. The technologies and forms of social organization associated with the "new economy" do indeed have the potential to improve productivity by compressing time spent in product design, reducing the time of deliveries of inputs from subcontractors, speeding up the production process, initiating a faster delivery of finished commodities to distributors and final consumers, and undertaking other measures to reduce the turnover time of capital (Hof et al. 1998; Reinhardt 1998). But the very measures that are rational from the standpoint of the individual enterprise can be irrational on the level of the global capitalist economy. The global economic slowdown in the 1970s was first and foremost a decline in profitability rather than a decline in productivity; declines in productivity followed the lower rates of investment that resulted from the decline in profitability (Brenner 1998; Webber and Rigby 1996). The very measures that improved productivity for individual firms resulted in overcapacity problems that lowered profit rates in the global economy as a whole. This simple and elementary point is overlooked by those who hold that the globalization of the "new economy" in the absence of contingent extrinsic factors can itself bring about a "long boom" in the twenty-first century. The history of capitalism shows that a future extended boom period cannot be ruled out *a priori*. But the history of capitalism also suggests that a precondition for such a long boom is a massive devaluation of capital of the sort that only extended global depressions and world wars have been able to accomplish in the past.

There is another consideration that is relevant to the impact of the diffusion of lean production on the global capitalist economy. In his masterwork *The Long Twentieth Century* (1994) Giovanni Arrighi distinguishes four systematic cycles of accumulation in the history of capitalism thus far, the periods dominated by Genoese capital, Dutch capital, British capital, and U.S. capital. The fourth cycle corresponds to what has been termed the era of "Fordism" in this work. At the conclusion of his book Arrighi inquires whether a fifth systematic cycle of accumulation is in the process of emerging in the Far East. His description of the Far East model coincides with the lean production model that has been our concern.

With the benefit of hindsight it is easy today to mock the suggestion that the Far East will be the center of global capitalism in the twenty-first century. This region is now mired in an extended economic depression that shows few signs of abating. This development, I believe, points to a significant disanalogy between the rise of the "new economy" and the expansionary periods in the systematic cycles of accumulation discussed by Arrighi.

In each successive systematic cycle of accumulation capitals in the hegemonic regions were able to appropriate surplus profits for an extended period of time. This was the absolutely crucial factor in the formation of a "virtuous circle" connecting surplus profits with high levels of investment, increased productivity, and extensive (if uneven) prosperity. Genoese merchants were able to use their control of silver markets to transfer to their coffers profits attained in circuits of capital extending throughout Europe and the "New" World. Later, the ability of Dutch chartered corporations to establish and protect trade routes allowed them to establish Amsterdam as a center for global trade, and also enabled Dutch capital to shift relatively quickly to profitable forms of production as they arose. Technological advances in large-scale capital goods provided comparable advantages to British capital during the long nineteenth century. And the economies of scale and speed of throughput enjoyed by the vertically integrated U.S. firms provided U.S. capital with means for appropriating high levels of surplus profits throughout much of the long twentieth century. In each case it proved immensely difficult over an extended period of time for competing capitals to duplicate the advantages of the hegemonic region. The surplus profits enjoyed by Genoese merchants were a result of their alliance with Spain, and merchants from competing Italian city states could not reproduce this alliance. Nor was it a simple matter for the competitors of Dutch capital in the long seventeenth century to copy the synthesis of territorial logic and capital logic attained by the Dutch East India Corporation. Similarly, it proved exceedingly difficult to duplicate the military empire and capital goods industry of nineteenth century Britain, or the vertically integrated corporations of twentieth-century U.S. capital.

Let us assume for the sake of the argument that the technical and organizational innovations of lean production are comparable in significance to the technical and social innovations of the Genoese, the Dutch, the British, and the U.S. systems at the dawn of the systematic cycles of accumulation they dominated. It does not follow that units of capital in any particular region introducing these innovations will be able to appropriate surplus profits for an extended period of time. *The technological and organizational innovations of lean production have had a far faster rate of diffusion than the innovations underlying previous systematic cycles of accumulation.* I do not mean to deny the tremendous variety on regional levels that continues to exist in capitalism in the age of lean production (Kochan et al. 1997, introduction). But once the decision was made to learn from Japanese firms, other corporations throughout the globe were able to begin immediately to increase their use of subcontractors within production chains across regional borders, to integrate the first and second tiers of subcontractors into the design process, to set up just-in-time deliveries, to set up work teams incorporating non–value adding activities (quality control, cleaning, etc.), to reduce the "pores" in the working day, to eliminate levels of middle management, to engage in mass customization, to employ information technologies to note smaller and smaller market niches, to monitor sudden shifts in consumer demands, and so on (Lester 1998, 81). Even if we assume that these measures significantly reduce the turnover time of capital, it does not follow that they are likely to set off a "long boom" of capitalist expansion in the twenty-first century. Arrighi's overview of the history of capitalism suggests that long booms commence when capitals in a specific region are able to appropriate surplus profits from technical and social innovations over an extended period of time. It does not seem likely that the innovations of the "new economy" will have this result.

Browning and Reiss, two leading theorists of the "new economy," implicitly refer to this conclusion with the question they pose in the following passage:

> [The new economy] means empowered consumers, accelerated market development, and shorter life spans for products and jobs . . . hypercompetition prevails and the victors win by adapting quickest

to change. Here lies an interesting dilemma: when its harder and harder to keep a grip, how do you sustain your competitive advantage? (Browning and Reiss 1998b, 95)

They offer three possible ways to avoid the problem: operate in a niche market too small to attract significant competition; innovate rapidly enough to stay ahead of competitors; or enjoy an old-fashioned monopoly (Browning and Reiss 1998a, 112). Regarding the first, the surplus profits enjoyed in small niche markets are surely not going to be sufficient to set off a new expanded cycle of capital accumulation on the level of the global capitalist system. The second option, rapid innovation over the long term, requires greater and greater expenditure in research and development, the constant scrapping of older facilities and their replacement with state-of-the-art production sites, higher levels of equipment per production worker, and so on. But this implies that funds that might otherwise have been appropriated as "surplus profits" and invested in new fields must instead be devoted to higher investments in the original area.[6] The high fixed costs that result suggest that future recessions might take a greater toll on corporate earnings than past downturns (Roach 1998, 53). All these considerations point away from a new period of rapid expansion in the capitalist global economy. Finally, rapid technological change also tends to undermine "old-fashioned monopolies," thereby removing Browning and Reiss's third option as well.

Another relevant consideration in this context has to do with the pressures on profits that result from instant access to price information around the globe. Consider Bill Gates's description of future consumer activity in the electronic marketplace:

> All the goods for sale in the world will be available for you to examine, compare, and, often, customize. When you want to buy something you'll be able to tell your computer to find it for you at the best price offered by any acceptable source or ask your computer to "haggle" with the computers of various sellers. (Gates 1995, 158)[7]

This arrangement works against the long-term appropriation of surplus profits. The short-term benefits to consumers fortunate enough to possess disposable income are obvious. But the resulting low profit margins eventually must tend to discourage capitalist expansion. While Browning and Reiss do not draw this conclusion, it appears to follow from the prominence of "churning" in their account of "new economy":

> Ever faster innovation means more possibilities for customers to decide they don't really like your product after all—or to realize that someone else has a cheaper, faster, or better version. And the new

economy's ever more efficient markets make it less costly—in money, time, or both—for consumers to make the move. (Browning and Reiss 1998a, 109; see Hof et al. 1998)

A final point concerns the tension between the reduction of turnover time in the circuit of capital and productivity gains. The lean production model leads corporations to devote considerable energy to design, advertising, and marketing to make one commodity appear different from others that it replaces or competes against. These efforts may reduce the turnover time of some investments of capital. But they do not necessarily increase the total output of commodities per unit of labor or capital in the given sector. If mass customization requires that more labor be expanded to hold onto and retain customers, then the "new economy" does not necessarily tend to lead to breakthroughs in productivity. If shorter production runs mean that increasingly more labor hours must be spent introducing and marketing products that are only slightly different from what has gone before, then it would be foolish to expect any great jump in productivity in the "new economy."

The conclusion of this chapter is that a "new economy" incorporating lean production will neither lead to a just global order, nor is it likely to inaugurate a new period of expansion in the global economy. This suggests that we ought to consider instituting a form of globalization that is beyond both lean production and the tyranny of the law of value. What might such a world look like? This is the main topic of the next and final chapter of this work.

CHAPTER SEVEN

Socialism:
An Alternative to Lean Production?

In the previous chapters of this work a number of serious criticisms have been directed against lean production. Let us suppose that these objections can withstand scrutiny. This in itself does not refute the new capitalist utopians. They could concede that some of the stronger claims for the "new economy" cannot be fully redeemed, yet still insist that this system remains the best feasible alternative. After all, no one wants to return to Fordism. And have not events in Eastern Europe and elsewhere shown that the socialist alternative has failed?

In order to deal with this weaker but still quite powerful claim I shall take a somewhat roundabout path. Some of the factors underlying the collapse of the so-called Soviet model are sketched in section A, concentrating on shortcomings regarding processes of technical change. Defenders of the "new economy" stress that technological innovation is one of the great strengths of contemporary capitalism, and so this seems an especially appropriate issue to emphasize here. In section B I ask what set of social transformations might fulfill the promises made by the defenders of lean production. A set of proposals are presented for a form of socialism in which in which the democratic planning of technical change plays a crucial role. In section C arguments are offered to show that this model of democratic socialism could in principle avoid the shortcomings regarding technical change that doom centralized bureaucratic planning. If this is the case, then there is reason to think a feasible and normatively attractive alternative to lean production may be found. In the final section of this work I contrast a form of globalization based upon socialist democracy with the perspectives on globalization considered in the previous chapter.

A. The Structural Contradictions of Bureaucratic Planning

A great variety of economic, political, and cultural factors played a part in the collapse of the bureaucratic command economies of Eastern Europe.

In the context of the present work the most relevant issues concern technological change and the socioeconomic framework within which such change occurs.

In bureaucratically planned economies, general plans for each economic sector are formulated by central ministers and then coordinated by the leading bodies of the ruling party. These plans are based upon information relayed by lower-level officials to those above. The plans are then transmitted through various intermediate strata to the managers of local enterprises. Successful passage to higher positions in the bureaucracy depends upon fulfilling quotas dictated from above. The outputs are then distributed either to other enterprises or to final consumers. These consumers, and those working in enterprises, have no active role in the formulation of the plan (Mandel 1989; Kagarlitsky 1990).

This arrangement has proven compatible with significant technological advances during periods of initial industrialization.[1] It has also proven compatible with continued advances in certain areas of basic scientific-technical knowledge, especially in areas of special interest to the central planners, such as arms and space (Evangeliste 1988). Bureaucratically planned economies, however, have great difficulty making the transition from extensive to intensive technologies. They also experience serious difficulties in moving from basic research to concrete applications of that research, and in nonpriority areas. These shortcomings cannot be blamed on contingent matters. A series of structural problems regarding technological change plague the model that has just been sketched.

1. Bureaucratic Planning Hampers Innovation in General

Bureaucracies operate according to routine, and routines function most smoothly when events follow a predictable course. Bureaucratic planning in principle could be efficient if technical innovation were predictable. But the less routine an activity is, the less likely it is to be administered effectively through bureaucratic procedures. Out of all human endeavors technological innovation is among the least predictable, the least subject to organizational routine. Hence it is among the areas where bureaucratic procedures are least likely to be effective.

2. The Plan Hampers Process Innovations in Specific

A process innovation is a new technique for producing an already existing product more efficiently. Process innovations generally require a shift in the ratios in which different factors of production are employed, or else the employment of new types of inputs that were not previously used. This demands a revision of the economic plan set by the ruling bureaucracy. If process innovations are introduced continually throughout the economy, the plan would soon be in shambles. Adherence to a plan throughout a given production period thus is equivalent to discouraging process innovation.

3. Economic Disincentives for Technical Change

In the bureaucratic hierarchy managers of firms are rewarded according to their ability to meet or surpass the output requested of them. However if they regularly surpass the requested output it is quite likely that the amount required of them will be increased in the next plan, making it more difficult to meet or exceed what is requested. This in turn makes it more difficult for managers to claim their rewards. Within this social framework it will not be in the interests of managers or workers to introduce new technologies whenever doing so threatens to set off such a chain of events.

4. Secrecy and Misinformation

Given the previous point, managers might still introduce new technologies if they felt that they would be able to keep new process innovations secret. However if this tactic is successful only the isolated firm benefits from the innovation; the process of diffusing the innovation throughout the economy breaks down.

Besides a tendency toward secrecy in the introduction of new technologies, there is also a general tendency to secrecy regarding the amount of resources actually required to produce a given level of output. If the promotion prospects of enterprise managers depend upon meeting the output quotas assigned them, they have every incentive to overstate the amount of labor, raw materials, machinery, and so forth, they require. Then if anything unexpected were to occur ample reserves would be on hand. Local managers also have a clear incentive to understate the amount of output their enterprises are capable of producing in order to maximize their chances of attaining the quotas set for them.

When all the incentives for secrecy on the local level are taken into account, we can see that there is a general tendency for plans to be formulated by upper-level officials without accurate information regarding actual production conditions.

5. Neglect of Communication Technology

Communications technology generates a unique set of difficulties within the bureaucratic command model. Since that model is premised on the rule of a single party elite, the formation of groups competing for political influence is by definition a threat to that elite. Communications technology allows various groups to be organized outside the control of the state apparatus. It is all but inevitable that some of these groups will be (or will be perceived to be) antagonistic to the ruling *nomenclatura*.[2] From this it follows that the ruling strata will be suspicious of the diffusion of communications technology throughout the society, and may take steps to hamper that diffusion.[3] This, of course, reinforces a problem mentioned above; without adequate communications technology it will be even harder for the central planners to employ accurate information.

6. Avoidance of Risk

If rewards are allocated to local officials according to their success at fulfilling the assigned quotas, then the rational manager would be wary of introducing risky technologies. If a technology did not make good on its promise and the firm failed to attain the output level specified in the plan, the position and reward of the manager of that firm would be threatened.

Another point reinforces this tendency. If rewards are allocated according to the fulfillment of the plan, then technical innovations may not be rewarded, since by definition they result from activities not specified by the plan. At the least we may say that the risks faced by those who engaged in innovative activity may not be rewarded in a manner that corresponds to these risks.

7. Neglect of Quality

Another feature of the plan is that output requests are generally formulated in quantitative terms. It is very difficult for the central planners to evaluate the quality of outputs. This implies that technologies that allow enterprises to meet or surpass quotas are acceptable to decision makers within firms, regardless of any negative effects on the quality of that output. Local managers have little incentive to undertake additional investments that might raise the quality of goods and services. And if attempts to improve quality threaten the quantitative output of the firm in any way, then there is an outright disincentive for them to be concerned with qualitative matters.

If there were no form of socialism that could avoid these problems, then the new capitalist utopians would have the last word. There would be no feasible and attractive socialist alternative either to capitalism in general, or to lean production in particular. Before accepting such a pessimistic conclusion, however, the possibility of a nonbureaucratic form of socialism ought to be considered seriously. This is the topic of the following section.

B. Socialism and the Democratic Planning of Technical Change

In chapters 3–5 I have argued that the normative claims made by advocates of the "new economy" regarding labor relations, consumer relations, and interenterprise relations in lean production cannot be sustained. What sorts of institutional changes would have to be made for the promises of lean production to be actualized?

The main result of chapter 3 can be summarized as follows: the promise of a fundamental transformation in labor relations can only be redeemed if structural coercion, exploitation, and alienation in the workplace are overcome to the greatest extent possible. The structural coercion that workers face in capitalist labor markets stems from lack of secure access to the means of subsistence and production. Secure access to the means of subsistence can only be guaranteed if all citizens are granted a right to share in the fruits of economic life. This could be accomplished through the direct provision of basic social needs, through a guaranteed basic income, or through some combination of the two (Mandel 1992, 205–10; Van Parijs 1989). In a similar fashion, access to the means of production demands an acknowledgment of the right to employment as a fundamental citizen right. Only then would decisions regarding whether to work for particular enterprises count as truly free decisions.

Reversing exploitation and alienation in the labor process would necessitate both public ownership of enterprises past a certain point in size and worker self-management. As long as firms are owned by private capital investors who appoint managers as their agents, technologies and forms of organization will be introduced first and foremost in order to further the interests of those owners and agents. And they will be employed in ways that tend to sacrifice other interests to that end. In contrast, if the management of an enterprise were democratically accountable to the workforce, other factors would determine the fundamental goals of technical and organizational change in the workplace. Far more economic surplus reinvested within the firm would be devoted to innovations that reduce work hours, enhance the creativity of workers, increase workplace safety, and so on.[4] After all, the first principle of democracy is that authority rests on the consent of those over whom authority is exercised. Exploitation and alienation in the workplace will only be overcome when this principle is applied to exercises of authority in labor relations.

This argument does not imply that everyone in the workplace should get to decide about everything all the time. It does indicate, however, that those who decide how economic resources are to be allocated within a firm, and how the labor process is to be structured, ought to be accountable to those over whom this authority is exercised. The collective body of workers must themselves delegate those who are to make these decisions, and have the power to recall them when occasion demands.[5]

If these institutional changes are necessary for overcoming antagonisms in the workplace, and if these changes are not part of the lean production model, then we may conclude once again that systematic antagonisms have not been overcome in the "new economy." Perhaps it is the case that the workforce as a whole experiences a net increase in skill levels with the transformation to the technologies and social organization of lean production. But it does not follow from this that the fundamental class conflict between capital and labor discussed by Marx is now a thing of the past. Structural coercion, exploitation, and the real subsumption of labor under capital remain in lean production systems. Eradicating this fundamental class antagonism demands an institutional transformation far deeper than the transition from the traditional mass production of Fordism to lean production.

What sort of social arrangements would have to be in place for institutionalized antagonisms in consumer relations to be truly overcome? First and foremost, the main source of the asymmetry of power between producing enterprises and consuming individuals and households must be addressed. This involves numerous factors outside the sphere of consumption. Public ownership of large enterprises, workplace democracy, and mechanisms allowing social accountability for investment decisions,[6] all work to dissolve the concentrated economic power that in capitalism distorts consumer relations no less than relations in production.

Other solutions specific to the realm of consumption must complement these measures. Well-funded consumer unions could take an active role in soliciting consumer products, in monitoring price markups, in transmitting information regarding these matters to consumers, and so on (Elson 1988). If these unions were democratically accountable to the consumers whose interests they represent, then the atomization of consumers would be overcome through political organization.

Consumer unions would also help guard against the real subsumption of consumers occurring when the objectification of their desires is used against them. These unions must have open access to the data bases collected on individuals and households. They must monitor how enterprises make use of these data bases, and they must ensure that consumers are fully informed of these tactics. They must also ensure that privacy rights are enforced, including the right to not have information about oneself be part of a data base without explicit consent.

Turning to questions of subjectivity, a major problem with consumption in the "new economy" concerns the systematic inducements to define one's identity through the consumption items one has purchased. In a different social context, different forms of self-definition would be encouraged.

If more participatory forms of decision making pervaded the workplace and the community, ample opportunities would be provided for active participation in social life. A significant reduction of the working day would allow working men and women to take advantage of these opportunities.[7] Under such social circumstances one's identity would tend to be defined more by one's active contributions to the community than by the items one passively consumes. A significant reduction in the working day would also allow more time to be spent in direct personal relations with partners, children, relatives, and friends. This too would result in the strengthening of other forms of identity besides those connected to the consumption of commodities.

This does not mean that individuals would cease altogether to define themselves through the items they purchase. The clothing, music, decor, and so on, a person chooses to buy would all continue to contribute to the sense of who that person is. But in a society of economic democracy and increased personal interactions, the consumption of commodities would provide just one dimension of the complex process of identity formation. This provides a clear contrast to life under the capital form, where we are barraged with ads telling us that what we buy defines who we are, where the freedom to select among consumer goods compensates for the drudgery and stress of labor, and where the lack of time to devote to pursuits outside the workplace encourages the instant gratification of shopping.

The failure to meet wants that do not take the commodity form is another tendency that remains in lean production. This failure could be reversed through an extensive and well-funded program of allocating public grants to community groups that set out to meet social needs in a noncommodifiable way. These grants must be coupled with regulations guaranteeing access to the technologies of distribution. For example, sufficient bandwidth must be set aside on the Internet for the transmission of information and entertainment produced by community groups, and ample funds should be made available to allow those groups to finance their projects.

We have seen in chapter 4 that a gulf between consumers and the objects of consumption arises whenever decisions to purchase commodities contribute to results inconsistent with the consumers' own considered judgments regarding the social good. This tends to occur when relevant information is not transmitted to consumers through the price mechanism. And so other mechanisms must be established. Information technologies certainly make it possible in principle to transmit at little or no cost information regarding the work conditions under which products were produced, the environmental consequences of using those products, and so on. We could imagine, for instance, consumer unions investigating these and other relevant matters. Enterprises would be required to collect and make available to the consumer unions the data required. Printouts of findings could then be made available on demand to consumers, through terminals at both the point of purchase and consumers' households. The results of these investigations might also be summarized in grades that would appear alongside the prices on display. Some of these findings and grades would no doubt contradict others. It would be the responsibility of the consumer unions to highlight the differences, tracing them back to divergent methodological assumptions, value judgements, and so on. Consumers would then have the opportunity to sort through this information. Having easy access to information regarding product availability and product features would also eliminate much of the need for advertisements.

There is thus a general congruence between the sorts of measures required if consumer interests are truly to be institutionalized, and the measures required to ensure that the interests of workers are adequately represented. As long as both sets of interests are ultimately subordinate to the imperatives of capital accumulation the promises made by the advocates of lean production will remain utopian fantasies.

Regarding relationships among economic enterprises, once again we need to ask what sorts of social transformations would have to occur for the claims of the new capitalist utopians to hold true. This question has been raised by Bennett Harrison, who has perhaps as deep a sense of the limitations of networks of lean production firms as any social theorist. And yet there is a huge gap between his description of what he terms "the dark side" of lean production and his specific policy proposals. He calls for a rejuvenation of the labor movement, along with a higher minimum wage, mandatory corporate training programs, a ban on the hiring of permanent replacement workers for strikers, and a long-term growth strategy led by public investment (Harrison 1994, 245). As laudable as these objectives are, especially in the present political climate, they do not begin to remove the difficulties discussed in chapter 5.

It is difficult to think that Harrison himself is unaware of the limits of his proposals. I suspect that he feared that if he had seriously addressed the shortcomings of lean production networks his work would be ignored in mainstream policy-making circles. The tremendous gap between his description of these shortcomings and his proposals to address them provides a striking measure of the limits of mainstream political discourse today.

Drawing on the work of Diane Elson, Hilary Wainwright, and David Schweickart, four suggestions can be proposed for bringing about greater harmony and trust among units of production and distribution. These suggestions directly address the four problems mentioned at the conclusion of chapter 5.

(1) The use of technologies within networks of firms is a function of the ownership and control of those firms. With public ownership of enterprises past a certain size, and with workplace democracy instituted in those enterprises, the interfirm communication and coordination enabled by ad-

vanced information technologies would take a quite different form from that in lean production networks. Large firms would not be able to use equity holdings in smaller firms to dictate production targets and prices. Nor could they insist on unreciprocated access to information. Decisions affecting networks of firms could be made by representatives of the different labor forces, who would be accountable to those groups of workers. Representatives of smaller firms would not be likely to agree to arrangements in which larger firms unilaterally appropriated cost savings made by smaller firms, or arrangements in which more and more economic burdens were placed on smaller enterprises, while larger ones received more and more economic benefits. And so these problems would not tend to arise.

(2) One factor ensuring that intercapital relations remain aggressively antagonistic is the "expand or die" nature of capitalist markets. This imperative is not weakened one iota in lean production. And so technical change in lean production tends to generate overproduction crises, which lead each intercapital network to frantic attempts to shift the costs of devaluation onto other networks. Publicly owned workers' cooperatives would escape this trap. As expansion proceeds, a point is reached where taking on any more people in the co-op would lessen the share of present members. When this point is attained these workers do not have an incentive to support the continued expansion of their enterprise (Schweickart 1994, chapter 4).

In order to lessen internetwork antagonisms significantly, however, much more is required. The activities of different networks must be coordinated together in a democratic fashion. In brief, there must be a greater role for the democratic planning of investment decisions in society as a whole. This planning has a number of objectives. Decisions must be made regarding the general direction of the economy. The background conditions for implementing those decisions must be provided. And the decisions must be implemented concretely. I shall soon attempt to sketch how a system of technology boards and community banks would contribute to these objectives. Of course the collapse of the Soviet Union has made all talk of planning extremely suspect, and this misgiving must be addressed. But if a system of technology boards and community banks could help attain the above goals, the danger of overproduction crises would be significantly lessened. Decisions to expand would be subject to public oversight to a certain degree. The need to devalue previous investments as technologies change and demands shift would not be eliminated, but it would be profoundly reduced. And most of the costs of the devaluations that did occur would be fairly shared. In this manner the forces generating interenterprise antagonisms would be diminished far more than in lean production or any other conceivable form of capitalism.

(3) In the model of socialized markets advocated by Elson, enterprises are required to disclose all information regarding production and distribu-

tion.[8] It would not be possible for anyone to monopolize a significant portion of this information, as executives of firms in lean production networks do at present. Further, if the management of enterprises in networks were democratically accountable to their workforce, horizontal links among workers in different enterprises would not be systematically discouraged as is the case today. Community oversight would also foster communication between enterprises and social movements. In this manner the bias in the sorts of information collected and transmitted within lean production networks would be overcome.

(4) If those making decisions regarding the management of a firm are democratically accountable to the workforce of the enterprise, and if decisions regarding the expansion of the enterprise are made by elected representative bodies and community banks following principles agreed upon in public debate, then there would not be a necessary tendency for the formation of interenterprise networks to conflict with the common good. For that tendency necessarily arises only if those making decisions affecting the public are able to shield themselves from public accountability.

I am well aware that this is no more than the briefest of sketches of an account of interfirm relations in an alternative social order. But I believe it is sufficient to establish the following point: uniting different units of capital in lean production networks does not by itself suffice to bring about trust, cooperation, and harmony in interenterprise relations, even if information technologies are used to promote greater communication and coordination within networks. Here too the new capitalist utopians are wrong. Fundamental changes in both property relations and production relations are required to realize the potential for greater trust and cooperation created by information technologies. These changes would inaugurate a historical break with capitalism, and not merely another variant of it (see Marsh 1995, chapters 15 and 16).

Democratic planning is one of the essential features of this historical break. As mentioned above, democratic planning has three dimensions, the determination of the direction of the economy as a whole, the fulfillment of the background conditions necessary to proceed in this direction, and the concrete implementation of the decisions that have been made. Regarding the last topic, David Schweickart (1994) has proposed that new investment funds be distributed to regions on a per capita basis. Community banks in these regions would then fund the expansion of present enterprises and the formation of new enterprises. These enterprises would then either provide goods and services directly, or compete in (socialized) markets.[9]

How should the direction of the economy as a whole be determined, and how should the background conditions necessary for developing in that direction be established? The idea of a comprehensive plan including each individual input and each unit of output is a fantasy, and must be unequivocally rejected. Even with the best intentions in the world and immense computing power at their disposal, central planners will simply lack too much relevant information. In the model defended here each enterprise decides for itself what set of inputs it will purchase from other enterprises in producer markets, and what set of outputs it will sell to other producers and final consumers. Similarly, consumers decide for themselves which goods and services they wish to purchase. But this does not imply that the idea of subjecting the general direction of the economy as a whole to social control ought to be rejected. To a considerable extent the general direction of the economy is a function of the path of technical change, and capitalist economies already provide amble evidence that the path of technical change can (must) be influenced as a result of decisions made by public authorities. Since World War II in the United States, between one half to two thirds of all research and development has been funded by the government, and two thirds of all basic research has been so funded (Mowery and Rosenberg 1989, 128, 130). The pattern of this funding has shaped the general direction of the U.S. economy.[10] The role of the government in determining the direction of technical change, and thus of the economy as a whole, is similar in all other technically advanced societies as well. The question really isn't "planning or the market?" but rather the sort of planning and the sort of market we should have. The problem in the United States and elsewhere is that this planning has been done behind closed doors. *To a large extent, democratic central planning is the democratization of technology policy.*[11] I shall now sketch one way this planning could be implemented, expanding on suggestions made by Diane Elson.

Central planning could be undertaken by a national technology board, whose actions would be coordinated with an international board. Organizations representing mass movements must play a crucial role in any truly democratic form of central planning (Fisk 1989). And so the board should consist of representatives from mass organizations of workers, consumers, environmental groups, collectives of scientists and technicians, and so on, along with representatives of the state. This board would have the duty of formulating a number of competing plans regarding the general allocation of resources for technological development, plans based on different estimations of the scientific-technical potential in the society, the risks associated with developing that potential, and the priority of social needs. These various plans could then be taken back to the base of the mass organizations and subjected to extensive discussion, making full use of the potential of the contemporary revolution in communications technology. At the conclusion of the discussion period, a society-wide vote could then decide which framework should be accepted.

The technology board would at that point have the responsibility of setting in motion the plan that had been agreed to. This would first involve allocating resources to various centers for research and development. These centers would work in conjunction with nearby universities and units of production and distribution, forming a "technological milieu."[12] These centers would then proceed through the different stages in the technology pipeline, from the most abstract and basic research to progressively more concrete applications.[13] At the conclusion of this process, the results would be provided to worker-run enterprises for final production and distribution, using either internally generated funds or investments made by local community banks.

For each local center a local technology board could be established, consisting of both local officials and local representatives of mass organizations. Among the main tasks of these local boards would be:

1. to ensure that local citizens and groups have continuous access to scientific and technological expertise so that they can educate themselves regarding new developments (unlike both bureaucratic socialist economies and capitalist market societies, where access to expertise tends to be restricted to elites);
2. to set up a series of science and technology courts, where scientists and technologists with different evaluations of predominantly technical matters relevant to economic development can be cross-examined;
3. to set up a series of public hearings, allowing local citizens and groups to articulate any questions or misgivings they may have regarding economic developments;
4. to modify or stop such developments if objections are serious enough; and
5. to forward appeals of their decisions to regional, national, and international technology boards, with the most controversial decisions ultimately to be left to society-wide discussion and vote.

In this manner local communities could ensure that local technological development is consistent with the democratic will (Sclove 1995).

These proposals are designed to transcend the lack of cooperation among units of production and distribution that generates overproduction crises and massive social disruptions in all forms of capitalism, including lean production. The institutionalization of national and international technology boards would eliminate the madness of a system in which each individual unit of production—or each network—desperately attempts to shift social costs onto its workforce, other enterprises, other networks, or the community at large. It would also overcome the limits set by capitalism to the flow of information regarding production and distribution.

If, as much of the rhetoric of lean production is designed to suggest, economic systems are to be judged by the extent to which they overcome social antagonisms, democratic planning would surely rank above the lean production model of capitalism . . . if it were feasible. How do we know that economic democracy provides a feasible alternative to the "new economy"? Are there any reasons to think that democracy in the workplace, in the realm of consumption, and in the planning of technological development could avoid the difficulties that plagued bureaucratic central planning?

In the present work advocates of lean production have repeatedly been referred to as "new capitalist utopians." It may strike many readers that the proposals outlined in this section deserve to be dismissed as utopian illusions far more than anything submitted by defenders of the "new economy." However sympathetic readers might be to the idea that the promises of lean production have been wildly overstated, the idea that there is a form of socialism that can redeem these promises may seem laughably absurd. For most social theorists, and for most citizens, the utter collapse of the Soviet model has proven conclusively that the best humanity can realistically hope for is a reasonably humane form of capitalism. In the following section I shall address this concern. I shall argue that the alternative to lean production sketched in this section is feasible as well as normatively attractive.

C. The Contrast between Democratic and Bureaucratic Planning of Technical Change

Seven difficulties regarding bureaucratic central planning were discussed in section A: Bureaucratic central planning (1) hampers innovation in general, (2) hampers process innovation in specific, (3) involves disincentives for technical change, (4) leads to secrecy and plans based on misinformation, (5) hampers the development of communication technologies, (6) leads to a fear of the risks connected with technological innovation, and (7) inevitably leads to a neglect of quality. Would the form of socialism just sketched be equally prone to these difficulties?

1. Flexibility

Democratic central planning need not involve the specification of rigid plans governing the entire economy. It concerns only the most general pattern of the allocation of the social surplus. Many remaining aspects of economic life are left to the (socialized) market, with its inherent flexibility. The members of society could decide to place greater priority on say, developing innovations to provide adequate housing rather than luxury condominiums, solar rather than nuclear energy, or sustainable rather than chemical agriculture. These decisions do not commit the housing sector, the energy sector, or the agricultural sector to adopt any specific technique. Nor do they demand that one set of techniques alone be employed by these sectors over the course of an entire planning period. These sorts of decisions can be decentralized, that is, left to local enterprises working in conjunction with local technology boards and community banks. In this manner, democratic central planning does not involve the structural tendency toward predictable routine that characterizes bureaucratic planning.

2. Process Innovation

When new processes are introduced, they typically require new inputs. In bureaucratically deformed economies if a firm makes such an innovation the central plan is disrupted, with the effect that suppliers often cannot be found to provide the required inputs for the innovating enterprises. Two factors in the democratic central planning of technical change suggest that this difficulty would not arise. As already noted, central planning in this model leaves considerable scope for decentralized decision making. Also, research on local and regional levels is performed in centers that are part of a "technological milieu." Those engaged in pure and applied research interact both formally and informally with those engaged in assembly as well as with their suppliers. The local and regional technology boards overseeing the innovation process include representatives of all these groups. This arrangement would allow a change in the mix of inputs used by assemblers to be planned in conjunction with a simultaneous change in the output mix of the relevant suppliers. The flexibility inherent in (socialized) markets can be relied upon to take things from there.

3. Incentives

The issue of incentives for technical change is perhaps the most crucial of the seven points discussed in this section. It will be discussed at somewhat greater length than the other six matters.

Bureaucratic central planning proved capable of guiding the initial process of industrialization, albeit at great personal and political cost. Beyond that, however, it failed to provide sufficient incentives to institutionalize technical change throughout the economy. If the same shortcoming held for democratic central planning as well, then the case for lean production would be much stronger. Whatever its other limitations, there is a strong case for considering lean production to be "innovation-mediated production" (Kenney and Florida 1993), at least for firms of the "core."

In all forms of capitalism the owners and controllers of capital generally have strong material incentives to introduce changes in technology. In lean production, the expansion of intellectual property rights provides an extra incentive to develop technical knowledge, the fruits of which can then be privately appropriated. If in the model of socialism sketched in the previous section there is public ownership of firms past a certain size, and if there are no intellectual property rights in this model, then who exactly has an incentive to undertake technical change?

The general answer to this question is straightforward enough. Within the workplace the members of the workforce have a clear incentive to seek new techniques that lessen their toil. Workplace democracy provides an institutional mechanism to carry out this objective. They can elect managers who will institute a search for such new techniques, and who will introduce them when they are found; they can vote out managers who fail to act in this manner. On the community level a similar point holds. It is plausible to assume that citizens wish to have social needs provided for in as efficient a manner as possible. They can be expected to elect representatives to technology boards who will direct the search for innovations that meet socially articulated needs in a more adequate fashion, and who will encourage the introduction of such innovations when they are found. Since these planners are recallable, accountability can be continuously enforced.

What of the lack of intellectual property rights? Their absence may allow the free flow of knowledge that has already been produced. But if you cannot privately appropriate the fruits of your innovation, where is the incentive to produce new forms of knowledge? I find Elson's response to this question persuasive (1988). In her model of socialism the technology board provides grants to research institutes to fund the search for new knowledge, provides rewards when this search is successful, and takes the past track record of institutes into account when providing new funding. These arrangements appear to be more than sufficient to provide an institutional context in which knowledge workers can flourish.[14]

In this context it is also worth stressing that democratic planning is compatible with both private property and a certain degree of inequality in its distribution. While defenders of this model are against the private ownership of large-scale productive resources, they are not against the private ownership of individual consumption goods.[15] A democratically planned society can reward innovative individuals and research teams with greater material compensation in order to provide incentives for further innovation. This would not contradict the principles of that society, so long as the society collectively agreed that the resulting increase in inequality was more than compensated by the positive effects of providing these incentives.

Even if certain incentives for technical change were provided in our alternative to lean production, however, they might be outweighed by even more powerful disincentives. Consider the force of habit. A workforce that has become comfortable with a certain way of doing things may resist attempts to change established procedures. A community may resist attempts to upset its established patterns of life. Bureaucratic central planning overcomes this problem through bribery and the threat of direct physical coercion. Capitalistic markets rely on the structural coercion connected with forced unemployment and disinvestment in communities. There does not appear to be any analogous mechanism at the disposal of democratic socialist planning to break the weight of past habits.

For the defenders of socialist democracy this is a pseudo-problem. The minimization of toil and the better satisfaction of social needs are social goods. The minimization of personal and social disruptions are also social goods. The correct trade-off between these two sets of benefits cannot be determined *a priori*. We certainly cannot trust either bureaucratic officials or the impersonal dictates of capitalistic markets to attain the proper balance. The appropriate trade-off is that which the affected workers and communities would decide for themselves in an uncoerced decision process. The democratic planning of technical change institutionalizes such a process. It should also be noted that economic democracy includes numerous local centers for small-scale, experimental innovation. This provides a reason to expect that the pace of technical change may not slow down at all compared to the current multinational-dominated economy.

Another possible disincentive for technical change stems from the extensive oversight processes defining democratic planning. It might be said that the series of boards, public hearings, science and technology courts, community banks, public votes, and so on that accompany the democratizing of economic development provide a powerful disincentive to those engaging in innovative activities. Would these hurdles not require considerable amounts of time and energy to jump? And would this not result in a structural tendency for innovators to be discouraged from introducing advances that they might otherwise have introduced?

It must be recalled that in capitalist market societies technical choices typically must also pass through an extensive series of hurdles. In the United States the military apparatus often must favorably assess the weapons potential of a proposed technical innovation for it to receive crucial initial funding. When it comes to commercial applications by start-up firms, venture capitalists must favorably assess the short- and long-term profit potential of the innovation. And an innovation generally becomes extensively diffused only if large multinationals either take over completely, purchase equity in, or reach marketing agreements with, small firms at the cutting edge of the new technology. These things only occur after the multinationals have completed extensive strategic deliberations. Somehow technical change continues in market societies at a fairly rapid rate despite being subjected to such scrutiny. There is no *a priori* reason to think that the pace of technical change will be significantly affected just because this scrutiny is made by publicly accountable representatives rather than by military officials and the owners and controllers of capital.

However, even if we accepted for the sake of the argument that the pace of technical change might lessen somewhat under democratic planning, this in itself would not be telling. Surely any adequate evaluation of the technical innovation process in different social systems must consider the *direction* as well as the pace of technical change. From the standpoint of the public interest a shift in direction can in principle compensate for any slackening in the pace of technical change. The measures introduced in the previous section are designed to ensure that the direction of technical change will further the social good to the greatest possible extent.

4. *The Avoidance of Secrecy and Misinformation*

Under the model of democratic planning, those engaged in the implementation of technological change win social acknowledgment, economic reward, and access to future career opportunities if they successfully introduce process innovations reducing the toil (or enhancing the creativity) of the labor force, or product innovations serving democratically articulated social needs. This provides ample motivation for innovators to publicize their innovations, and to transmit to the various technology boards accurate information regarding available technological capacities. Further, the processes of public hearings, science and technology courts, and appeals would by themselves be sufficient to ensure that there would not be a structural tendency towards secrecy and misinformation. The abolishing of intellectual property rights serves this same end as well.

5. *Communications Technology*

Obviously the entire model of the democratic socialist planning of technology requires quite developed communications technology. The coordination of activities along the technology pipeline, the social oversight of these activities by the various boards, and the accountability of these boards to the various mass organizations, all demand a continual flow of communication. While there are systematic reasons for the neglect of communications technology in bureaucratic command economies, a structural tendency for this area of technological development to receive first priority can be derived from the structural mechanisms of a democratic technology policy.

6. *Risk*

Under bureaucratic planning local officials tend to be wary of introducing untested technical innovations, since they will be held personally responsible for failing to fulfill quotas imposed by higher level officials. In contrast, under democratic planning innovations are developed as a result of a collective decision, and responsibility for any subsequent problems will therefore be collectively shared. If a technology does not fulfill its promise, a search for scapegoats would be pointless, and it would be obvious that energy would be better spent on correcting the error. Under these circumstances a person or team suggesting an innovation would not face the sort of risks faced in command economies.

7. Quality

The problems with quality under bureaucratic planning all stem from a single structural fact, the lack of feedback between producers and consumers. The heads of production facilities are accountable to intermediate strata in the bureaucratic hierarchy as well as to the central ministries, but they are not accountable to the particular end-users of their products. Since higher level officials are only concerned with whether assigned quotas have been fulfilled, while it is consumers who are concerned with the quality of the produced goods, this institutional framework has a built-in tendency to neglect qualitative matters connected with production technologies.

The point to stress here is that it is the lack of feedback between producers and consumers that is the problem, rather than anything inherent in planning per se. Under the democratic centralized planning of technical change there is direct accountability of the planners to consumers. If planners regularly develop technologies that lead goods and services to be produced that do not meet the community's standards of quality, democratic mechanisms grant the community a direct recourse: elect new planners. And the presence of socialized markets provides a second important feedback mechanism to ensure that technical change results in products and services meeting satisfactory standards of quality.

A feedback relation between producers and consumers is also found in capitalist market societies, of course. But capitalist markets are based on the principle one dollar, one vote, and vast inequalities are allowed to persist. The extent of the feedback provided by specific consumers is directly proportional to their disposable wealth. In socialized markets the provision of basic needs, price commissions, wage commissions, and so on, all help ensure that wealth is more equally distributed (Elson 1988, 27–30). Democratic planning provides a further feedback mechanism that bypasses the market entirely. As a result there is every reason to believe that quality considerations could be institutionalized in a deeper and more extensive fashion than in capitalist markets.

This completes the reply to those who hold that the collapse of the Soviet model proves conclusively that any attempt to seek an alternative to lean production that goes beyond capitalism is doomed to fail. No attempt has been made here to provide a complete picture of such an alternative; the model of socialism sketched above no doubt requires extensive refinement and revisions. Nonetheless, I believe that this model is sufficient to justify the following judgment: it is possible to conceive a democratic form of socialism that is both normatively attractive and feasible. History has not ended with the failure of bureaucratic planning and the resurgence of capitalist market societies. Our responsibility to future generations demands that we begin to grope towards some third alternative that the world has not yet seen, an alternative beyond the limits of the "new economy."

There is one last question to consider before bringing this work to a close. As noted in chapter 6, the diffusion of lean production is a central feature of what has come to be called "globalization." How does the socialist alternative to the "new economy" defended here fit into the globalization debate?

D. Marxian Internationalism and the Globalization Debate

In many ways socialist democracy appears to be consistent with the "new protectionism" called for by many populists (see the articles collected in Hines and Lang 1996). The goal of this policy is to encourage the most extensive regional self-sufficiency possible. Trade across regions would be reserved for those cases where economic activity within a given area simply could not provide needed goods and services. If this policy were implemented, regional populists assert, local communities and the regional governments democratically accountable to them would flourish. Environmental wastes generated when goods and services that could be produced locally are transported vast distances would also be eliminated.

Despite the attractiveness of much of this vision, I believe it ought to be rejected. There is a dangerous indeterminacy to populism; progressive populist positions may have the unanticipated consequence of strengthening right-wing xenophobia. Workers in the so-called First World, angry about stagnant or declining real wages, could easily direct that anger against the peoples of the Third World. In fact, however, relatively little of the downward pressure on wages in the United States and elsewhere can be explained by imports from low-waged countries (Webber and Rigby 1996, chapter 7). The antilabor offensive of the U.S. capitalist class and the austerity program of its chief general, Alan Greenspan, are far more significant explanatory variables in the United States. The story is the exactly same in Europe, as Robert Went has documented (Went 1996). The more the globalization narrative of the regional populists diverts attention from this state of affairs, the greater the danger that the new protectionism will degenerate to just another variant of the old xenophobia protectionism, defining the enemy as those outside "our" nation.

A strong case can be made for regional self-sufficiency in some areas of food production, given the centrality of nutrition to human well-being. But a generalization of the principle of self-sufficiency has a number of implications that appear troubling from the perspective of regional populists' own normative commitments. If a policy of regionalism were ever implemented, it would freeze the present uneven distribution of resources for investment. Regionalization would offer little redress for the plunder of poorer countries over the centuries. Technology transfer would be discouraged, cutting off enterprises and consumers in poorer regions from potentially beneficial state-of-the-art innovations.

Another set of problems arises from the fact that there are certain issues of interest to the global community as a whole. Should regions be free to set low environmental standards, despite the fact that environmental practices have "spill-over effects" that can spread throughout the world? Should different regions be free to set different labor standards, despite the fact that standards holding in some areas might fall well behind what the remainder of the human community considers the minimal safeguards of human dignity? What of other economic, civil, and political rights? Why shouldn't global homogenization at a high level be struggled for and enforced in these areas?

These considerations strongly suggest that any attempt to bring to life the promises left unfulfilled in lean production ought to aim at a new form of globalization, one in which the law of value is superseded. Once again we may turn to David Schweickart's model of economic democracy for clues.

Schweickart locates ownership rights to productive resources past a certain size in the community as a whole. One practical upshot of this is that the members of worker cooperatives do not have the right to treat their enterprises as their private "cash cows." They cannot run them into the ground while distributing the resulting revenues among themselves. A portion of revenues must be set aside as depreciation funds in order to maintain the value of the enterprise's productive resources. Decisions regarding the investment of these depreciation funds are to be made by the responsible authorities in those enterprises, subject to external social audits.

This leaves the question of new investment in the economy, including both the expansion of existing enterprises and the formation of new ones. Schweickart proposes that funds for new investments be collected from a flat tax on the capital assets of all worker cooperatives (he estimates that this should amount to 10-to-15 percent of GNP). A democratically elected body operating on the international level would have the responsibility of allocating this money.[16] After a period of open discussion and debate, these revenues would then be divided into three parts. One portion would be allocated to democratically elected bodies operating on national/regional levels. These funds would be distributed on a per capita basis, that is, more populous regions would receive proportionally more resources. A second would be devoted to the provision of public goods on an international level (education, transportation, health, cultural production, research and development, etc.). The final portion would be set aside for investment in new industries (or the expansion of old ones) addressing the social needs granted the highest priority at the conclusion of the democratic decision making process.[17]

Elected national/regional representative bodies would then have the duty to make the same three allocations. Funds for new investment would be allocated to local representative bodies on a per capita basis. Other funds would be directed toward public goods on the national/regional level. The remaining funds would be set aside for new investment in industries addressing needs having the greatest social priority within the given area. Local representative bodies, finally, would be elected to allocate funds for public goods on the local level and to provide grants to worker cooperatives addressing the needs most pressing in the local community.

The funds for new investment allocated to particular localities would then be distributed by community banks in those areas. Enterprises that wished to expand, or people who wished to set up new firms, would apply for grants from these banks. Banks would allocate funds based upon their estimates of the likelihood of economic success, the likelihood of new employment opportunities in the community, and consistency with the set of social priorities democratically set on the local, regional, and international levels. External social audits would measure the record of these community banks by these criteria. Community banks with documented success would be allocated greater funds to distribute in the future, while less successful ones would shrink over time.

How does this vision of a global economy contrast with that advocated by defenders of the other perspectives on globalization? I would argue that this postcapitalist form of globalization combines their strengths while avoiding their weaknesses. The regional populists are correct that the technological dynamism of global capitalism comes at a horrific cost: the threat of capital flight is used to blackmail workers and communities; ever more economic power is concentrated in fewer and fewer hands; more and more crucial decisions regarding the rules of intentional commerce are transferred to international bureaucracies unaccountable to those affected by their decisions. A postcapitalist global order of the sort described above would avoid each and every one of these ineluctable features of capitalism. With no class of capitalists, there is no possibility of capital flight. With decisions regarding new investment priorities made by democratically elected representatives at international, national/regional, and local levels, there is no possibility of vast concentrations of economic power, or of unaccountable trade technocrats decreeing the rules of global life behind closed doors. This policy would also significantly lessen the danger that globalization will result in the homogenization of social life across the planet. Community banks are far more likely to be sensitive to regional differences than multinational corporations, whose executives and leading investors increasingly inhabit a world of pseudo-cosmopolitanism (Daly and Cobb 1994, 234).

These goals of the regional populists can be accomplished without any retreat to merely local economies, which from the standpoint of Marxian internationalism would count as a retreat from one of the most profoundly progressive features of capitalism. We ought not to lament that the fate of every region is intertwined with the fate of all others. The proper question is not whether there should be a global community, but what form it should take. The eradication of hunger and disease, the fostering of economic and political democracy, and the avoidance of species-suicide through environmental crises, all require a mobilization of economic and political resources on a global level.

The neoliberals discussed in chapter 6 are correct to emphasize the importance of technological dynamism, and of a global order allowing all regions access to the latest product and process innovations. The above model of economic democracy provides ample mechanisms for the funding of basic and applied research and development, clear incentives for worker cooperatives to introduce innovations, and an absence of legal and economic barriers to the diffusion of innovations, topics discussed in section C.

Turning to the competitive regionalists discussed in the previous chapter, they rightly point to the continued importance of governments in the global economy, an emphasis consistent with the Marxian internationalism perspective. They are correct as well to stress the spatial dimension of economic activity; there are many respects in which the rise of a more globalized economy makes the formation of local clusters of firms, farms, universities, research labs, governmental agencies, and so on, even more significant. Schweickart's model of economic democracy would foster the development of such clusters; community banks would form hubs around which networks of complementary enterprises and institutions would form. But competitive regionalists myopically refuse to confront one ineluctable fact: strategies that are rational for individual regions to pursue taken singly may generate irrational results from the standpoint of the human community. The vision of a global economy in which a relatively few areas enjoy success and insecurity in equal measure, while remaining regions stagnate or decline, is not very inspiring. Capitalist development has always been profoundly uneven, and the strategies of the competitive regionalists would, if anything, exacerbate this tendency. Here lies the profound importance of the proposal to allocate funds for new investment strictly proportional to regional populations. If this proposal were implemented on a global level, the regional imbalances generated in the course of five hundred years of capitalism would begin to be reversed. No longer would a crazed rush of investment to some regions be mirrored by an absence of economic resources in the regions most in need.

Finally, global underconsumptionists reflect seriously on the systematic problems of the global capitalist economy. And they are to be applauded for understanding how the perversity of capitalism simultaneously generates overcapacity and poverty. But they misdiagnose both the problem and the solution. In their view, the source of the problem is restricted consumption power, and the solution is an expansion of effective demand. But the true source of global instability is the alien power of the law of value over social life, a power imposed blindly as the unanticipated collective result of individual responses to "the rules of the game." Under the value form, the accumulation process insanely pushes forward until far more capital has been accumulated than can find a profitable outlet. This structural tendency necessarily holds in capitalism *whatever* the consumption powers of the populace might be. Upon reaching the point of overaccumulation the law of value, like Moloch, demands its sacrifice. A more or less massive devaluation of capital must commence so that the process of accumulation may begin again, devaluation that inevitably places the greatest burdens on precisely those social groups that benefited least from previous capital accumulation. Shifting some purchasing power from one class of consumers to another may sometimes be humane, but it does not address this underlying power of the law of value. And adding extra consumer power though deficit spending merely extends the time scale in which this dynamic is played out.

For Marxian internationalists, if the root problem of contemporary globalization is the alien power of the law of value, the only solution commensurable with the problem is to free humanity from subjugation to this law. This does not imply the abolition of markets; it is not the presence of markets that establishes the alien power of the value form, but the institutionalization of the drive to accumulate surplus value to the greatest extent possible, whatever the cost to social life.[18] The law of value is abolished in the model of democratic socialism described above by three structural transformations. First, the class relationship upon which the law of value is based, the capital/wage labor relation, is abolished. There are no capital markets; no one has a right to sell shares in ownership rights to private investors. And there are no labor markets; persons who labor are not commodities with a price tag.[19] Second, the drive to accumulate as an end in itself is abolished. Decisions regarding the rate of new investment (the level at which the flat tax on the assets of cooperatives is set) are now a matter for democratic debate and decision, and worker cooperatives break free from the "grow or die" imperative of capitalist enterprises. Third, the overall direction of the economy is subject to social oversight, rather than handed over to profit imperatives. Globalization after such transformations would be far different from the globalization that threatens us all today. Unfortunately, democratic socialism is not on the immediate agenda. In the meantime, the push to institute lean production will only get stronger. How ought we to respond to this? Criticisms of the ideology of the "new economy" are no more than a small part of the story. The biggest part concerns the creative tactics and strategies devised in the course of concrete struggles in the realms of production, consumption, and community life (see McCarney 1990). In his recent work *Workers in a Lean World* (1997) Kim Moody provides a comprehensive synthesis of the lessons for the future to be learned from past struggles against lean production. Interested readers are urged to consult this important book. In conclusion I would like to state briefly what I take to be the four most important practical lessons that follow from the present work.

The first point is the most obvious one. If there is no reason to think that the interests of capital and labor are automatically reconciled in lean production, working men and women must be prepared to engage in struggles in defense of their interests. This in turn implies the need to form (or preserve) organizations that can effectively carry out such struggles. In other words, there is a clear need for independent labor organizations controlled by the workforce itself. Given the continued existence of capital/wage labor antagonism, the imperative to avoid company unions is as strong as it has ever been.

Second, the self-organization of labor must be on the same scale as the organization of capital. This means that the basic unit of organization cannot be a single firm or even a national industry. As capital is organized into unified networks of firms, so labor organizations must unite workers in assembly firms with those employed by subcontractors and distributors. As capital is organized across borders, labor organizations must become truly international as well. As one and the same process of capital accumulation creates both employment and unemployment, both sectors of the working class must be united in the same organizations. All of this demands a complete and unequivocal break from the agenda of lean production firms, which "are opposed to forms of alternative worker identification . . . which create a separate sphere of identity for workers and disrupt the alignment between worker and company" (Kenney and Florida 1993, 285).

Third, the struggle against the shortcomings of the lean production system also demands the setting up of alternative networks to those that unite lean production firms, networks that unite those engaged in struggles at the point of production with those engaged in struggles in other social arenas. The work of trade union committees must be closely integrated with community health and safety projects, with coalitions of oppressed groups, with consumer activist organizations engaged in the monitoring and critique of corporate advertising campaigns, with groups concerned with question of local, regional, and global ecology. and so on. All of these struggles concern the working class, and none can be successfully resolved as long as the reign of capital persists.

Finally, networks of information exchange are only an intermediate step. The struggle against lean production ultimately requires a revolutionary movement, committed to internationalist principles, and dedicated to the materialization of the utopian impulses lean production so cynically abuses.

NOTES

Preface

1. The "indeterminate, abstract, desert-like . . . waiting" Derrida speaks of appears to be but a variant of a Heideggerian waiting for "Being" to "reveal itself" in a new manner.

2. There is an immense and ever-growing literature in the scholarly and popular business press advocating this point of view. The following is a small but representative sample of writings in which the "new economy" thesis is defended: Boyett and Conn's *Workplace 2000* (1992), Peter Senge's *The Fifth Discipline* (1991), Hammer and Champy's *Reengineering the Corporation* (1993), Tom Peters's *Liberation Management* (1992), Davidow and Malone's *The Virtual Corporation* (1992), Don Tapscott's *The Digital Economy* (1996), Tapscott and Caston's *Paradigm Shift: The New Promise of Information Technology* (1993), Bill Gates's *The Road Ahead* (1995), Nicholas Negroponte's *Being Digital* (1995), Michael Dertouzos's *What Will Be: How the New World of Information Will Change Our Lives* (1997), Richard Lester, *The Productivity Edge* (1998), and Kevin Kelly's *New Rules for the New Economy* (1998).

3. Other aspects of the "new economy," such as the convergence of the telecommunications, computer, and media industries, will not be examined here. For a critical analysis of this development see Davis and Stack (1997) and the collection of papers in McChesney et al. (1998).

4. As we shall see in chapter 3, the question of deskilling is but one of the issues falling under the category of real subsumption.

Chapter One

1. This is a different type of question than the others, and so warrants special comment. Throughout the history of capitalism—indeed, throughout the history of class societies—advantaged groups have employed three quite distinct strategies when the legitimacy of the social order is questioned. The first is to remind the populace of the coercive apparatus under their control, and their willingness to employ this apparatus against attempts to resist the established order (Abercrombie et al. 1980). This may be combined with a second response, which attempts to legitimate the existing distribution of advantages by referring to special qualities found in those possessing these advantages, qualities ranging from purity of blood and divine bless-

ing to intelligence and initiative. The third strategy is quite distinct. The goal here is not to force the disadvantaged to acquiesce to their fate out of fear or a sense of inferiority. The goal is instead to convince them that they themselves enjoy more benefits from existing arrangements than they would from any feasible alternative. In the course of making this sort of argument a model of the social order must be presented. If the model most often employed in this context in a particular histori-cal period does not coincide with the model(s) most relevant to answering the pre-vious three questions listed in the main text, there is little reason to take it seriously as a candidate for defining a specific period in economic evolution. But if this fourth consideration leads us to the same model as one or more of the others, this strength-ens the case for the historical significance of the model in question.

2. Other criticisms of the concept of "Fordism" go outside the scope of the pres-ent work. For instance, many theorists of the so-called Fordist state employ a func-tionalism that can be severely questioned on methodological grounds, as Bonefeld (1991) correctly points out.

3. I would like to stress that from the standpoint of the present work very little depends upon the claim that "Fordism" counts as a distinct stage in the economic evolution of capitalism. The continuities between "machinofacture" as described by Marx in *Capital* and the Fordist model are numerous and profound. If the reader chooses to see the latter as a mere variant of the former he or she is free to do so. For our purposes the more essential issue is whether a break is now being made from the form of social organization in place in leading sectors and regions of the mid-twentieth-century capitalist economy, however one chooses to categorize it.

4. The following description of Fordism holds in broad outline for the office as well as for the factory. The Fordist office, like the Fordist factory, was devoted to the mass production of standardized commodities, had an extensive bureaucratic ap-paratus, and so on (Guiliano 1990).

5. A more complete account would also have to incorporate the state form, specifically the Keynesian state. See the articles collected in Bonefeld and Holloway (1991) and note 7 below.

6. This must be interpreted as a refusal to acknowledge the intellectual com-ponent always present in manual labor, rather than as the successful elimination of this component. It is worth noting that there were many respects in which "scientific management" treated so-called mental labor and manual labor similarly. According to Kenney and Florida, traditional mass production "was based simply on pumping physical work out of workers and pumping plans and specifications out of researchers and engineers" (Kenney and Florida 1993, 15).

7. The role of the state was of crucial importance in this context. In all stages of capitalism the state has enforced legal contracts, implemented fiscal and monetary policies, provided public goods, and purchased commodities. The particular fea-tures of the Fordist state included the codification and enforcement of extensive la-bor regulations, the granting of tax subsidies for suburbanization, the institution of easy credit policies, the rise of expenditures in scientific and technical areas (often

in a military context), and various other "Keynesian" expenditures designed to keep up levels of effective demand (the highway system, social welfare programs, and so on). Mass consumer markets would not have developed so extensively without such state activities. From the standpoint of individual consumers, suburbanization was an especially crucial factor. As privatized dwellings in suburbs replaced the collectivized living arrangements in urban tenements for more and more families, consumer expenditures on housing, automobiles, washers and dryers, refrigerators, and so on, rose, establishing a "demand pull" for the technologies of mass production.

8. This general point masks considerable diversity in the economic history of particular nations. A fairly comprehensive account of these national divergences is found in Webber and Rigby (1996), chapter 8.

9. "Constant capital" is a technical term employed in Marxian economics to refer to means of production that do not add value to the final product. It is being employed here simply as a way to organize a series of topics considered in both mainstream and heterodox accounts of Fordism.

10. The routinization of class conflict agreed to by the bureaucracy of the labor movement did not prevent such "wildcat" actions from occurring regularly.

11. Any complete picture of the crisis of Fordism would also have to stress how this crisis included the crisis of the Keynesian state, sometimes referred as "the crisis of crisis management." The very Keynesian policies instituted to stabilize capital accumulation (credit expansion, for example) eventually led to inflation and fiscal crisis (O'Connor 1973; Hirsh 1991; Clarke 1991).

12. At one time or another all four of the positions to be examined have been referred to under the heading "post-Fordism." This is one reason why I have avoided the use of that term here. A second reason has to do with the fact that in Britain the term is associated with the political perspective of the (now defunct) journal *Marxism Today*, which counseled the labor movement to condemn militancy and abandon ambitious demands. It is certainly possible to hold that capitalism is evolving beyond Fordism in certain respects without drawing these political conclusions. In general it is important to keep in mind just how fluid terminology remains in this area of study. The term "neo-Fordism," for instance, has been used to refer to what I shall term "flexible specialization," a quite different usage from that employed here (Clarke 1991, 132 n. 4).

13. The same point holds for sudden shifts in input prices and available designs.

14. Florida and Kenney formulated this argument in the course of a critique of the Silicon Valley model of innovation, where private venture capital is devoted to small start-up companies searching for technical breakthroughs. But the point is easily generalized to include the worker cooperative model of Piore and Sabel.

15. According to Hof, in the mid-1990s it cost up to $100 million to design a new computer chip, and another $1 billion for the factory to produce it (1994, 96). The figures have increased substantially since then.

16. Japanese electronics firms provide the paradigm here. They include divisions devoted to consumer electronics, semiconductors, computers, office equipment, in-

dustrial equipment, telecommunications technology, industrial robots, electric power and transmission systems, with a semiconductor unit supplying computer and consumer electronic units. Hewlett-Packard is the closest example in the United States (Hof 1993, 72 ff.). Other examples include the auto and steel industries, where companies incorporate software, integrated circuits, programmable logic controllers, advanced robotics, machine tools, and AI systems together (Kenny and Florida 1993, 305).

17. This point holds for both the factory and the office, according to advocates of lean production. While the model was first introduced in automobile manufacturing, it has subsequently spread to telecommunications, health care, retail trade, and the public sector (Parker and Slaughter 1994).

18. The term "value" is used here in the loose sense found in the lean production literature, not in the technical sense given to it in Marx's theory of value.

19. These are former units of the company granted formal organizational independence.

20. Joint ventures arise when two or more companies contribute staff and funding to a new firm, formally separate from them both.

21. See Kenney and Florida (1993, 302–3) for examples of compressed product life cycles in a number of different industries.

22. Economies of scale play the biggest role in the production of modules that can go into a range of different sorts of final products (Reich 1991, 112).

23. Reich shows how the most profitable firms in steelmaking, plastics, tool and die casting, semiconductors, software, telecommunications, trucking, rail, and air freight, and finance all exemplify this principle (Ibid., 82–83).

24. A full account of lean production would have to include the profound role of the state in the shaping of lean production (see note 34 below). Some remarks on the effects of lean production on the capital/state relation will be made in chapters 5 and 6.

25. A specific example may help here. In an International Assembly Plant Study undertaken by MIT researchers of the auto industry it was discovered that in 1993 U.S. lean production plants averaged 4 suggestions per employee, as opposed to 0.4 in traditional plants. The rate of implementation of suggestions in the two types of plants was 60 percent and 25 percent respectively (Macduffie 1995, 67 n. 6). Is this a "minor" modification of Fordist procedures? Defenders of lean production insist it is more plausible to say that the traditional Fordist dualism between conception and execution is in principle called into question here in a qualitatively new way.

26. This is a point where terminological confusions could easily arise. Appelbaum and Batt themselves contrast the "high performance workplace" (which fits the description of the labor process in lean production given in subsection 3 above) with "lean production," which in their usage refers to what I have been calling neo-Fordism.

27. Defenders of lean production insist that this point holds for both factories and offices. A General Electrics plant that changes product models a dozen times a

day introduced a team system in which employees were cross-trained to perform all tasks. Productivity increased by 250 percent over G.E. plants producing the same products that had not adopted these lean production practices. AT&T Credit Corp. found that a team structure allows 800 lease applications to be processed a day rather than 400 under the old system (Hoerr 1989, 58–59). This matter will be further discussed in the following chapter.

28. One part of this story is the time required to retool a factory to produce a new model. While a Honda Accord required 3 days and a Toyota Camry 18, the comparable Ford Contour and Chevy Lumina took 60 and 87 days, respectively. One advantage of lean production methods here is that it frees up to 45 percent of factory space, allowing new gear to be tested before it is needed in the change-over (*Business Week,* July 11, 1994, 112).

29. Organizational structures provide one sign of this: "In 1993, for example, 11.6 percent of manufacturing employment worked in administrative and managerial occupations in the United States and only 4.1 in Japan" (Gordon 1996, 45).

30. It is also worth noting that during this period the ratio of productivity growth to wage growth was higher in the more cooperative economies than in the more conflictual economies (Ibid., 161).

31. See Moody (1997), 103–4. Leading this development in Germany is a G.M. subsidiary, Opel. According to *Business Week,* after introducing lean production practices such as teamwork and just-in-time delivery from suppliers, Opel cut inventories by 60–80 percent and space requirements by 30–50 percent (Miller and Kerwin 1993, 68). The irony here is that in the U.S. General Motors has been a laggard in the introduction of lean production practices.

32. According to figures provided by the National Labor Relations Board, employers fired 1 out of 36 union supporters illegally in the late 1980s, as opposed to 1 in 110 in the late 1970s and 1 in 209 in the late 1960s (Bernstein 1994, 78).

33. Toyota has cut color and option combinations by 20 percent. Nissan and Mazda have made similar moves (Miller, Woodruff and Peterson 1992, 82).

34. Appelbaum and Batt (1994) believe that both neo-Fordism and lean production (in their terminology, the lean system and the team system, respectively) can be successful from the standpoint of corporate interests. They conclude that the path that is eventually selected will depend on government actions. In their view, governmental policies that promote employee participation, worker training, unions, intercapital cooperation, and so on, make the adaptation of what is being called "lean production" here more likely, while the absence of these policies allows neo-Fordism to become entrenched (see also Pollert 1988; Hirsch 1991; Vanarella 1996; Green 1996; Jarboe and Yudken 1997).

35. This is a global phenomenon, as Moody's discussion of the leadership body of various national and international labor organizations shows (Moody 1997, chapter 10).

36. Some theorists argue that any use of ideal types such as "Fordism" or "lean production" prevents proper acknowledgment of the openness of history. Bonefeld

writes that "the ambiguity, and the disarticulation of structure and struggle, in the concept of Fordism . . . leaves it open for the argument that struggle is not possible in the present situation" (Bonefeld 1991, 37; see also Holloway 1991, 101; Psychopedis 1991, 191). I am completely unconvinced by this argument. In the study of natural evolution it is certainly possible to trace a particular path of development while keeping in mind both the role of past contingencies in selecting one path rather than another, and the future contingencies that may push that path in completely unexpected directions. In tracing a path of economic evolution in capitalism I see no reason whatsoever why the use of concepts such as "Fordism" or "lean production" necessarily rules out an appreciation of the contingencies of this evolution, including especially those resulting from class struggles. As Jessop writes, "there are different national Fordisms, different national roads to post-Fordism, and different possible post-Fordist futures; and . . . these national specificities are the result of the balance of class forces in specific national conjunctures" (Jessop 1991, 77).

37. This by no means implies that vertical integration disappears in lean production. Vertical integration lowers input costs, everything else being equal. The final cost of a machine produced within an enterprise is simply the total of the costs required to produce it; if the same machine is purchased in the market from another firm, however, its price includes the profits of that firm as well as the costs of production. David Harvey (1982) concludes that there must be some equilibrium point at which the trade-off between centralization and decentralization is optimal for accumulation, that is, where lower input costs from further vertical integration would no longer outweigh the increase in circulation time that this further vertical integration would generate. Fordism can be seen as an organizational structure that pursued the benefits of vertical integration past the point where they compensated for the increase in circulation time. Lean production is an attempt to correct this imbalance; the disaggregation of production speeds up the circulation process, which allows more capital to be accumulated in a given unit of time. This is compatible with simultaneously attempting to enjoy as many of the benefits of vertical integration as possible in the new context.

38. The relevance of lean production to the normative social theory of Jürgen Habermas is explored in Smith (1995b).

39. The "received view" in social theory today is that Marxian theory is already in shambles as a result of the degeneration and collapse of the Soviet Union. But defenders of Marx could always point out that Marx's own work was first and foremost an analysis of capital. If recent developments in capitalism have made this analysis completely irrelevant, there would surely be little left of the theory to save. (I shall have more to say about the prospects for socialism in face of the collapse of the Soviet model in the final chapter of this work.)

Chapter Two

1. This question is obviously relevant to the debate between those who hold that lean production is a new stage in the economic evolution of capitalism and the neo-

Fordists who deny this. The stronger the tendency to deskilling in lean production, the greater the continuity with traditional Fordism, that is, the stronger the case for neo-Fordism.

2. As we shall see presently, Zuboff herself does not consider deskilling the dominant tendency in work relations today. She does, however, present the arguments for the deskilling thesis ("automating," in her vocabulary) exceptionally clearly.

3. "If an operator does not have access to the assumptions that are the basis for a model's calculations, then it is difficult to critically judge its output" (Zuboff 1988, 277).

4. "Workers [in lean production] take on the role of super-technicians who monitor, review data, and adjust and control the process. These super-technicians have skill levels that are equivalent to electrical engineers of two decades ago" (Kenney and Florida 1993, 304).

5. It is surprising to note that the authors of the article cited above admit this themselves. They write later in the same article that "dislocation is not the only serious problem caused by technology. Some workers complain about being de-skilled; others say their employers use the computer as a control device" (Hoerr et al. 1989, 360). The authors appear to be oblivious to the fact that this undermines their earlier claim that deskilling is "obsolete" in the computerized workplace.

6. Another category of indirect workers that can be reduced in the lean production model is that of lower-level managers and supervisors. This too results in significant cost savings. It also modifies the entire organizational dynamic of the enterprise, as we shall see below.

7. From the standpoint of survival in the market, a catastrophe can occur well short of the physical destruction of plant, persons, or machines. Extensive downtime is by itself quite expensive due to the cost of high technology production systems.

8. Gordon also suggests, however, that skill increases in manufacturing have not been matched in office occupations (ibid., 184).

9. Aronowitz and DiFazio attempt to defend a version of the deskilling thesis by denying that these capacities count as an increase of skill, in their definition of the term: "[T]here is a break between knowledge and skill. Computer-aided design, computer-aided manufacturing, computer-integrated manufacturing, and other computer-mediated technological innovations have taken over the skill component. In this sense there has been deskilling. The twentieth century, the industrial-capitalist era, is marked by the displacement of skill by knowledge. It is the knowledge component—the conceptual, the theoretical—that is now the basis for the scientific, technological, and social relations of production" (Aronowitz and DiFazio 1994, 95). This refusal to count the intellective skills discussed by Zuboff as skills rests upon the question-begging linguistic fiat that the only skills in the social world are craft-based skills.

10. See note 4 above.

11. One different sort of argument should be mentioned, however. Aronowitz and DiFazio propose a feminist deconstruction of the very concept of skill: "Women

are the disruption of the privileged realm of skill—a male property, guarded closely, always at a disadvantage, not because they were inferior, incompetent, not strong or intelligent enough but because the skill fields themselves were structured by men. Skill is a male discourse. If women were to succeed they had to change the field of discourse. In these gendered fields they could not win. If women forced their way in, the skill was devalued" (Aronowitz and DiFazio 1994, 96). This line of argument appears to be inconsistent with the passage quoted in the note 9, which made use of a nongendered (if ultimately inadequate) notion of skill. It also appears to be internally inconsistent. One cannot assert that women were not "inferior, or incompetent, or strong or intelligent enough" without appealing to some implicit notion of skill that is more than a male category. It is worth noting in passing that without such a notion feminist comparable worth proposals would be meaningless.

12. In the course of arguing that Japanese management strategies regarding transplant facilities in the United States follow those employed in periphery firms in Japan, Delbridge writes, "[I]t is in more complex production processes involving newer technology for more complex products that improvements are anticipated. These processes are carried out by the parent company, which expects its core employees to contribute their ideas for improving the system in an ongoing series of innovations. On the other hand, the 'mature' technologies which management does not expect to be the source of innovation are subcontracted out to subsidiaries with lower labour costs. It is the level of maturity and complexity of the technology, products, and production processes, and the relative centrality of innovation which explain the difference in management expectations for labour" (Delbridge 1998, 207–8). The enhanced skilling of the core workforce stressed by proponents of the "new economy" is thus inseparably united with its absence in the peripheral workforce.

13. "Studies show that group assembly not only makes workers feel better but also produces higher quality" (Hoerr et al. 1989, 364).

14. Kenney and Florida also adhere to the dialogic model of lean production. In their description of a lean production steel mill they write, "The workers themselves monitor, modify, and program the computers that guide the steelmaking process. Some even carry mobile computer packs so they can control the process from anywhere within the plant. They do so with assistance from, but not the interference of, managers and engineers. These workers, engineers, and supervisors are constantly discussing new ways to improve the process and make it more efficient" (Kenney and Florida 1993, 3).

15. "Consensus decision making provides an environment where ideas can surface, ensures thorough dissemination of information, and mitigates problems associated with lack of commitment to new decisions" (Kenney and Florida 1993, 42).

Chapter Three

1. The term "structural coercion" is used to distinguish the sort of situation described in the text from the form of coercion in which one individual forces another

to do his or her will under an implicit or explicit threat of direct violence. It should be noted that structural coercion is a matter of degree. It is present in a high degree when the alternative to waged work is immediate starvation, and in a lower degree when social welfare programs provide guarantees of physical subsistence. Structural coercion still exists in the latter case whenever mere physical subsistence is less than the minimally acceptable standard of living in the given society (Graham 1992). It is also worth mentioning that structural coercion does not prevent those who own and control capital from attempting to evoke a high degree of voluntary compliance from their employees through systems of promotions, higher wages, and so on. Such compliance does not in itself establish that there is no fundamental antagonism between labor and capital, as I shall attempt to establish in section C below.

2. Marx discusses the distinction between "real subsumption" and "formal subsumption" at length in "Results of the Immediate Process of Production" (Marx 1976, 1023ff.), the text originally intended as a concluding chapter to volume I of *Capital*.

3. For years during the recovery of the 1990s—that is, during a period when lean production practices were diffusing rapidly—job loss in the United States was actually higher than during the worst post–World War II recession in 1981–83 (Kutter 1996).

4. Defenders of this viewpoint must grant that the very studies referred to in chapter 1 that establish the empirical importance of lean production also document that the diffusion of lean production practices has not been accompanied by a diffusion of employment guarantees (Kochan et al. 1997, 7). And so their argument must rest on an appeal to the long-term dynamic of this system.

5. At any given point in time it will be fairly easy to note which regions and firms are part of the core and which part of the periphery in global capitalism. Over time, however, things may change. Patterns of investment and disinvestment may lead some regions and firms to switch positions with others, a complication that is not relevant to the point being made here.

6. In France, part-time and short-term employment have both increased by 50 percent since the '80s. Seventy percent of the jobs created in Spain in 1995 were temporary. Thirty percent of the British workforce now holds temporary jobs (Templeman et al. 1996). Nearly 60 percent of the jobs created in the United States in the first half of 1993 were part-time (Rifkin 1995, 167). While correlation does not prove causality, it is surely noteworthy that lean production practices were spreading rapidly in these countries during these periods (see note 20 below).

7. "What happens as lean producers . . . encounter heavy seas . . . ? A General Motors executive gave us one answer: . . . 'When the Japanese producers encounter these gigantic market waves, they will quickly become as mediocre as we are. They will have to start hiring and firing workers along with suppliers . . .' We aren't so sure, but we do feel this is a vital issue" (Womack et al. 1990, 249–50) Given the importance of the topic, this last sentence is remarkably insubstantial. There is considerable evidence that job guarantees in Japan are indeed in the process of eroding. As *Business Week* reported, "Already unnerved by four years of economic stagnation,

many Japanese multinationals want more freedom to shed capacity and workers" (Bremner et al. 1995, 31; see also Kamada 1994). By 1998 the real unemployment rate in Japan was estimated to be as high as 10 percent (Thornton 1998).

8. Paul Adler's rhetoric seems to suggest otherwise when he refers to the flexible production firm as the "property" of everyone working within it (Adler 1993, 102). This is quite misleading. Ownership rights in lean production firms remain concentrated in the hands of investment capital. Workers in these enterprises are merely delegated certain use rights, rights that can be revoked at any moment.

9. Capital mobility can also be restricted by reliance on a network of suppliers in a given region, or by state regulations on the flow of capital. It should be noted here that many state regulations on capital flow have been dismantled (Smith 1993c).

10. In Japan, which serves as a picture of where countries adopting lean production may be heading in the absence of strong oppositional social movements, the figures are quite striking. 6.3 vacation days are taken on average, as opposed to 19 days in the United States (Fucini and Fucini 1990, 155). On the whole, workers in Japanese industry average roughly 200 to 500 more hours at work per year than workers in the United States and Europe. It is hardly surprising that a 1986 survey by the All Toyota Union discovered that 124,000 out of 200,000 members suffer from chronic fatigue (Kenney and Florida 1993, 10).

11. Other trends are worth noting as well. While unemployment tends to reduce poverty rates, in the 1990s the effect of low unemployment rates on the poverty rate has significantly weakened in comparison to previous economic cycles. And while the poverty rate declined between 1996 and 1997, those in poverty have become poorer, and the number of the "very poor" has increased (Henwood 1998).

12. In August of 1998 planned job cuts were up 37 percent from the previous year (Koretz 1998). By the end of October 1998 announced job cuts were up 60 percent from the previous year (Bernstein 1998b).

13. "Most employees at all levels in Japanese companies receive a large part of their compensation—up to a third—in the form of bonuses" (Womack et al. 1990, 250).

14. I am referring here only to the portion of the surplus product allocated within the given enterprise. Other aspects of the allocation of the total surplus product are discussed in the final chapter of this work.

15. "[T]he new industrial revolution exploits the worker more completely and totally than before" (Kenney and Florida 1993, 17).

16. This point has been illustrated in a discourse analysis of team meetings at lean production facilities (Gee et al. 1996, chapters 4–5).

17. In this light the following statement is truly astounding: "American managers both see themselves and are seen as agents of the owners or stockholders of the firm, whereas in Japan the manager is far more a representative of the employees of the firm (i.e., those who constitute the value-producing members of the company)" (Kenney and Florida 1993, 288–89). How this can be true when top management in

Japan continues to be appointed by those who own and control capital, rather than democratically elected by employees or their representatives, is something Kenney and Florida do not explain.

18. All of these media have been used by lean production firms to combat union organizing drives (Kenney and Florida 1993, 276).

19. Kenney and Florida also point out that single union plants "ensure that the union remains relatively weak vis-à-vis management" (Kenney and Florida 1993, 256). This reinforces the difficulty of forging "a separate sphere of identity for workers." Defenders of lean production in the business press generally advocate single union plants—when they do not deny the need for unions altogether.

20. "The 80% of the total workforce in the US that hold working-class jobs saw their real average weekly earnings slip by 18% from 1973 through 1995. Real hourly earnings in that period fell by 12%, indicating that the growth of part-time work had reduced the average weekly income of US workers by another 6 percentage points. Indeed, part-time jobs grew from 15.6% of the total workforce to 18.6% in that same period" (Moody 1997, 188). 27% of all net-wage and salary jobs created in the United States between January 1993 and June 1996 were part-time or temporary (ibid., 191). In Japan, 16 percent of the workforce was part-time and temporary in the early 1980s, a figure that jumped to 31 percent by the mid-1990s (ibid., 188).

21. In firms in Japan, and in Japanese transplants operating in the U.S., wages in supplier firms are only 70 percent of those paid by assemblers (Kenney and Florida 1993, 138; see Lester 1998, 67).

22. Of course, this always holds in capitalism. What is new in lean production is the rate at which innovations are introduced allowing higher levels of production to be maintained with fewer workers. Even if layoffs are avoided and "downsizing" is accomplished solely through attrition, this still results in constant recruitment into the ranks of the unemployed.

23. There is also a strong gender component to the distinction between full-time and part-time workers; in developed industrialized nations women make up between 70 percent and 90 percent of the part-time workforce (Moody 1997, 99).

24. In the United States, most lean production plants have been located on greenfield sites, far from the urban areas where minorities are concentrated. Only 11 percent of workers in transplant suppliers are minorities, and just 9 percent of management (Kenney and Florida 1993, 136, 137).

25. Lifetime employment guarantees do not guarantee that you will work for the same firm. The retirement age in Japanese industry is between fifty-five and sixty. Few workers in Japan can afford not to work when they reach this age. Most are forced to take deep pay cuts to work for suppliers networked to the core enterprises.

26. Perhaps the clearest sign of this power is the ability of management to shift at will from the rhetoric of labor-management cooperation to unabashed aggression. In the United States, policies at A.E. Staley, Caterpillar, Firestone, and many other corporations fit the following description: "[A]ll the talk about cooperation and

competitiveness [was] a prelude to even more demands for concessions as well as [a] means to disarm the unions" (Moody 1997, 25).

27. This is obviously relevant to the issue of structural coercion. A "lifetime" guarantee of a job means little if it is attached to a job that cannot be performed by people in their fifties or sixties. "Because most assembly line jobs are so demanding in traditional auto plants, workers look to the off-line 'desirable' jobs as a form of job security. If they cannot keep up the pace when they get older, they can hope that they will have enough seniority to select a job that matches their capabilities. [In lean production plants] these jobs do not exist" (Parker and Slaughter 1988 105). Eighty-one percent of the workers surveyed at a Mazda lean production facility thought they would not be able to sustain their current work intensity until retirement (Babson 1996, 89).

28. One example is provided by a General Motors sheet metal plant in Lordstown. In 1992 workers went on strike over the issue of job security. Within a day the Saturn plant in Tennessee suspended production, as the just-in-time system left it without necessary parts. Within a week the actions of 240 people at Lordstown left 30,000 G.M. workers idle (Aronowitz and DiFazio 1994, 305; numerous other examples are discussed in Moody 1997, chapter 5, and Moody 1998).

Chapter Four

1. This is subject to the proviso that the development of new needs does not place unacceptable burdens on the ecosystem. For an influential argument that it need not do so, see Commoner (1993).

2. "The challenge of the new business era, with its virtual products, is to adapt the product to the consumer, not the consumer to the product" (Davidow and Malone 1992, 219; see Lester 1998, 83, 314–15).

3. "Mass customization of markets means that the same large number of customers can be reached as in the mass markets of the industrial [that is, Fordist T.S.] economy, and simultaneously they can be treated individually as in the customized markets of pre-industrial economies" (Davis 1989, 169).

4. To some extent shorter runs of more diverse products can be accomplished with conventional technologies. While U.S. manufactures chased the dream of full automation, the Japanese learned how to create what were in effect "multifunctional" machines through combining low-cost conventional machines in manufacturing cells (Warner 1989, 276). It is also clear, however, that lean production systems tend to evolve such that conventional machines are replaced by programmable multifunctional machines, capable of switching from one production application to another at low cost (Ohno 1988; Maleki 1991).

5. See Kenney and Florida (1993) 302–3 for other examples of compressed product life cycles.

6. Cf. Marx (1978) 225ff., 327, and 329 for discussion of how a tendency to de-

velop transportation technologies can be derived from the capital form. This tendency is amply illustrated in lean production.

7. This is a central feature of the management approach termed "quality function deployment," the goal of which is to reconcile what consumers want with what engineers can build (Hauser and Clausing 1988; see also Womack et al. 1990, 181).

8. "During its circulation time, capital does not function as productive capital, and therefore produces neither commodities nor surplus-value. . . . The more that the circulation metamorphoses of capital are only ideal, i.e. the closer the circulation time comes to zero, the more the capital functions, and the greater is its productivity and self-valorization" (Marx 1978, 203; see also 326, 388–89, 391–92).

9. "The circuit of capital proceeds normally only as long as its various phases pass into each other without delay. If capital comes to a standstill in the . . . last phase, C'-M', unsalable stocks of commodities obstruct the flow of circulation" (Marx 1978, 133; see also 18 ff., 222ff., 331).

10. "According to the varying speed with which the capital sheds its commodity form and assumes its money form, i.e. according to the briskness of the sale, the same capital value will serve to a very uneven degree in the formation of products and value, and the scale of the reproduction will expand or contract" (Marx 1978, 124).

11. Another social relation relevant here is established by transactions among different units of capital. Buying and selling among units of capital will be considered in the next chapter. In the present context I shall also ignore the consumption activities of those who own and control capital. I take the claim that consumption is a site where their interests tend to be reconciled with the interests of capital to be trivially true.

12. "Often incumbency—being the first one in the door—is a special advantage as the customer invests in learning a specific application, achieves benefits from it, and forms the ties that bond with the supplier" (Tapscott and Caston 1993, 105).

13. Indeed, from the standpoint of many business theorists the consumer relation is by far the most important dimension to the "new economy," referred to as "fast capitalism" in the following passage: "[T]he fast capitalist literature is deeply devoted to what we call 'consumer determinism.' These texts lead one to believe that all the effects of the new capitalism are caused, not by complex economic, technological, and global issues, and certainly not by the compounding effects of greed and technology, but *by consumers' desires*. The consumer is seen as the transformative agent and cause of our current economic upheavals" (Gee, et al. 1996, 41).

14. They provide a specific example later: "The Japanese automobile industry is moving toward marketing techniques that resemble those of the high-fashion industry, with constantly changing designs and enforced scarcity through artificially limited numbers or limited time periods in which to order the car" (Kenney and Florida 1993, 321–22). This "fashion mentality" has spread to other sectors as well, such as consumer electronics.

15. It is possible to categorize advertising as a pervasive system of manipulation without following Adorno and others in the assumption that ads (and other artifacts of the culture industry) have all but eliminated the possibility of autonomous action. Recipients of ads are not passive automatons; they are often able to negotiate their way through the maze of advertising images, formulating meanings for ads that do not necessarily coincide with those intended. But this does not imply that the notion of manipulation is not applicable here. An attempt at manipulation does not suddenly become something else when the attempt fails or succeeds only partially.

16. As more and more of our social transactions are mediated by digital transmissions across the internet, amassing these sorts of data bases becomes immensely easier (McWilliams 1998).

17. Future developments along these lines can be anticipated. Suppose it is discovered that color preferences are genetically linked to personality such that people who respond to the color red may be more predisposed to consider messages presented in a laid-back fashion, while those who prefer blue are more likely to be persuaded by intimidating messages. We could then expect color-coded direct-mail campaigns based on this information. As more and more genetically linked behavioral traits are discovered, advertisers and marketers will amass vast genographic data bases of their customers analogous to the demographic and psychographic data bases used today (Schrage 1993).

18. This has political dimensions as well. Politicians are increasingly able to customize a different version of their agenda to different voters, based on data bases collecting information on what individual voters have watched and purchased on multimedia information systems.

19. This claim rests upon an implicit philosophical anthropology, that is, a position regarding the conditions of the possibility of human flourishing and self-realization. There is not space here to develop such an anthropology explicitly. For steps in this direction, see Geras (1983).

20. Assume that there are x workers, each of whom is paid $100. As Marx wrote, "With this capital of x times 100, the capitalist class buys a certain quantity of labour-power, or pays wages to a certain number of workers—first transaction. The workers use this sum to buy a certain value of commodities from the capitalists—second transaction. This process is constantly repeated. The sum of x time 100 can therefore never enable the working class to buy the part of the product which contains the constant capital, let alone the surplus-value which belongs to the capitalists. The workers can buy with x times 100 only a portion of value which represents the value of the variable capital advanced" (Marx 1978, 422; see also 155, 194, 197–98, 290–91, 454ff., 515–24).

21. Kenney and Florida write that in Japan, where the lean production model has been instituted the longest, "automation is not an immediate threat to consumer demand because of the long-term employment commitment" (Kenney and Florida 1993, 317–18). In this passage they suddenly forget what they otherwise know quite well: in Japan and elsewhere only a relatively small percentage of the workforce in

lean production systems enjoy job guarantees. Even in these societies unemployment continues to occur due to technical changes, shifts in demand, opportunities for speculation, and cyclical downswings; it is simply shifted to smaller firms on the periphery of the "core" firms. Regarding the global capitalist system as a whole, the figures are truly striking: "Of the 5.4 billion people on earth, almost 3.6 billion have neither cash nor credit to buy much of anything. A majority of people on the planet are at most window shoppers" (Barnet and Cavanaugh 1994, 16).

Chapter Five

1. In the previous chapter the close connection between industrial capital and merchant capital in lean production was discussed. For a general discussion of the central importance of finance capital in the "new economy," see Harvey (1982) and Henwood (1997a). For an specific illustration of the importance of finance capital in lean production networks, see Gerlach's (1992) discussion of Japan.

2. Regarding industrial capital, we need to distinguish two forms of lean production networks (or *keiretsu*, to use the now-standard Japanese term): horizontal networks connecting firms of different sectors, each of which holds a roughly comparable place in its industry, and vertical networks uniting enterprises within a single sector. The latter will be our main concern here.

3. The manner in which research and development was structured in Fordist organizations was of great significance for the question of innovation too. Typically, it would be centralized in a separate department of the core assembly firms. Walls were set up between innovation, production, and distribution. Researchers would throw discoveries over the walls, but all too often there wasn't anyone on the other side to catch them. Also, the more operations Fordist firms attempted to integrate, the more competing demands were placed on their R&D departments, leading in many cases to a lack of focus. Here too the advantages to capital of vertical integration came at a significant cost.

4. These centers formally remain branches of the parent company, while being granted significant autonomy in decision making.

5. Moving to lean production networks generally requires reducing the numbers of suppliers with which a core firm deals directly. Xerox, for instance, cut the number of their suppliers from five thousand to five hundred (Davidow and Malone 1992, 139). It can be noted in passing that a number of different types of suppliers that can be distinguished. Some supply inputs directly to a stage of assembly process (windshields, for example); others produce replacement parts; yet others are capital goods manufacturers (Kenney and Florida 1993, 126).

6. According to Kenney and Florida, in the auto industry suppliers provide up to 70 percent of components in Japan, as opposed to 30–50 percent in the United States prior to the conversion to lean production (ibid., 1993, 45, 130). Gerlach estimates that in Japan automobile makers rely on outside suppliers for 80% of added value in production (Gerlach 1992, 89). Some other percentages of parts outsourced

by core companies in Japan: Fuji-Xerox, 90%; NEC and Epson, 70%; Canon, 65% (Kenney and Florida, 1993, 75).

7. There is a seven hour drive from Toyota's supplier in Michigan to its Kentucky plant. Nonetheless, orders are received from Kentucky every hour in Michigan, and deliveries from Michigan are made every hour in Kentucky (Kenney and Florida 1993, 140). It is worth noting that synchronized delivery is more important for some parts (seats, for instance) than for others (such as steel and other materials).

8. "The importance of an ongoing interaction and an intimate familiarity among technology collaborators, as well as the peculiar public-goods character of information, raises the transactions costs associated with relying on arm's length markets to govern transactions. At the same time, the uncertainties born of technological discontinuities in many sectors have ensured that no single firm can expect to be master of more than a fraction of its production inputs, and the diffuse demands of contemporary technological and market development have surpassed the capability of single firms to accomplish the required coordination of interdependent processes on their own." (Gerlach 1992, 205)

9. In general, when a technology demands complementary developments in a number of sectors, risks are reduced if complementary enterprises join in single program of development (Lockwood 1968, 227).

10. In 1992 the average age of U.S. equipment was around fourteen years, around double of the figure for Japan. Part of the explanation for this discrepancy has to do with the way large manufacturers in the United States played suppliers off against each other to get the best price, thereby leaving suppliers without sufficient capital to modernize regularly (Kelly et al. 1992, 54).

11. Xerox was able to reduce product development time in half after moving to concurrent engineering (Davidow and Malone, 140). Concurrent engineering also tends to lower costs, as designers upstream become more aware of the downstream consequences of their decisions. In the networks set up by Japanese transplant firms in the United States, 50 percent of first-tier suppliers participate closely in new product designs (Kenney and Florida 1993, 142).

12. The distribution of specific firms to the core and ring of a network is not immutable. There have been cases where small start-ups grew large enough to become truly independent from the parent firm; in a few instances they have then even become major shareholders in the parent. In the evaluation of core/ring networks that follows, however, I shall concentrate on what is generally the case, not the exception.

13. Toyota, for example, sends three to six representative directors to each of its first-line satellites (Gerlach 1992, 135).

14. This can occur even if trade secrets are respected. The business press is replete with warnings against the danger of transferring technical information to firms that might later become competitors (Hamel et al. 1989).

15. Consider the rise in the number of suits for alleged violations of intellectual property rights. Between 1985 and 1988, for example, Intel's total litigation expenses increased tenfold (Harrison 1994, 111).

16. The fact that business espionage is one of the fastest growing sectors in the economy is also worth mentioning in this context.

17. "This is life at the bottom of Japan's corporate food chain. Small operators traditionally bear the brunt of recessions as blue-chip companies press suppliers for bone-crunching price cuts, and those suppliers in turn press subsuppliers" (Holyoke et al. 1994, 52; see Lester 1998, 67).

18. "Wired corporations find themselves armed to play suppliers off one another and get lower prices or better service. General Electric Co. bought $1 billion worth of supplies via the Net last year. That saved the company 20% on materials costs because its divisions were able to reach a wider base of suppliers to hammer out better deals" (Hof et al. 1998, 125).

19. This strategy has been adopted by Compaq, among many other core firms (Burrows 1994, 141).

20. This dynamic is also relevant to the question of skills. See note 12, chapter 2.

21. According to Peter Drucker, lean production firms in Japan attempt to develop three competing products simultaneously: improvements of an existing product; new products that evolve out of the old; and breakthrough innovations that initiate a new path of technical development (Drucker 1991, A12). The more successful the third endeavor is, the more precarious the present network configuration.

22. See Holyoke et al., for a description of the pressure the economic recession of the '90s has placed on lean production networks in Japan. "This recession is different: Its magnitude is severing some long-term supplier relationships at the core of Japanese industrial prowess. . . . In electronics. . . nearly every major company is forging new partnerships—and not just for parts. . . . While they still rarely use foreign suppliers in Japan, auto makers are redrawing traditional supply patterns to slash costs" (Holyoke et al. 1994, 52–53).

23. There is also an inherent tendency to seek productivity advances in order to increase the rate of exploitation, but that has more to do with the capital/wage labor relation than with intercapital relations.

24. "Who would pay money for a computer that had 18,000 vacuum tubes and failed once a day on average? Only the military. Defense paid for development of the ENIAC and provided a market for many of the computers developed in the 1940s and early 1950s. It wasn't until the late 1950s that a significant commercial market for these machines developed. Likewise, the military and NASA snatched up the first crude integrated circuits at $100 a pop in the early 1960s, when no one else would. DARPA paid for the worlds's first switching network in the 1970s, advancing a technology that has become the staple of datacommunications. This decade's spin-off examples include expert systems, which derived from rule-based programming work sponsored by DARPA in the late 1970s. And you can thank DARPA for Unix-based workstations, as well. . . . 'The field of computer science, pure and simple, was invented and fueled by DARPA,' says Dan Dimancescu, technology policy consultant and author of several books of R&D policy" (Leibowitz 1989, 54–58). In Japan, the

Ministry of International Trade and Industry has played a role analogous to that of the Department of Defense in the United States

25. Superb accounts of critical theory are found in Marsh (1995) and Feenberg (1991).

26. Reich's own term is "high value" production.

Chapter Six

1. It should also be noted in passing that neoliberals appear to overestimate the decline in the nation-state's capacities in other ways as well. The role of governments in the newly industrializing countries (NICs), for instance, has hardly been limited to guaranteeing loans for international finance capital. They have also protected local industries, subsidized the agricultural sector, actively intervened in labor markets to control real wages, and undertaken many other forms of industrial policy. The neoliberal view that savings must come before economic growth is directly refuted by the experience of the NICs; successful growth strategies were instituted by nation-states, after which high rates of savings resulted (Webber and Rigby 1996, chapter 10). Further, organizations such as the World Trade Organization, the International Monetary Fund, and the World Bank have no powers to tax, and no coercive apparatus of their own to enforce decisions. The powers they do have are delegated to them by nation-states, along with their funding and much of their leading personnel. Nor have recent technological developments made it impossible for nation-states to monitor global flows of money, as even periodic and half-hearted investigations into the flow of drug money show (Helleiner 1996, 203). It is also the case that many nation-states maintain a set of symbols and rituals that effectively reproduce beliefs in the legitimacy of the social order within a significant portion of the populace. No institution of transnational capital is remotely capable of duplicating this function (Hirst and Thompson 1996). Finally, it is worth mentioning that most of the neoliberals theorists and politicians who justify dismantling the social state on the grounds of the erosion of state capacities themselves insist that nation-states bail out banks, corporations, investors, and international lending agencies when financial crises break out in the world economy. Surely this is hypocrisy of the highest order.

2. The capitalist state has always included divisions that have been shielded from public in order to pursue the interests of capital accumulation without the nuisances of democratic accountability. The international agencies of the global economy should be seen as forums in which representatives of these departments of the "protected state" coordinate their activities. The rise of these international agencies (and of international speculators as well) thus need not imply the impotence of the nation-state in general, but rather a consolidation of the power of one part of the state apparatus over others.

3. This is a very compressed account of an exceedingly complex story. Close attentions to historical specificities must be paid if it is to have any concrete explanatory force. In some contexts the expression of the drive to accumulate in a drive to

appropriate technological rents is of central importance. This results in the "moral depreciation" of previous investments in fixed capital, which can lead to a falling rate of profit with the right sort of stratification among units of capital. (On technological rents, see Smith 2000; for a discussion of falling rates of profit centering on the stratifications of capital, see Reuten 1991.) In certain historical periods rapid capital accumulation may encourage the formation of less productive units of capital, bringing about an overall decline in profits throughout the economy. (This is how Webber and Rigby [1996] explain the demise of the—partly mythical—"golden age" of post–World War II capitalism.) A third factor concerns the way the drive to accumulate may be expressed in a tendency for more and more investment in unproductive labor, which *ceteris paribus* will lead to a falling rate of profit (Moseley 1997). As far as I can tell, these approaches are mutually consistent. Each one shifts attention away from declining consumption power as the main factor explaining crises in capitalism. And all three fit within the most basic dynamic underlying overaccumulation crises. The drive for technological rents and the entry of new units of capital are mechanisms leading to an increase in accumulated capital; the low level of productivity in new units of capital and an increase in unproductive labor contribute to explanations for why the rate of surplus value (and thus the rate of profit) does not grow at the same rate as the mass of capital.

4. "[T]he only possible reason why [capital accumulation] should suddenly be halted is a lack of surplus-value; and this lack must have arisen within and despite the accumulation process. In reality, of course, it seems to be the other way around; it appears that the surplus-value is unrealizable due to an abundance of use-values (commodities). And to the individual capitalist it is indeed lack of demand which hinders the sale of his commodities and which induces him not to increase production by additional investments. But his apparent dependency of accumulation on market demand merely reveals the individual capitalists' reactions to the social dearth of surplus-value . . . to the decrease of the exploitability of labor in comparison with the profit requirements of a progressive capital accumulation" (Mattick 1969, 78–79).

5. A random list of sectors suffering from serious levels of excess productive capacity today includes oil, steel, commodity chemicals, autos, and computer printers (Melcher 1998).

6. "Between 1990 and 1997, corporate America spent $1.1 trillion (current dollars) on information technology hardware alone, an 80 percent faster rate of investment than in the first seven years of the 1980s. . . . [A] large portion of these outlays is written off quickly. Nevertheless, with their tax-based service lives typically clustered over three to five years, about $460 billion still remains on the books. . . . This is hardly an insignificant element of overall corporate costs; by way of comparison, total U.S. corporate interest expenses are presently running at about $400 billion annually" (Roach 1998, 53). To this we must add the costs of software, training, repairs, and support. It has been estimated that a $2,500 PC costs a typical big business $6,000 to $13,000 a year in these "secondary" costs (Henwood 1997b). Such figures go a

long way toward explaining why all of the advantages of the "new economy" have not yet appeared as significant and lasting improvements in productivity statistics. See also the penultimate paragraph of this chapter below.

7. This description obviously contradicts the views of the defenders of the "new economy" discussed in chapter 4. A contingent interaction between a consumer and "any acceptable source" hardly counts as a "co-destiny" relationship!

Chapter Seven

1. The rate of technological change is at least roughly reflected in growth rates. It is often forgotten today that between 1929 and 1975 the Soviet Union grew at an average of over 5 percent per year, while the United States averaged under 3 percent during this period (Meurs and Schauffler 1990, 6). This advance is often credited to technology transfer from the west. An argument against this interpretation is found in Apostolakis (1988).

2. The "nomenclatura" consists of those whose names appear on the list of those approved for appointment and promotion within the bureaucratic system.

3. Romania under Ceausescu offered a particularly extreme case of this. According to a Romanian manager, the word "computer" was even banned from official publications for a period (Foley 1990, 5; see also Graham 1992).

4. This does not necessarily mean that innovations will never be introduced that speed up the work process. It may well be the case that a workforce democratically decides that it would prefer a shorter work day of more intense labor to a longer work day at a more relaxed pace (Slaughter 1998).

5. This does not mean that workers in a particular enterprise would experience no external pressures once worker self-management has been instituted. Institutional mechanisms must be set up that encourage enterprises to respond to social needs in an efficient manner. In the alternative to lean production presented here competition in producer and consumer markets (there are no labor or capital markets) and the oversight of community banks and representative political bodies ensure that this tends to occur. I shall also refer later to the portion of the economic surplus that is allocated outside of particular enterprises. This too must be subject to democratic control for exploitation to be absent.

6. Elson (1988) proposes that social audits be performed at each step in the production and distribution process. Another possibility would be to have representatives of consumer interest groups sit on the boards of directors of enterprises (Devine 1988). Schweickart (1994) calls for publicly owned community banks that allocate new investment funds according to criteria formulated in a democratic process. See below.

7. In 1969, workers in the United States annually labored 1,786 hours on average. By 1987 the figure was 1,949. This means that the average worker put in roughly one month (163 hours) of extra work each year (Schor 1991).

8. This implies that there are no intellectual property rights of any sort. The effects this might have on innovation are discussed in the following section.

9. I do not think there is any way to fix once and for all the goods and services that should be provided directly as public goods and those that should be distributed through (socialized) markets. The appropriate mixture depends upon the given cultural and historical context, although we can expect the public goods sector to exceed that found in any variant of capitalism. I would also like to note that Diane Elson (1988) has discussed a number of institutional arrangements that further the socialization of the market besides those mentioned here. These include organizations of users of public services, wage commissions, price commissions, public regulators, and network coordinators.

10. To give only one example, David Noble (1984) has shown how capital/labor relations in the civilian sector have been profoundly affected by the Pentagon's role in the development of computerized manufacturing.

11. Another part of this planning concerns the setting of priorities for new investments, a topic discussed further in section D below.

12. Under capitalism, technological innovation has been most successful where a "technological milieu" combines people with expertise in different facets of the innovation process, such as those engaged in basic science, applied engineers, production workers, subcontractors, and so on (Storper and Walker, chapter 4). The same point would hold under a different set of social relations. In fact, we could expect technological milieus to flourish under socialism. Production workers would be given far more opportunity to familiarize themselves with the theoretical principles of science and engineering if a significant reduction in the work day were combined with democracy at the workplace.

13. In reality, this is not a linear process. Each stage in the pipeline proceeds simultaneously, and provides feedback to every other stage.

14. It should also be recalled that in capitalism the people actually generating new scientific-technical information are generally not the ones who benefit the most from intellectual property rights. One of the first things a new researcher hired by a corporation typically has to do is sign away all patent rights to the corporation.

15. Marx insisted unequivocally on this point in his essay, "Critique of the Gotha Programme" (Marx 1977).

16. Schweickart himself does not extend the idea of pooling funds for new investment to the international level; this proposal is an extrapolation from his discussion of economic democracy on the national level.

17. The assumption here is that markets left to themselves systematically tend to underinvest in both public goods and industries with high positive externalities, due to familiar free-rider problems.

18. It is important to remember that there have been markets of tens of thousands of years, while the dominance of the value form can be measured in centuries.

19. It may be worth mentioning that few advocates of "free markets" fail to put restrictions on what are appropriate matters for market transactions. No one today laments the fact that as a society we have drawn a line and said that there will no markets in which property rights to the ownership of human beings are exchanged. Nor do even the fiercest libertarians advocate setting up a market for political offices granting private ownership of those offices to those willing to pay the highest price. The democratic version of socialism advocated here simply shifts the line defining where legitimate market transactions end, based on the assumption that private ownership of another's labor power or of large-scale productive resources is strictly analogous to private ownership of a person or a political office. This argument, needless to say, does not rule out private ownership of items for personal consumption.

Selected Bibliography

Abegglen, James. 1985. *The Japanese Factory*. Cambridge, Mass.: MIT Press.

Abercrombie, Nicholas, S. Hill, and B. Turner. 1980. *The Dominant Ideology Thesis*. London: Allen & Unwin.

Adler, Paul. 1987. "Automation and Skill: New Directions." *International Journal of Technology Management*, Vol. 2.

———. 1988. "Automation, Skill and the Future of Capitalism." *Berkeley Journal of Sociology*, Vol. 23.

———. 1990. "Marx, Machines, and Skill." *Technology and Culture*, Vol. 31, No. 4.

———. 1992a. "The "Learning Bureaucracy": New United Motor Manufacturing, Inc." In Straw and Cummings.

———. ed. 1992b. *Technology and the Future of Work*. New York: Oxford University Press.

———. 1993. "Time and Motion Regained." *Harvard Business Review*, January-February.

———. 1995. "'Democratic Taylorism': The Toyota Production System at NUMMI." In Babson 1995b.

Adler, Paul, and B. Borys. 1989. "Automation and Skill: Three Generations of Research on the NC Case." *Politics and Society*, Vol. 17, No. 3.

Aoki, Masahiko. 1988. *Information, Incentives, and Bargaining in the Japanese Economy*. Cambridge: Cambridge University Press.

Apostolakis, Bobby. 1988. "The Role of Technology Transfer in Soviet Development." *Review of Radical Political Economy*, Vol. 20, No. 4.

Appelbaum, Eileen, and R. 1994. Batt. *The New American Workplace: Transforming Work Systems in the United States*. Ithaca: ILR Press.

Aronowitz, Stanley, and W. 1994. DiFazio. *The Jobless Future: Sci-Tech and the Dogma of Work*. Minneapolis: University of Minnesota Press.

Babson, Steve. "Lean Production and Labor: Empowerment and Exploitation." In Babson 1995a.

———, ed. 1995b. *Lean Work: Empowerment and Exploitation in the Global Auto Industry*. Detroit: Wayne State University.

———, 1996. "UAW, Lean Production, and Labor-Management Relations at Auto Alliance." In Green and Yanarella 1996.

Barnet, Richard, and J. 1994. Cavanagh. *Global Dreams: Imperial Corporations and the New World Order*. New York: Touchstone.

Bass, Thomas. 1996. "The Future of Money." *Wired,* Vol. 4, No. 10.

Batt, Rose, and E. Appelbaum. 1993. "Labor's New Agenda," *Dollars and Sense,* September/October.

Beckett, Beverly, B. 1990. Knill, T. Rohan, and G. Werner. "New Wizards of Management." *Industry Week,* March 19.

Beniger, John. 1986. *The Control Revolution: Technological and Economic Origins of the Information Society.* Cambridge, Mass.: Harvard University Press.

Berger, Suzanne, and R. 1996. Dore, eds. *National Diversity and Global Capitalism.* Ithaca: Cornell University Press.

Berggren, Christian. 1992. *Alternatives to Lean Production: Work Organization in the Swedish Auto Industry.* Ithaca: ILR Press.

Bernstein, Aaron. 1994. "Why America Needs Unions But Not the Kind It Has Now." *Business Week,* May 23.

———, 1995. "The Wages Squeeze." *Business Week,* July 17.

———, 1997. "Sharing Prosperity." *Business Week,* September 1.

———. 1998a. "Now Workers Are Getting the Gravy." *Business Week,* June 22.

———. A Strong Economy Needs Strong Wages." *Business Week,* November 16.

Bessant, John, and A. Chisholm. 1989. "Human Factors in Computer-integrated Manufacturing." In Forester 1989.

Blinder, Alan, ed. 1990. *Paying for Productivity.* Washington, D.C.: The Brookings Institution.

Bluestone, Brry, and I. Bluestone. 1992. *Negotiating the Future: A Labor Perspective on American Business.* New York: Basic Books, 1992.

Bonefeld, Werner. 1991. "The Reformulation of State Theory." In Bonefeld and Holloway 1991.

Bonefeld, Werner and J. Holloway. 1991. *Post-Fordism & Social Form: A Marxist Debate on the Post-Fordist State.* London: Macmillan.

Bosworth, Brian, and S. 1993. Rosenfeld, eds. *Significant Others: Exploring the Potentials of Manufacturing Networks.* Chapel Hill, N.C.: Regional Technology Strategies.

Botwinick, Howard. 1993. *Persistent Inequalities: Wage Disparity under Capitalist Competition.* Princeton: Princeton University Press.

Boyer, Robert, and D. Drache. 1996. *States Against Markets: The Limits of Globalization.* New York: Routledge.

Boyett, Joseph, and H. 1992. Conn. *Workplace 2000: The Revolution Reshaping American Business.* New York: Penguin.

Braverman, Harry. *Labor and Monopoly Capital.* 1974. New York: Monthly Review Press.

Bremner, Brian, W. Holstein, A. Borrus, and L. Bernier. 1995. "Rougher Trade: The U.S.-Japan Chasm Widens." *Business Week,* July 17.

Brenner, Robert. 1998. *The Economics of Global Turbulence.* Special Issue, *New Left Review,* No. 229.

Brouwer, Steve. 1998. *Sharing the Pie: A Citizen's Guide to Wealth and Power in America.* New York: Henry Holt and Company.

Brown, Charles, J. Hamilton, and J. Medoff. 1990. *Employers Large and Small.* Cambridge: Harvard University Press.

Browning, John, and S. Reiss. 1998a. "Encyclopedia of the New Economy, Part I." *Wired,* March.

_____. 1998b. "Encyclopedia of the New Economy, Part II." *Wired,* April.

Burrows, Peter. 1984. "Compaq Stretches for the Crown." *Business Week,* July 11.

Byrne, John. 1993. "The Horizontal Corporation." *Business Week,* December 20.

Cappelli, Peter. 1993. "Are Skill Requirements Rising? Evidence from Production and Clerical Jobs." *Industrial and Labor Relations Review,* Vol. 46, No. 3.

Carchedi, Guglielmo. 1991. *Frontiers of Political Economy* London: Verso.

Castells, Manuel. 191989. "Social Movements and the Informational City." *Hitotsubashi Journal of Social Studies* Vol. 21.

Clark, Kim, and T. 1989. Fujimoto. "Reducing the Time to Market: The Case of the World Auto Industry." *Design Management Journal,* Fall.

Clarke, Simon. 1991. "Overaccumulation, Class Struggle and the Regulation Approach." In Bonefeld and Holloway.

Cohen, Stephen, and J. Zysman. 1987. *Manufacturing Matters: The Myth of the Post-Industrial Economy.* New York: Basic Books.

Commoner, Barry. 1993. "Population and Poverty." In Fisk 1993.

Cooke, William. 1990. *Labor-Management Cooperation: New Partnership or Going in Circles?* Kalamazoo, Mich.: W. E. Upjohn Institute.

Cox, Kevin, ed. 1997. *Spaces of Globalization: Reasserting the Power of the Local.* New York: Guiliford.

Daly, Herman, and J. Cobb. 1994. *For the Common Good: Redirecting the Economy Towards Community, The Environment, and a Sustainable Future.* Boston, Beacon Press.

Dassbach, Carl. 1996. "Lean Production, Labor Control, and Post-Fordism in the Japanese Automobile Industry." In Green and Yanarell 1996.

Davidow, William, and M. Malone. 1992. *The Virtual Corporation: Structuring and Revitalizing the Corporation for the 21'st Century.* New York: Edward Burlingame Books/HarperBusiness.

Davies, Stephen. 1979. *The Diffusion of Process Innovations.* Cambridge: Cambridge University Press.

Davis, Jim, and M. Stack. 1997. "The Digital Advantage." In Davis et al. 1997.

Davis, Jim, T. Hirschl, and M. Stack. 1997. *Cutting Edge: Technology, Information, Capitalism and Social Revolution.* New York: Verso Press.

Davis, Mike. *Prisoners of the American Dream.* 1986. New York: Verso.

Davis, Stanley. *Future Perfect.* 1987. Reading, Mass.: Addison-Wesley.

_____, 1989. "From 'Future Perfect': Mass Customizing." *Planning Review,* March/April.

Delbridge, Rick. 1998. *Life on the Line in Contemporary Manufacturing: The Workplace Experience of Lean Production and the 'Japanese' Model.* New York: Oxford University Press.

Derrida, Jacques. 1994. "A Lecture on Marx." *New Left Review,* No. 205, May-June.

Dertouzos, Michael. 1997. *What Will Be: How the New World of Information Will Change Our Lives.* New York: HarperEdge.

Dertouzos, Michael, R. Lester, R. Solow, and the MIT Commission on Industrial Productivity. 1991. *Made in America: Regaining the Productive Edge.* Cambridge, Mass.: MIT Press.

Devine, Pat. 1988. *Democracy and Economic Planning.* Cambridge: Polity Press.

Dohse, Knuth, U. Jurgens, and T. Malsch. 1985. "From 'Fordism' to 'Toyotism'? The Social Organization of the Labor Process in the Japanese Automobile Industry." *Politics and Society,* Vol. 14, No. 2.

Dosi, Giovanni, C. Freeman, R. Nelson, G. Silverberg, and L. Soete, eds. 1988. *Technical Change and Economic Theory.* New York, Pinter Publishers.

Drucker, Peter. 1991. "Japan: New Strategies for a New Reality." *The Wall Street Journal,* October 2.

Elger, Tony and C. Smith, eds. 1994. *Global Japanization? The Transnational Transformation of the Labour Process.* London: Routledge.

Elliott, Larry, and D. Atkinson. 1998. *The Age of Insecurity.* London: Verso Press.

Elson, Diane, ed. 1979. *Value: The Representation of Labour in Capitalism.* Atlantic Highlands, N.J.: Humanities Press.

———, 1989. "Market Socialism or Socialization of the Market?" *New Left Review,* No. 172.

Ermann, M. David, M. Williams, and C. Gutierrez, eds. 1990. *Computers, Ethics, & Society.* New York: Oxford University Press.

Evangeliste, Matthew. 1988. *Innovation and the Arms Race: How the United States and the Soviet Union Develop New Military Technologies.* Ithaca: Cornell University Press.

Feenberg, Andrew. 1991. *Critical Theory of Technology.* New York: Oxford University Press.

Fisk, Milton. 1989. *The State and Justice: An Essay in Political Theory.* Cambridge: Cambridge University Press.

———, ed. 1993. *Justice.* Atlantic Highlands, N.J.: Humanities Press.

Florida, Richard, and M. Kenney. 1990. *The Breakthrough Illusion.* New York: Basic Books.

Foley, Gerry. 1990. "After Ceausescu"s Overthrow," *International Viewpoint,* No. 177, Jan. 29.

Forester, John, ed. 1989. *Computers and the Human Context.* Cambridge Mass.: MIT Press.

Froebel, F., J. Heinrichs, and O. Kreye. 1980. *The New Industrial Division of Labour: Structural Unemployment in Industrialized Countries and Industrialization in Developing Countries.* Cambridge: Cambridge University Press.

Fucini, Joseph, and S. Fucini. 1990. *Working for the Japanese: Inside Mazda's American Auto Plant.* New York: The Free Press.

Garland, Susan, and E. Thornton. "Justice's Cartel Crackdown." 1998. *Business Week,* July 27.

Gates, Bill. 1995. *The Road Ahead.* New York: Viking Press.

Gee, James Paul, G. Hull, and C. Lankshear. 1996. *The New Work Order: Behind the language of the New Capitalism.* Boulder: Westview Press.

Geras, Norman. *Marx and Human Nature.* 1983. London: Verso.

Gerlach, Michael. 1992. *Alliance Capitalism: The Social Organization of Japanese Business.* Berkeley: University of California Press.

Glick, Mark, and R. Brenner. 1996. "The Regulation Approach: Theory and History." *New Left Review,* No. 188.

Gordon, David. 1996. *Fat and Mean.* New York: The Free Press.

Goto, Akira. 1982. "Business Groups in a Market Economy." *European Economic Review,* Vol. 19.

Graham, Keith. 1992. *Karl Marx Our Contemporary.* Toronto: University of Toronto Press.

Graham, Laurie. 1994. "How Does the Japanese Model Transfer to the United States? A View from the Line." In Elger and Smith 1994.

Graham, Loren. 1984. "Science and Computers in Soviet Society." In Hoffman 1984.

_____, 1996. "The Myth of Egalitarianism: Worker Response to Post-Fordism at Subaru-Isuzu." In Green and Yanarell 1996.

Green, William. 1996. "The Transformation of the NLRA Paradigm: The Future of Labor-Management Relations in Post-Fordist Auto Plants." In Green and Yanarell 1996.

Green, William, and E. Yanarella. 1996. *North American Auto Unions in Crisis: Lean Production as Contested Terrain.* Albany: State University of New York Press.

Greenbaum, Joan. 1995. *Windows on the Workplace: Computers, Jobs, and the Organization of Office Work in the Late Twentieth Century.* New York: Cornerstone Books.

Gros, Neil. 1998. "The Supply Chain." *Business Week,* June 22.

Gros, Neil, and I. Sager. 1998. "Caution Signs Along the Road." *Business Week,* June 22.

Guiliano, Vincent. 1990a. "The Mechanization of Office Work." In Ermann et al. 1990.

Hamel, Gary, Y. Doz, and C. K. Prahalad. 1989. "Collaborate with Your Competitors—and Win." *Harvard Business Review,* January-February.

Hammonds, Keith, K. Kelly, K. Thurston. 1994. "The New World of Work." *Business Week,* October 17.

Handy, Charles. 1994. *The Age of Paradox.* Cambridge, MA: Harvard Business School.

Hapoienu, Spencer. 1990. "The Rise of Micromarketing." *The Journal of Business Strategy,* December.

Harrison, Bennett. 1994. *Lean and Mean: The Changing Landscape of Corporate Power in the Age of Flexibility.* New York: Basic Books.

Harvey, David. 1982. *The Limits to Capital.* New York: Oxford University Press.

_____, 1989. *The Condition of Postmodernity.* Cambridge: Blackwell.

_____, 1996. *Justice, Nature & the Geography of Difference.* Oxford: Blackwell.

Hauser, John, and D. Clausing. 1988. "The House of Quality." *Harvard Business Review,* May-June.

Helleiner, Eric. 1996. "Post-Globalization: Is the Financial Liberalization Trend Likely to be Reversed?" In Boyer and Drache 1996.

Henriksson, Lars. 1994. "The Swedish Model." In Parker and Slaughter.

Henwood, Doug. 1976a. *Wall Street.* New York: Verso.

———. 1997b. "Where's the Payoff?" *Left Business Observer,* No. 79.

———. 1998. "Prosperity Breaks Out!" *Left Business Observer,* No. 86.

Hines, Colin, and T. Lang. "In Favor of a New Protectionism." In Mander and Goldsmith 1996.

Hirsch, Joachim. "Fordism and Post-Fordism: The Present Crisis and its Consequences." In Bonefeld and Holloway 1991.

Hirschhorn, Larry. 1984. *Beyond Mechanization: Work and Technology in the Post-Industrial Age.* Cambridge Mass.: MIT Press.

Hirst, Paul, and G. Thompson. 1996. *Globalization in Question.* Cambridge: Polity Press.

Hoerr, John. 1989. "The Payoff From Teamwork." *Business Week,* July 10

Hoerr, John, M. Pollock, and D. Whiteside. 1989. "Management Discovers the Human Side of Automation." In Forester 1989.

Hof, Robert. 1993. "Hewlett-Packard Digs Deep For a Digital Future." *Business Week,* October 18.

———, 1994. "Can This Chip Make the Next Quantum Leap?" *Business Week,* November 21.

Hof, Robert, G. McWilliams, and G. Saveri. 1998. "The 'Click Here' Economy." *Business Week,* June 22.

Hoffman, Eric, ed. 1984. *The Soviet Union in the 1980's.* Special issue of *Proceedings of the Academy of Political Science,* Vol. 35, No. 3.

Holyoke, Larry, W. Spindle, and N. Gross. 1994. "Doing the Unthinkable: Japan Inc.'s Suppliers Gasp as It Buys Abroad." *Business Week,* January 10.

Hounshell, David. 1984. *From the American System to Mass Production, 1820–1932.* Baltimore: Johns Hopkins Press.

Howard, Robert. 1985. *Brave New Workplace.* New York: Viking Press.

Howell, David. 1984. "The Skills Myth." *American Prospect,* Summer.

Howes, Candace. 1995. "Are Japanese Transplants Restoring U.S. Competitiveness or Dumping Their Social Problems in the U.S. Market?" In Babson 1995b.

Ichniowski, Casey, T. Kochan, D. Levine, C. Olson, and G. Strauss. 1996. "What Works at Work: Overview and Assessment." *Industrial Relations,* Vol. 35, No. 3.

Imai, Masaaki. 1986. *Kaizen.* Cambridge MA: McGraw-Hill.

Ishida, Mitsuo. 1997. "Japan: Beyond the Model for Lean Production." In Kochan et al. 1997.

Jarboe, Kenan, and J. Yudken. 1997. "Time to Get Serious About Workplace Change." *Issues in Science and Technology,* Summer.

Jenson, Jane. 1989. "The Talents of Women, the Skills of Men: Flexible Specialisation and Women." In Wood.

Jessop, Bob. 1991. "Regulation Theory, Post-Fordism and the State: More than a Reply to Werner Bonefeld." In Bonefeld and Holloway.

Kagarlitsky, Boris. 1990. *Dialectics of Change.* London: Verso.

Kamada, Toshiko. 1994. "'Japanese Management' and the 'Loaning' of Labour: Restructuring in the Japanese Iron and Steel Industry." In Elger and Smith 1994.

Kantor, Rosabeth Moss. 1995. *World Class: Thriving Locally in the Global Economy.* New York: Touchstone.

Kawanishi, Hirosuke. 1992. *Enterprise Unionism in Japan.* London: Kegan Paul.

Kelly, Kevin. 1998. *New Rules for the New Economy.* New York: Viking.

Kelly, Kevin, O. Port, J. Treece, G. DeGeorge, and Z. Schiller 1992. "Learning from Japan." *Business Week,* January 27.

Kelley, Maryellen. 1986. "Programmable Automation and the Skill Question: A Reinterpretation of the Cross-National Evidence." *Human Systems Management,* Vol. 6, No. 3.

Kelley, Maryellen, and B. Harrison. "Unions, Technology, and Labor-Management Cooperation." In Mishel and Voos 1992.

Kenney, Martin, and R. Florida. 1993. *Beyond Mass Production: The Japanese System and Its Transfer to the U.S..* Oxford: Oxford University Press.

Kerwin, Kathleen. 1998. "GM: Modular Plants Won't Be A Snap." *Business Week,* November 9.

Kline, Stephen. 1993. *Out of the Garden: Toys, TV and Children's Culture in the Age of Marketing.* New York: Verso Press.

Kloppenberg, Jack. 1988. *First the Seed: The Political Economy of Plant Biotechnology 1492–2000.* New York: Cambridge University Press.

Kochan, Thomas, H. 1986. Katz, and R. McKersie. *The Transformation of American Industrial Relations,* New York: Basic Books.

Kochan, Thomas, R. Lansbury, and J.P. MacDuffie. 1997. *After Lean Production.* Ithica: ILR (Cornell University) Press.

Koike, Kazuo. 1988. *Understanding Industrial Relations in Japan.* New York: St. Martin's Press.

Koretz, Gene. 1998. "Which Way Are Wages Headed?" *Business Week,* September 21.

Krafcik, John. 1989. "A New Diet for U.S. Manufacturing." *Technology Review* January.

Kumazawa, Makoto and J. 1989. Yamada. "Jobs and Skills under the Lifelong Nenko Employment." In Wood.

Kuttner, Robert. 1996. "Happy Labor Day, Joe Six-Pack. Have Some Crumbs." *Business Week,* September 9.

Lane, Robert. 1993. "Does Money Buy Happiness?" *The Public Interest,* Vol. 111.

Lawler, Edward, S. Mohrman, and G. Ledford. 1992. *Employee Involvement and Total Quality Management.* San Francisco: Jossey-Boss.

Leibowitz, Michael. 1989. "Does Military R&D Stimulate Commerce or the Pork Barrel?" *Electronic Business,* February 6.

Lester, Richard. 1998. *The Productivity Edge: How U.S. Industries Are Pointing the Way to a new Era of Economic Growth.* New York: W.W. Norton.

Levine, David, and L. Tyson. 1990. "Participation, Productivity and the Firm's Environment." In Blinder 1990.

Lifson, Thomas. 1992. "Innovations and Institutions: Notes on the Japanese Paradigm." In Adler.

Lockwood, William. 1968. *The Economic Development of Japan.* Princeton: Princeton University Press.

Lundvall, Bengt-Ake. 1988. "Innovation as an Interactive Process: From User-producer Interaction to the National System of Innovation." In Dosi et. al. 1988.

MacDuffie, John. 1995. "Workers' Roles in Lean Production: The Implications for Worker Representation." In Babson.

MacDuffie, John, and F. Pil. 1995. "The International Assembly Plant Study: Philosophical and Methodological Issues." In Babson 1995b.

———. 1997. "Changes in Auto Industry Employment Practices: An International Overview." In Kochan et al. 1997.

MacKenzie, Donald, and J. Wajcman, eds. 1985. *The Social Shaping of Technology.* Philadelphia: Open University Press.

Maleki, Reza. 1991. *Flexible Manufacturing System.* New York: Prentice-Hall.

Mandel, Ernest. 1975. *Late Capitalism.* London: Verso.

———, 1989. *Beyond Perestroika.* London: Verso.

———, 1992. *Power and Money.* London: Verso.

Mander, Jerry, and E. Goldsmith. 1996. *The Case Against the Global Economy.* San Francisco: Sierra Club Books.

Mann, Keith. 1994. "Class Struggle, Skill and the Productive Process Today." *International Marxist Review,* No. 15, Spring.

Manske, Fred, and H. Wolf, eds. 1990–91. *The Future of Industrial Work in Changing Capitalism.* Special issue of the *International Journal of Political Economy,* Vol. 20, No. 4.

Marsh, James. *Critique, Action, and Liberation.* 1995. Albany:State University of New York Press.

Marx, Karl. 1973. *Grundrisse.* New York: Vintage Press.

———, 1976. *Capital: Volume I.* New York: Penguin.

———, 1977. *Karl Marx: Selected Writings,* ed. by David McLellan. New York: Oxford University Press.

———, 1978. *Capital: Volume II.* New York: Penguin.

———, 1981. *Capital: Volume III.* New York: Penguin.

Marx, Karl, and F. Engels. 1983. *Letters on 'Capital'.* London: New Park.

Matsu, Kono. 1994. "From Advertising to Subvertising." *Adbusters* Winter.

Mattick, Paul. 1969. *Marx & Keynes: The Limits of the Mixed Economy.* Boston: Porter Sargent.

Mayer, Martin. 1990. "Scanning the Future." *Forbes,* October 15.

McCarney, Joseph. 1990. *Social Theory and the Crisis of Marxism.* New York: Verso.

McChesney, Robert, E. W. Wood, and J. B. Foster, eds. 1998. *Capitalism and the Information Age: The Political Economy of the Global Communication Revolution.* New York: Monthly Review Press.

McDonough, John. 1988. "A Culture of Choice." *Advertising Age,* Nov. 9.

McWilliams, Gary, and M. Stepanek. 1998. "Taming the Info Monster." *Business Week,* June 22.

Melcher, Richard. 1998. "The Party is Getting Quieter." *Business Week,* February 2.

Meurs, Mike, and R. Schauffler. 1990. "Not According to Plan: The Collapse of the Soviet Planned Economy." *Dollars & Sense,* No. 195, July/Augusst.

Miller, Karen, D. Woodruff, and T. Peterson. "Overhaul in Japan." 1992. *Business Week,* December 21.

Miller, Karen and K. Kerwin. 1993. "GM's German Lessons." *Business Week,* December 20.

Mishel, Lawrence, and P. Voos, eds. 1992. *Unions and Economic Competitiveness.* Washington, D.C.: Economic Policy Institute.

Moody, Kim. 1997. *Labor in a Lean World.* New York: Verso.

———, 1998. "After the General Motors Shutdown: 'What Means This Strike'?" *Against the Current,* September/October.

Morgan, Kevin. 1993. "Do Networks Result in Innovations? The Automotive and Machine Tool Industries in Europe." In Bosworth and Rosenfeld 1993.

Moseley, Fred, ed. 1993. *Marx's Method in 'Capital'.* New York: Humanities Press.

———, 1997. "The Rate of Profit and the Future of Capitalism." *Review of Radical Political Economics.* Vol. 29, No. 4.

Moseley, Fred, and M. Campbell. 1997. *New Investigations of Marxian Method.* Atlantic Highlands, N.J.: Humanities Press.

Mowery, David, and N. Rosenberg. 1989. *Technology and the Pursuit of Economic Growth.* New York: Cambridge University Press.

Murray, Fergus. 1983. "The Decentralisation of Production—the Decline of the Mass-Collective Worker?" *Capital and Class,* No. 19.

———, 1987. "Flexible Specialisation in the 'Third Italy'." *Capital and Class,* No. 33.

Nader, Ralph, and L. Wallach. "GATT, NAFTA, and the Subversion of the Democratic Process." In Mander and Goldsmith 1996.

Neff, Robert. 1992. "For Bankrupt Companies, Happiness is a Warm *Keiretsu.*" *Business Week,* October 26.

Negroponte, Nicholas. 1995. *Being Digital.* New York, Knopf.

Nelson, Richard, and S. Winter. 1977. "In Search of Useful Theory of Innovation." *Research Policy,* Vol. 6.

Neuborne, Ellen, and R. Hof. "Branding on the Net." 1998. *Business Week,* November 9.

Nobel, Barbara Presley. 1993. "More Than Labor Amity at A.T.& T." *New York Times,* March 14.

———, 1994. "Must It Be No Pain, No Gain?" *New York Times,* May 8.

Noble, David. 1984. *Forces of Production.* New York: Knopf.

O'Connor, James. 1973. *The Fiscal Crisis of the State.* New York: St. Martin's Press.

Ohno, Taiichi. 1988. *Toyota Production Systems.* (Cambridge MA.: Productivity Press.

Ohtani, Nobuoki, S. Duke, and S. Ohtani. 1997. *Japanese Design and Development.* Brookfield, Vermont: Gower.

Ollman, Bertell. 1993. *Dialectical Investigations.* New York: Routledge, Chapman and Hall.

Parker, Mike, and J. 1988. Slaughter. *Choosing Sides: Unions and the Team Concept.* Boston: South End Press.

———, 1994. *Working Smart: A Union Guide to Participation Programs and Reengineering.* Detroit: Labor Notes.

Pelaez, Eloina, and J. Holloway. 1991. "Learning to Bow: Post-Fordism and Technological Determinism." In Bonefeld and Holloway.

Perez, Carlota, and L. Soete. 1988. "Catching Up in Technology: Entry Barriers and Windows of Opportunity." In Dosi et al. 1988.

Peters, Tom. 1992. *Liberation Management: Necessary Disorganization for the Nanosecond Nineties.* New York, Fawcett.

Piore, Michael, and C. Sabel. 1984. *The Second Industrial Divide.* New York: Basic Books.

Pollert, Anna. 1988. "Dismantling Flexibility." *Capital and Class,* No. 34.

Porter, Michael, ed. 1986. *Competition in Global Industries.* Boston: Harvard Business School Press.

Porter, Michael, and M. Fuller. 1986. "Coalitions and Global Strategy." In Porter 1986.

Powell, Walter. 1990. "Neither Market nor Hierarchy: Network Forms of Organization." In Straw and Cummings.

Preo, Eugenio. 1994. "Industrial Transformation and the Employers' Offensive." *International Marxist Review,* No. 15, Spring.

Price, John. 1992. "Workers Are Put Second in Japan's Economy." *Labor Notes,* June.

Psychopedis, Kosmos. 1991. "Crisis of Theory in the Contemporary Social Sciences." In Bonefeld and Holloway.

Pyke, Frank, and W. Sengenberger, eds. 1992. *Industrial Districts and Local Economic Regeneration.* Geneva: International Institute for Labour Studies.

Rank, Hugh. 1994. "Serious Ads and Other Channel Grazing Hazards." *Adbusters,* Winter.

Reich, Robert. 1991. *The Work of Nations: Preparing Ourselves for 21st Century Capitalism.* New York: Knopf.

Reinhardt, Andy. 1998. "Log On, Link Up, Save Big." *Business Week,* June 22.

Reinhart, James, D. Robertson, C. Huxley, and J. Wareham. 1994. "Reunifying Conception and Execution of Work Under Japanese Production Management? A Canadian Case Study." In Elger and Smith.

Reuten, Geert. 1991. "Accumulation of Capital and the Foundation of the Tendency of the Rate of Profit to Fall." *Cambridge Journal of Economics,* Vol. 15, No. 1.

Rifkin, Jeremy. 1995. *The End of Work.* New York: Tarcher/Putnam.

Roach, Stephen. 1998. "No Productivity Boom for Workers." *Issues in Science and Technology,* Summer.

Robertson, David, and others. 1993. *The CAMI Report: Lean Production in a Unionized Auto Plant.* Willowdale, Ontario: CAW-Canada Research.

Ross, Sherwood. 1998. "Employee Involvement Key to Better Returns." *Des Moines Register,* September 8.

Sabel, Charles. 1992. "Studies Trust: Building New Forms of Co-operation in a Volatile Economy." In Pyke and Sengenberger.

Sassen, Saskia. 1998. *Globalization and Its Discontents.* New York: The New Press.

Sayer, Andrew. 1986. "New Developments in Manufacturing." *Capital and Class,* No. 30.

Sayer, Andrew, and R. Walker. 1992. *The New Social Economy.* Oxford: Blackwell.

Schmidt, Stefan, and M. Shelley, eds. 1993. *Readings in American Government and Politics Today.* Belmont, CA: West Publishing Company.

Schoenberger, Erica. 1989. "Multinational Corporations and the New International Division of Labour: A Critical Appraisal," in Wood 1989.

Schor, Juliet. 1991. *The Overworked American.* New York: Basic Books.

Schrage, Michael. 1993. "Will DNA Be the Next Marketing Tool?" *San Francisco Chronicle,* December 12.

Schumann, Michael, V. Baethge-Kinsky, U. Neumann, and R. Springer. 1990–91. "The Spread of the New Model of Production—A Halting Transformation of the Structures of Work." In Manske and Wolf 1990–91.

Schwartz, Peter, and P. Leyden. "The Long Boom." 1997. *Wired,* July.

Schweickart, David. 1994. *Against Capitalism.* New York: Cambridge University Press.

Scitovsky, Tibor. 1992. *The Joylesss Economy: The Psychology of Human Satisfaction.* New York: Oxford University Press.

Sclove, Richard. 1995. *Democracy and Technology.* New York: Guilford.

Senge, Peter. 1991. *The Fifth Discipline: The Art and Practice of the Learning Organization.* New York: Doubleday.

Sennett, Richard. 1998. *The Corrosion of Character: The Personal Consequences of Work in the New Capitalism.* New York: W.W. Norton.

Shaiken, Harley. 1985. *Work Transformed: Automation and Labor in the Computer Ages.* New York: Holt, Reinhart and Winston.

———, 1990. *Mexico in the Global Economy: High Technology and Work Organization in Export Industries.* San Diego: Center for U.S.-Mexican Studies Monograph Series, 33.

Sheridan, John. 1990. "Suppliers: Partners in Prosperity." *Industry Week,* March 19.

Shimada, Haruo, and J. MacDuffie. 1986. *Industrial Relations and "Humanware".* Cambridge, Mass.: Sloan School of Management.

Slaughter, Jane. 1988. "We Have a Right to Work Fast Sometimes." *Labor Notes,* October.

Smith, Tony. 1990. *The Logic of Marx's Capital.* Albany: State University of New York Press.

————, 1992. *The Role of Ethics in Social Theory*. Albany: State University of New York Press.

————, 1993a. *Dialectical Social Theory and Its Critics*. Albany: State University of New York Press.

————, 1993b. "Marx's Capital and Hegelian Dialectical Logic." In Moseley.

————, 1993c. "The Free Trade Agreement: Who Gains? Who Loses?" In Schmidt and Shelley.

————, 1994a. "Flexible Production and the Capital/Wage Labour Relation in Manufacturing." *Capital and Class*, No. 53.

————, 1994b. *Lean Production: A Capitalist Utopia?* Amsterdam: The International Institute for Research and Education.

————, 1995a. "The Argument Against Free Market Environmentalism." *The Journal of Environmental and Agricultural Ethics*, Vol. 8, No. 2.

————, 1995b. "Flexible Production and Habermasian Social Philosophy." *International Studies in Philosophy*, Vol. 27, No. 4.

————, 1997. "Marx's Systematic Dialectic and Lakatos' Methodology of Scientific Research Programs." In Moseley and Campbell 1997.

————, 1999. "Marx's Theory of Technological Rents." *Radical Philosophy Review*, Vol. 1, No. 1.

Spekman, Robert. 1988. "Strategic Supplier Selection: Understanding Long-Term Buyer Relationships." *Business Horizons*, July-August.

Spenner, Kenneth. 1983. "Deciphering Prometheus: Temporal Changes in the Skill Level of Work." *American Sociological Review*, Vol. 48.

Stefanides, E. J. 1989. "Turning Suppliers into Partners." *Design News*, January 18

Storper, Michael, and R. Walker. 1989. *The Capitalist Imperative: Territory, Technology, and Industrial Growth*. New York: Blackwell.

Straw, Barry, and L. Cummings. 1990. *Research in Organizational Behavior*. Greenwich, Conn.: JAI Press.

Streeck, Wolfgang. 1996. "Lean Production in the German Automobile Industry: A Test Case for Convergence Theory." In Berger and Dore.

Szakonyi, Robert, ed. 1992. *Technology Management: Case Studies in Innovation*. Boston: Auerbach Publications.

Taffel, William. 1993. "Advantageous Liaisons." *Technology Review*, May/June.

Tapscott, Don. 1996. *The Digital Economy*. New York: McGraw-Hill.

Tapscott, Don, and A. Caston. 1993. *Paradigm Shift: The New Promise of Information Technology*. New York: McGraw-Hill.

Teece, David. 1986. "Profiting from Technological Innovation: Implications for Integration, Collaboration, Licensing, and Public Policy." *Research Policy*, Vol. 15.

Templeman, John, M. Trinephi, and S. Toy. 1996. "A Continent Swarming with Temps." *Business Week*, April 8.

Thornton, Emily. 1998. "Japan: Hidden Jobless." *Business Week*, August 17.

Toffler, Alvin. 1980. *The Third Wave*. New York: William Morrow.

Tolliday, Steven, and J. Zeitlin. 1992. *Between Fordism and Flexibility*. New York: St. Martin's Press.

Tomaney, John. 1990. "The Reality of Workplace Flexibility." *Capital and Class*, No. 40.

Van Parijs, Phillippe. 1989. "In Defense of Abundance." In Ware and Nielsen 1989.

Vlasic, Bill. 1986. "Get Big—Or Get Out." *Business Week*, September 2.

Wainwright, Hilary. 1994. *Arguments for a New Left*. Oxford: Blackwell.

Walker, Richard. 1989. "Machinery, Labour and Location." In Wood 1989.

Ware, Robert, and K. Nielsen. 1989. *Analyzing Marxism: New Essays on Analytical Marxism*. Calgary: University of Calgary Press.

Warner, Timothy. 1989. "Information Technology as a Competitive Burden." In Forester.

Watanabe, Ben. 1992. "Sudden Death From Overwork." *Labor Notes*, June.

Webber, Michael, and D. Rigby. 1996. *The Golden Age Illusion: Rethinking Postwar Capitalism*. New York: Guilford Press.

Weber, Max. 1959. *Methodology of the Social Sciences*. Chicago: Free Press.

Weiss, Linda. 1998. *The Myth of the Powerless State*. Ithica: Cornell University Press.

Went, Robert. 1996. "Globalization: Myths, Reality and Ideology." *International Journal of Political Economy*, Vol. 26, No. 3.

Williams, Karel, T. Cutler, J. Williams, and C. Haslan. 1987. "The End of Mass Production?" *Economy and Society*, Vol. 16, No. 3.

Williams, Karel, C. Haslam, S. Johal, J. Williams, and A. Adcroft. "Against Lean Production." 1992. *Economy and Society*, Vol. 21, No. 3.

_____, 1995. "Beyond Management: Problems of the Average Car Company." In Babson 1995b.

Williamson, Oliver. 1975. *Markets and Hierarchies*. New York: The Free Press.

Winger, Richard and D. Edelman. 1990. "The Art of Selling to a Segment of One." *Business Month*, January.

Womack, James P, D. Jones, and D. Roos. 1990. *The Machine that Changed the World: The Story of Lean Production*. Cambridge Mass.: MIT Press.

Wood, Stephen, ed. 1982. *The Degradation of Work?* London: Hutchinson.

_____, ed. 1989. *The Transformation of Work?* London: Unwin Hyman.

Wysocki, Bernard. 1995. "Big Corporate Layoffs are Slowing Down." *The Wall Street Journal*, June 12.

Yanarella, Ernest. 1996. "Worker Training at Toyota and Saturn: Hegemony Begins in the Training Center Classroom." In Green and Yanarella.

Zuboff, Shoshana. 1988. *In the Age of the Smart Machine: The Future of Work and Power*. New York: Basic Books.

INDEX

Adler, Paul, 18, 39, 68–9, 71, 170n. 8
Adorno, Theodor, 38, 87, 174n.15
alienation. *See* consumption; real subsumption
Aronowitz and DiFazio, 167nn. 9, 11
Arrighi, Giovanni, 131–2

Baudrillard, Jean, 38
Benjamin, Walter, 87
Braverman, Harry, 34, 39, 42
Brenner, Robert, xi, 129–30

Castells, Manuel, 116
computer technology: and consumption, x, 78–80, 86, 140–1; costs of, 11–2, 133, 163n.15, 179n. 6; and Fordism, 5; and globalization, 120–1; and government funding, 177n. 24; and lean production, 13, 14, 15, 29, 42–3, 50; and management control of labor process, 35–6, 39, 41, 50, 71; and networks, x, 98; and new skills, 40, 44, 167n. 9; and the postindustrialist thesis, 9, 10; and small firms 103
consumption: and alienation, 77, 81, 140–1; and consumer sovereignty, x, 75–8, 82–91, 173n. 13; and feedback to production, 152; in Fordism, 6, 7, 10, 76–8, 84; in lean production, 14, 30, 77–91, 180n. 7; and mass advertising, 84–5, 174n. 15; and surplus profits, 133–4. *See also* underconsumption crises

Derrida, Jacques, vii
deskilling, ix, 33–51; 54, 69, 167n. 5; and women, 167n. 11. *See also* mulitskilling
devaluation, 111, 131, 143, 157

Elson, Diane, 140, 142–5, 149, 152, 180n. 6, 181n. 9
exploitation, 53–4, 59–64, 65–6, 67; overcoming of, 139–40, 180n. 5

Fisk, Milton, 145
flexible specialization, 9–12
Fordism, viii, 3–6, 131, 162n. 3; bureaucracy in, 5, 6, 94; crisis of, viii, 1, 6–8, 114; labor relations in, 4–5, 7, 17; markets and hierarchies in, 93–6, 102; and the office, 162n. 4; and science, 7; and the state, 162n. 7, 163n. 12. *See also* consumption, vertical integration
Foucault, Michel, 69

globalization, 23, 58, 64, 119–34; divergent views on, xi, 120–6, 155–6; a socialist version of, 153–8
Gordon, David, 24, 44

Habermas, Jürgen, 114
Harvey, David, 16, 87, 93, 125, 129, 166n. 37
Heidegger, Martin, vii, 161n. 1

Parker and Saughter, 35, 41, 56
Piore and Sabel. *See* flexible specialization
Postindustrialism, 9
Postmodernism, 55, 97
Proudhon, Pierre, 9

Real subsumption, 54, 67–73, 85–6, 139; and
    alienation in production, 69–71
Reich, Robert, 114–5
Reuten, Geert, 178n. 3

Sayer, Andrew, 15–6
Schweickart, David, 142, 144, 154–5, 180n. 6
scientific management, 4, 34, 41, 68–9, 76,
    162n. 6
Shaiken, Harley, 36–7, 56, 58, 90, 125
Smith, Adam, 42
socialism, xii, 38–9, 62, 135–59; democratic
    model of, 139–47, 182n. 19; and glob-
    alization, 153–8; and technological
    change, 147–52, 181n. 12
Soviet Model: and bureaucratic planning,
    136; collapse of, vii, xi; and techno-
    logical change, 136–8, 180n. 1
state, 127–8, 162n. 7, 178n. 2; and globaliza-
    tion, 121, 123, 124–5; 178n. 1; and
    lean production, 25, 114–7; 165n. 34;
    and research and development, 145,
    181n. 10
structural coercion, 53, 54–9, 139, 168n. 1

Taylorism. *See* scientific management

uneven development, 124, 125–6, 157
underconsumption crises, 127

value, xi, 111, 128–9, 157–8
vertical integration, 3, 29–30, 93–6, 106,
    131–2, 166n. 37
virtual corporation, 109–10

Wainwright, Hilary, 142
Walker, Richard, 1, 9, 15–6, 77, 123, 181
Went, Robert, 153
Womack, James, 12, 58–9
Work teams, 22, 27, 49–50, 68, 80, 123; limits
    of, 62–3, 69–70, 73; and peer pres-
    sure, 64–5, 70, 72
Wriston, Walter, 115–6

Zuboff, Shoshana, 35, 39–40, 45–6, 50, 62–3,
    167nn. 2, 3